# Migrating Modernist Performance

Claire Warden

# Migrating Modernist Performance

## British Theatrical Travels Through Russia

palgrave
macmillan

Claire Warden
De Montfort University
Leicester, United Kingdom

ISBN 978-1-137-38569-7 ISBN 978-1-137-38570-3 (eBook)
DOI 10.1057/978-1-137-38570-3

Library of Congress Control Number: 2016953100



Printed on acid-free paper

This Palgrave Macmillan imprint is published by Springer Nature
The registered company is Macmillan Publishers Ltd. London

*For Olga Taxidou and Roger Savage, with sincere thanks*

# Acknowledgements

Many colleagues and friends provided assistance as I wrote this book. I want to extend my thanks to those associated with the Anglo-Russian Research Network, the Russian Theatre Network and many other communities who have been so unequivocally supportive during this project. A number of people deserve special mention: Andrzej Gasiorek who invited me to give a talk at the Northern Modernism Seminar when this project was in its infancy; Jonathan Pitches whose assistance and advice I have valued so much; Amy Skinner who set up the Russian Theatre Network and helped me find a home for this work; Steve Nicholson whose publications and chats have been enormously inspiring; Anna Vaninskaya and those associated with the Scottish-Russian Forum where I was able to share some early thoughts on Joseph Macleod. A number of other kindly and eminent people have answered questions and guided me on the right path: in this regard I particularly thank Laurence Senelick, Michael Walton, Edward Braun, Martin Banham, Robert Leach, Ramsay Burt and Mike Huxley. Particular thanks must go to Alec Baron's family for so generously sharing his unpublished autobiography with me. I want to thank my departmental colleagues at De Montfort University and, previously, at the University of Lincoln for their support. As usual Adrian Curtin proved the most wonderful reader, and I wish to particularly thank him for his time and friendship.

Two publications pre-empted this book and proved vital starting points for my thoughts. I would like to thank *Theatre Survey* and *Comparative Drama* for publishing this early work. Many archivists and librarians have helped along the way and I want to thank all those at the British

Library, the National Library of Scotland, the John Rylands Library, Newnham College, the V&A Theatre Collection, the Working Class Movement Library, the Labour History Archive, the Cadbury Research Library (University of Birmingham), Southern Illinois University and the Brotherton Collection (University of Leeds) for their assistance.

This project received funding from three institutions and I am grateful to the Amiel and Melburn Trust (for a 2012 grant that sent me on my way), the Society for Theatre Research who awarded this project the Anthony Denning Prize in 2014, and the British Academy who generously saw fit to fund archival visits and travel in 2015. As always I want to express my thanks to all at Palgrave Macmillan who have been so patient and helpful. I particularly want to thank Paula Kennedy who has helped so many of us in the world of performance studies over the past few years, and April James for all her editorial assistance.

And finally I extend thanks to my family and friends who give encouragement, keep out of my way when necessary and send useful newspaper clippings in the post. Of course, my final thanks go to David who is definitely one of the best.

# Contents

# List of Figures

# Introduction

In 1920 author H.G. Wells made his second trip to Russia, and found destruction and destitution that would not have looked out of place in his seminal 1898 alien-invasion novel *The War of the Worlds*; in his words, 'a vast, irreparable breakdown'.[1] His subsequent reflections on his trip, published as *Russia in the Shadows* (1921), simultaneously lament the poverty and ruination he found while at the same time, with caveats, backing the Bolshevik government's attempts to initiate positive changes. Not only has Russia suffered economic and societal collapse, he cries; there has also been a serious cultural breakdown. And yet, amidst this picture of wretchedness stands a peculiar anomaly:

> For a time the stablest thing in Russia [sic] culture was the theatre. There stood the theatres, and nobody wanted to loot them or destroy them; the artists were accustomed to meet and work in them and went on meeting and working; the tradition of official subsidies held good. So quite amazingly the Russian dramatic and operatic life kept on through the extremest storms of violence, and keeps on to this day.[2]

While books remained unprinted, pictures unpainted, and poetry rejected as obscure and precious, theatre endured.[3] For Wells the theatre seemed unbreakable, a steadfast cultural presence in a country where everything else seemed fractured, damaged or desecrated. Here we begin: a British traveller to Russia, discovering that theatre abides in even the harshest



C. Warden, *Migrating Modernist Performance*,
DOI 10.1057/978-1-137-38570-3_1

environment, providing a creative outlet regardless of the socio-political tumult beyond its walls, acting as a refuge for bewildered foreign travellers.

## Russia and Britain: Untangling the Relationship

'Russia' and 'Britain' are by no means settled concepts; in fact they exist as both individual, denotional abstractions and as tangible, geographically designated yet tentatively definable spaces with shifting borders. I will employ the lexicon of performance from the off and suggest that Russia and Britain, along with other nation states, enact a sort of dance, occasionally coming closer or moving further apart, politically, socially and even geographically.[4] This is unsurprising if one reads space in light of Michel de Certeau's definition that 'a *space* exists when one takes into consideration vectors of direction, velocities and time variables. Thus space is composed of intersections of mobile elements.'[5] If space is defined by fluidity rather than stasis then, inevitably, the relationships between and across spaces will be equally malleable. In the early to mid twentieth century, British perceptions of Russia oscillated between perceived threat and supportive ally, negative exemplar and model to emulate. These differing opinions appeared simultaneously across the socio-political spectrum. Inevitably in global diplomatic relations, other countries interrupted and transformed the enacted geographical dance between these two European superpowers. The rise of fascism, for example, significantly altered British attitudes to Russia; left-leaning activists felt compelled to shift their focus from setting up a political utopia in the image of Soviet Russia to fighting against fascism, first in the Spanish Civil War and later against Nazi aggression. The effect of fascist expansion was as keenly felt in the corridors of Whitehall as the union committee halls, eventually engendering an alliance that would see Stalin sit alongside Churchill and Roosevelt. The difficulty in defining the changing relationship between Russia and Britain patently remains in the contemporary context with referenda, foreign affairs, shadowy stories of spies and poisonings, economic antipathies/accords and wars. A tense (and mutable) alliance continues just as it did during the early to mid twentieth century.

This shifting relationship on a broad, political scale is complicated further by the subjective, interpretative reflections of its citizens. How can one make sense of the cultures, histories and identities of another country? Throughout this book, this remains an issue, particularly when understood through varying political prejudices and media agendas. A scan through historical newspaper articles illustrates the complexity. The *Daily Mail*, for instance, mentions Russia on numerous occasions and, like so many mainstream outlets, seems to fluctuate between effusive praise and exasperated (even fearful) condemnation. It describes the early days of the Soviet Union in ambivalent terms, simultaneously decrying the treatment of the Tsar while also celebrating the First World War victories of the new Russian army. The 1930s are full of denunciations of the new Russian state. By 1943 Russia and Britain had established a wartime pact and the newspaper reverberated with celebratory tributes in an editorial entitled 'Russia and Ourselves', a piece that focuses on British citizens' admiration for their Russian allies and their desire to materially support their comrades:

> They have studied the soldiers and the people of Russia under their own great ordeal, and have drawn the right conclusions for themselves.[6]

Not only does this article bask in the glory of the Red Army, it gives a strong sense of the working people of Britain uniting in spirit with their Russian counterparts.

The experiences and conclusions of prominent British socialist figures Beatrice and Sidney Webb provide another brief (and alternative) case in point. Journeying to Russia in 1932, the couple wrote two subsequent books: *Soviet Communism: A New Civilisation?* (1936) and *The Truth About Soviet Russia* (1942). Like many Britons on both sides of the political divide, they arrived in Russia with a partisan attitude: in their case, a one-sided admiration of Russian Communism. Neither spoke Russian and this proved a barrier to a fuller understanding of culture, as it did for many of the figures in this book. Their reflections are full of odd, ill-informed assumptions, including the remarkable proclamation in the 1942 volume (written some ten years after their original trip and following Stalin's infamous Purges) that Soviet Russia 'is the most inclusive and equalized democracy in the world'.[7] Historian A.J.P. Taylor who, it must be remembered, was not without his own biases,[8] described *Soviet Communism: A New Civilisation?* as 'the most preposterous book ever written about Soviet Russia'.[9] Without wishing to unkindly vilify the Webbs (or predictably and unfairly point the finger solely at the *Daily Mail*), these examples reveal some of the inherent difficulties in comprehending the relationship between Britain and Russia: the prejudices, political motives, misunderstandings and limited experiences (as often caused as much by travel restrictions put in place by Soviet governments as by unwillingness on the part of journalists or commentators) make historical accuracy a difficult thing to find. This absence of objective fact does not prove a barrier for this enquiry. For *Migrating Modernist Performance*, in a sense, the stories created and performances enacted are more important than unearthing presumed realities or truths. This book is less an analysis of historical fact than an unpacking of the various British responses to Russian culture, and theatre in particular.

While the relationship between the two countries, particularly in a modernist context, is difficult to assess, many scholars are currently attempting to untangle it. This book engages with the work of two recently established networks: the Anglo-Russian Research Network and the Russian Theatre Network (UK). In addition, it is indebted to (and I hope sits alongside) a number of new reassessments of Russian and British culture: Rebecca Beasley and Philip Ross Bullock's edited collection *Russia in Britain 1880–1940* (Oxford UP, 2013) (and their 2011 special edition of *Translation and Literature*), Anthony Cross's edited *A People Passing Rude: British Responses to Russian Culture* (Open Book, 2013), Jonathan Pitches's edited *Russians in Britain: British Theatre and the Russian Tradition of Actor Training* (Routledge, 2012) and Caroline MacLean's *The Vogue for Russia: Modernism and the Unseen in Britain 1900–1930* (Edinburgh UP, 2015) among others. David Ayer's forthcoming *Modernism, Internationalism and the Russian Revolution* (Edinburgh UP) and Matthew Taunton's future book on the resonances of the Russian Revolution in Britain confirm the ongoing interest in this artistic relationship between modernist Russia and Britain. This book aims to engage with this current trend, evident in both modernist studies and performance studies.

## Modernist Spatiality and the "Expanding" Fields

The comprehensive reassessment of prominent figures in these recent books has given me licence to approach the work of more marginal Britons, many of whom remain under-researched, their innovations and reflections 'lost' to theatre history. Most of them prove rather difficult to situate; I am interested in theatre-makers and commentators and, while they might categorise themselves as actors, directors, playwrights or choreographers (or even filmmakers, poets, painters or travel writers) at certain moments, most of them adopt a number of these roles at various points in their careers. Their performances sometimes strongly exhibit influences from the Russian stage but, at other times, seem to be consciously rebelling against the constructivism of Vsevolod Meyerhold or the later optimistic similitude of socialist realism, or else constructing (deliberately or accidentally) distinctly 'British' appropriations of Russian methods and texts. Some are identified with the established theatre (and therefore often falsely dismissed as formally conservative), some are better known in reference to other artistic genres (cinema particularly) and others have been simply ignored, their work regarded as too marginal, regional, esoteric or artistically unsuccessful. Further, some disassociated themselves from the modernist art scene, making it difficult for future scholars to know quite how to categorise them or intelligibly narrate their careers. A combination of all these barriers has prevented a full assessment of these figures, particularly their connections with the Russian stage.

In this study I use the term 'modernist' not only because of its chronologically specific (though notoriously fluid) associations, but also because of its suggestion of innovation, both politically and aesthetically. It is a term that has always provoked questioning and debate but, in recent years, new perspectives have led to an even more inclusive and dynamic field. Indeed Michael Whitworth concedes that modernism 'is not so much a thing as a set of responses to problems caused by the conditions of modernity'.[10] While the figures in this book differ considerably in character, intention and artistic practice, all are responding to the conditions of modernity, aesthetically and/or socio-politically.

There are two particular disciplines explored in this book: modernism and performance. Both fields have experienced significant and far-reaching growth over recent years, to the point where 'modernism' and 'performance' have become almost indefinable. Much of this extension of the disciplines is welcome. However, simultaneously, new obstacles have been erected. For example, unhelpful barriers have appeared between 'theatre' and 'performance', the former (along with 'drama') regarded as rather old-hat compared with the perceived broad inclusivity of the latter. I include both terms in the title of this book, actively resisting the obstructive barriers often put up between them. In this I am following the lead of scholars like Erika Fischer-Lichte and Benjamin Wihstutz whose *Performance and the Politics of Space* 'aims to bridge the gap between the artistic and academic disciplines of theatre and performance'.[11] Actually the theoretical approaches of both theatre studies and performance studies influence this book, whether discussing the onstage techniques of directors or the everyday performance of travellers in unfamiliar cities. 'Modernism', too, has become increasingly broad; it is no longer simply a chronological delineator or select collection of aesthetic choices. Indeed we are now, following Peter Nicholls, confronted with 'modernisms' in the plural[12] and our definition is challenged afresh by what Andreas Huyssen refers to as 'alternative modernisms'.[13]

In her analysis of planetarity and modernism Susan Stanford Friedman acknowledges the problem: 'the danger of an expansionist modernism lapsing into meaninglessness or colonizing gestures is real.'[14] In response to this trap scholars advocate a geographically broader approach. There is a desire to reassess modernism in more global terms and, as part of that, to challenge the Western-centric. This is a central intention of recent volumes like Stephen Ross and Allana Lindgren's *The Modernist World*, which 'addresses the various ways *modernism* signifies across the disciplines and around the world'.[15] Geographical and disciplinary expansions go hand in hand here. Simon Gikandi recognises a particular postcolonial transformation in the way modernism is constructed: 'a second narrative of global modernism is evident in the rerouting of modernity through a set of texts that might initially appear to be marginal to its economy.'[16] While *Migrating Modernist Performance* does not directly tap into these welcome postcolonial narratives, it remains focused on the act of 'rerouting' or discovering new journeys and reinterpreting the dynamics between Britain and Russia through them.

The fascination with spatiality is evident even in the language used to describe these changes in modernist and performance studies, with Douglas Mao and Rebecca Walkowitz, like Friedman, referring to the central effect of new modernist studies as 'expansion'.[17] If 'expansion' is an effect, it is also an action, a conscious decision to extend the territory of the field. A similar undertaking can be identified in performance studies where scholar/director Richard Schechner suggests that '(in)direction is characteristic of performance studies'.[18] Both approaches rely on the syntax of geography and movement across spaces. This expansion does not only occur in the theoretical terminology but is embedded in the search for new spaces of cultural production to be brought alongside more established modernist or performance spaces. Indeed, many recent scholars follow Peter Brooker and Andrew Thacker in *Geographies of Modernism* in asking 'where was modernism?'[19] A similar question preoccupies theatre studies and performance studies with Schechner, in his seminal textbook *Performance Studies: An Introduction*, asking 'where do performances take place?'[20] and Paul Rae, grounding his question in global spatiality, pondering 'where is the cosmopolitan stage?'[21]

But this is by no means simply a retrospective imposition of theoretical narrative; early twentieth-century artists were also fascinated by space and the way one moves between spaces. It is no wonder; their worlds were expanding and growing ever more complex as they did so. While recognising that much of the world's population remained trapped by economic circumstances, the defining objects of modernity – cars, trains, steamboats, aeroplanes – engendered the potential for travel. Casey Blanton suggests that, through the gradual 'democratization' of these symbols of urban, industrial expansion, more people than ever started to travel, experiencing new cultures, landscapes and ideas.[22] Coupled with the growth in literacy, technology (telegraphy, telephony, radio and eventually television) and media outlets that focused on international affairs, however one-sided their journalism could be, national barriers began to break down even as they were reconstructed by economic meltdown, the rise of dictators and subsequent wars.

## Spatiality, Subjectivity and Movement

In *The Soul of London* (1905) Ford Madox Ford famously concludes that 'we live in spacious times'.[23] Too often, however, Ford's well-known proclamation of spaciousness is read without reference to the rest of *The Soul of London*. It is worth returning to the preceding sentence:

> Humanity is on the march somewhere, tomorrow the ultimate questions shall be solved and the soul of man assuaged.[24]

These are not just 'spacious times', they are 'moving times': we are marching, questioning and satisfying our 'souls' in the process. Ford is ultimately interested in the way communities and individuals move across spaces and the way spaces like London are transformed into kinetic, shifting landscapes by the addition of people. Thacker picks up on this defining characteristic of modernist space, beginning his 2003 book *Moving Through Modernity: Space and Geography in Modernism* with Ford's proclamation of 'spacious times' before suggesting a 'connection between space, geography and movement' that forms the basis for his own studies.[25] Thacker is by no means alone in his corporeal understanding of space. Jessica Berman, for example, identifies a change in perceptions of space during the modernist period when 'cultural geography diverged from cartographic and physical geography by focusing on the interaction between human communities and their natural contexts'.[26] Even when mapping does occur in modernist studies, it often defies easy borders or boundaries, and suggests a greater sense of movement, reflecting Friedman's idea of circulation, 'a polycentric model of global modernities and modernisms based on circular or multidirectional rather than linear flows'.[27] I am reminded here of Bonnie Kime Scott's 'A Tangled Mesh of Modernists' or of that quintessential modernist cartographic image, Harry Beck's Tube map, based less on accurate geography than on usability. It seems that even mapping (whether historically modernist or embedded in contemporary modernist studies) becomes tied up with subjective, bodily understandings of space.

In this book I have chosen the term 'migrating' to describe the activity, intention and aesthetic approach of my key figures. It also describes the transference of modernist techniques and ideas following Brooker and Thacker's introductory comment to *Geographies of Modernism* in which they identify 'the *transnational* character of modernisms, whereby modernist practices travel and migrate across nations and are, in turn, transformed by encounters with indigenous national cultures'.[28] Although, as this suggests, texts can migrate, the term 'migration' also intimates subjective, corporeal associations. While I mention more text-based communication between Russia and Britain, this book is primarily interested in the act of travel, in the difference that physical interaction can make to an individual's theatrical output and perspective on a country. According to Christopher Schedler, the prevalence of the moving body (the wandering, exiled, restless) in modernism means that 'modernism and migration are inextricably linked'.[29] 'Migrating' also suggests movement between spaces without making those spaces too settled or determinable. I return here to de Certeau's idea of the '*migrational*, or metaphorical city', a space defined by an intrinsic sense of mobility rather than stasis.[30]

Brigid Cohen, while focusing primarily on precarious movements of people during times of war and upheaval, builds on this by suggesting that 'migration' is a 'directionally ambiguous term'.[31] Although this study has two European superpowers at its heart, the way people (and indeed ideas) move between these spaces is indeed 'directionally ambiguous'. Individuals moved through other countries in order to make this journey, arrived in obscure way stations, found themselves stranded in Riga or Kiev, or included a visit to Russia as part of more expansive trips. The same is true for theatrical ideas, which often arrived and developed alongside avant-garde aesthetics in Paris, or merged with artistic practices originating in Germany, or even crossed the Atlantic only to find their way back to Europe. Despite the clear focus on two nations, this book takes a multidirectional approach, revealing Britain and Russia less as two centre-points than as locations in a shifting confluence of people and ideas.

While in our globalised world 'migration' has taken on specific political associations, this book attempts to re-energise the term as, in Emma Cox's conception, 'migration is, at its heart, about encounters with foreignness – with foreign people, and with foreign places. These are, it may be supposed, ingredients of good storytelling'.[32] 'Migration' seems to centralise corporeal encounters and emphasise the unfamiliar, the culturally contrastive. There is also the direct connection of the term with subsequent storytelling, whether through written narratives, spoken reflections or, indeed, theatre-making. Furthermore, 'migration' brings a welcome sense of messiness that the more stable (and hierarchically political) 'international' potentially negates. In developing a 'cosmopolitan style', Walkowitz suggests 'replacing static models of modernist exile with more flexible, dynamic models of migration, entanglement and mix-up'.[33] While this approach is less straightforward, and certainly harder to manage, it better reflects the fluid toing and froing between cultures, artistically and/or physically. The tangled openness of the term is as useful for modernism as for performance studies, for transnational interchange as for artistic interdisciplinarity: as Schechner suggests when considering the relationship between the avant-garde and the mainstream (a dialogue vital to the narrative of this book), 'particular genres migrate from one category to another'.[34]

## British Experiences of the Russian Stage: Translation, Texts and Travel

Given the recent postcolonial expansion of modernist studies it might appear a little regressive to focus on the relationship between two European superpowers:[35] Russia and Britain. Rebecca Beasley and Phillip Bullock identify this problem in their introduction to *Russia in Britain*. While it might seem a 'somewhat old-fashioned topic, affiliated to an earlier methodology', actually the complex relationship between these two influential geographical spaces and cultures is often overlooked and remains 'largely absent from the discussions about the "global turn"'.[36] Uncovering this relationship, as we will see, can be a difficult, bewildering task. In addition, this reconfiguration of Russia and Britain can be understood through Laura Doyle's dialectic, 'regional transnationalism' with its 'particular regions and their transnational economic and discursive formations, *across borders and yet within a certain circumference*'.[37] This model fits rather better with the Russia-Britain dialogue than broader postcolonial frameworks.

While this book centres on travel and direct embodied experience of Russian theatre, such journeys should be contextualised within a literary, text-based transnationalism. The early decades of the twentieth century witnessed the rise of a number of little magazines, journals, newsletters and pamphlets that significantly contributed to British theatre-makers' understanding of the Russian stage. These documents stretched across the whole spectrum of political and aesthetic convictions. The Workers' Theatre Movement (WTM), for example, produced *Red Stage* (entitled *New Red Stage* from June/July 1932 onwards), a magazine that promoted leftist theatre and aimed to create some sense of connectivity between the various nationwide WTM groups. Russian theatre is mentioned regularly and with unequivocal admiration. There are, for example, articles written by Russian theatre-makers associated with TRAM (Theatre for Young Workers) with whom the WTM had 'entered into a contract of Socialist competition (or better – emulation)'.[38] Other articles authored by WTM members wistfully celebrate Russian theatre, often comparing it to the situation across Britain where absence of communist governance, prominence of escapist music hall or well-made plays, and lack of support for local working-class theatre were constant vexations. The first article of the opening edition from November 1931 establishes this comparative approach, which continues through each of the subsequent volumes:

> In the Soviet Union, our brother organisation fights with the workers' State against the prejudices and relics of Czarism, against the enemies of the Soviet Union, and helps to inspire the workers to greater achievements for the Five Year Plan.[39]

The British groups enjoyed none of these circumstances. Comparisons between vibrant Russia and moribund, reactionary Britain can be found throughout *Red Stage* and *New Red Stage*. In April/May 1932, for instance, leading figure of the WTM Tom Thomas wrote an article entitled 'How They Do It Over There' lamenting that 'we cannot expect such plays in Britain until the social conditions have been established'.[40]

In September 1932 Russian theatre audiences were described in glowing terms:

> In the U.S.S.R. the theatre is the weapon of the working class. Happy proletarian faces crowd the comfortable circles. Instinctively you feel in touch with the crowd, and everybody in touch with one another, instead of being divided by the insuperable barriers of class and money, as in England.[41]

Clearly the perceived commonality of the Russian audiences versus the fragmented, hierarchical English theatre spaces enabled the WTM members to make broader political statements. Though partly founded on inaccurate, romanticised imaginings of Russian theatre and politics, the articles of *New Red Stage* negotiate national difference and create connections between the working-class dramas of these two European powerhouses.

Periodicals published in the Soviet Union and distributed in Britain substantiated the claims found in journals like *New Red Stage*. From 1929 onwards many travellers entered the Soviet Union on organised trips with Intourist, a government-endorsed travel agency. Intourist produced periodicals – *Soviet Travel* and, later, *Soviet Land* – in order to promote their trips. In 1934 the following description could be found in *Soviet Travel*:

> The lathe worker laid aside his newly made instrument, and while he prepared to make another turned to his neighbour at the next lathe and said: 'the wife and I went to the Beethoven Evening at the Conservatory yesterday"… Such conversations are no longer rarities among Moscow workers. Go to any factory and you can hear them discussing plays, operas, concerts, or criticizing the performances of the actors, their make-up, or the stage decorations.[42]

This Soviet-produced material presents a concrete example of the 'happy proletarian faces' described by *New Red Stage*.

More general magazines and journals with various (or, indeed, no explicit) political perspectives mentioned Russian theatre alongside their other interests. T.S. Eliot's *The Criterion*, for example, regularly referred to Russian culture, particularly the Russian ballet.[43] This was similarly true for magazines like *New Age*, in which drama critic John Francis Hope unequivocally rejected Anton Chekhov's *The Seagull* as 'a dreary study in self-pity',[44] or *The Egoist* where, in his analysis of Russian literature as the 'latest craze', M. Montagu-Nathan mentions playwrights like Chekhov and Ostrovsky alongside Pushkin, Tolstoy and Dostoevsky.[45] As so often in this book, the influence was not simply one-way. When Ballets Russes founder Sergei Diaghilev co-founded *Mir Iskusstva* journal in 1898 he looked to British magazine *The Studio* and figures like Oscar Wilde and Aubrey Beardsley for inspiration.[46] Furthermore, British theatre-makers increasingly enjoyed access to a number of important European theatre books. Many are mentioned in this volume. Books such as Huntly Carter's *The New Spirit in Drama and Art* (1912) and Leon Mousinnac's *The New Movement in Theatre* (1931), among others, included Russian innovations alongside work from elsewhere in Continental Europe, giving the impression that, across the Channel, exciting new methods were sweeping away traditional institutions and techniques. A number of new volumes appeared, aiming to give British readers a sense of the Russian stage: Alexander Bakshy's *The Path of the Modern Russian Stage and Other Essays* (1916),[47] for instance, provides an analysis of the Moscow Art Theatre and Meyerhold from a self-professed non-specialist. Again, the transmission of modern theatre techniques through the latest published books shifted both ways with texts such as Edward Gordon Craig's *The Art of Theatre*, translated into Russian in 1906.[48]

Thanks to the growth in translation, Russian playtexts, diverse in political intention and aesthetic attributes, became far more accessible to a general audience. Beasley claims 'translation from the Russian might be understood as *the* translation project of British modernism' and certainly the evidence bears this out.[49] This was not purely a literary revolution, however, and influenced the performance oeuvre of many companies and theatrical venues, with plays by Anton Chekhov, Maxim Gorky and Alexander Afinogenov presented alongside Shakespeare, Jonson, Shaw or Granville Barker. Indeed, in a sense, the act of translation is an act of performance, a process of 'acting out' a script, of transforming it into something intelligible and accessible for new audiences.[50]

Initial enquiries might suggest that British theatre companies attempted Chekhov's plays on a regular basis but largely overlooked other Russian plays deemed too experimental, incomprehensible or financially unworkable. However, on further reflection, it is clear that an enormous variety of Russian techniques inspired a generation of British artists, stretching to more experimental or formally challenging work. By way of example: Edith Craig's Pioneer Players showed a particular interest in Russian symbolism, producing Leonid Andreyev's *The Dear Departing* in 1915. This odd play narrates the story of a young man who appears to be about to commit suicide and the cosmopolitan crowd who have gathered to witness this event. Interestingly for the purposes of this book, *The Dear Departing* is a play of travel and voyeurism, some people viewing the scene for detached entertainment and others trying to intervene.[51] Andreyev's work received especial attention in Britain; plays like *The Seven Who Got Hanged* (1908) and *He Who Gets Slapped* (1916) can be seen in the performance lists of a number of British theatre companies despite Andreyev's brand of realist symbolism (or symbolic realism), which proved challenging for potential audiences.[52] *He Who Gets Slapped* (produced at Birmingham Rep in 1926 and at the Everyman, London in 1927) seemed to be particularly contentious. Reviewers' issues with this play were grounded in their understanding of Russian theatre history: 'where Tchehov [sic] succeeds in making dull people interesting, Andreyev, in this piece, succeeds only in making potentially interesting people most abominably dull.'[53] The *Daily Graphic*'s reviewer continues by criticising the play through issues of national identity, issues that reappear throughout this book:

> Every producer who feels in danger of being swept along into the Russian revival should see this production. It is Andreyev through English eyes; whereas M. Komisarjevsky is giving us in town Tchehov through Russian eyes. And the latter is the more satisfying fare.[54]

The question of authenticity compels this reviewer to make his comparison. The inference is that Russian theatre is better produced 'through Russian eyes' (in this case the eyes of Russian émigré Theodore Komisarjevsky), as if 'English eyes' find it tricky to really grasp the subtleties of the Russian stage. Again this tension acts as a backdrop to many productions mentioned in this book: can 'English eyes' ever satisfactorily 'view' (or creatively interpret) Russian theatre either as part of travel experiences or as practitioners engaging with Russian plays and aesthetics in a British context?

In March 1915 the Pioneer Players grappled with another Russian symbolist play: Nikolai Evreinov's *Theatre of the Soul*, translated by Christopher St John and Maria Potapenko and performed at the Little Theatre, London. Evreinov had welcomed the October Revolution, orchestrating one of the most memorable and influential theatrical achievements of Bolshevik theatre: *The Storming of the Winter Palace* (1920). However, his brand of symbolist experimentalism soon attracted the ire of the Soviet government and he emigrated from Russia to Paris where he struggled to gain the sort of recognition his innovations surely deserved. Such a fate awaited Andreyev, too, who ended his days in Finland, a fervent anti-revolutionary, grief-stricken at the Bolshevik takeover of his homeland.

Evreinov's *Theatre of the Soul* dramatises prominent psychological theories, presenting three aspects of human consciousness: M1 (rational entity), M2 (emotional entity) and M3 (subliminal entity). After some typical wrangling with the Lord Chamberlain, Craig produced the play and St John describes the performance as follows:

> The heart was represented by a glowing red space which appeared to pulsate owing to an effect of light... The whole effect was thrilling and beautiful, and helped enormously to create a dramatic atmosphere.[55]

Such experiment was rare on the British stage and such work was far less celebrated than productions of Chekhov plays. Stuart Young suggests 'although there was a grudging recognition of Evreinov's dramatic skills, his plays were generally dismissed as pretentious, portentous and humourless' and certainly there is merit in this appraisal.[56] However, *Theatre of the Soul* has an interesting performance history that reveals broader issues about the British reception of such experimental Russian plays. After the initial March performance, Craig's production was due to move to the Alhambra theatre as part of a November celebration entitled *Russia's Day*. Such events occurred with remarkable regularity during the early to mid twentieth century, though often fraught with socio-political or aesthetic issues. However, *Theatre of the Soul* did not appear as part of this event; it was withdrawn late on with very little explanation.[57] The play appeared the next month, however, as part of a charity matinee for British troops at the Shaftesbury Theatre. The commentator in *The Times* seems in two minds about *Theatre of the Soul*; on the one hand, he concludes that Evreinov has a 'dramatic gift' and his presentation of the split mind is 'theatrically effective'; on the other, he suggests, the playwright uses 'a crude and easy method of characterization'.[58] Certainly such experimental Russian work engendered some audience confusion. However, it was not simply rejected. And, in this case, it found a new audience of soldiers and sailors. Whether they enjoyed the peculiarly obscure play we cannot know, but (and this will be a running theme throughout this book) modernist avant-garde Russian performance was by no means restricted to the Oxbridge-educated or the well-heeled frequenters of the West End. In fact some of the most innovative responses to Russian theatre actually occurred in front of predominantly working-class audiences.

Meanwhile, at the Festival Theatre (Cambridge), Terence Gray built his theatrical vision on Continental avant-garde foundations for, he concluded, 'European culture represented the birthplace of the modern theatre art'.[59] In 1931, as part of this project, he decided to produce *Roar China!* by Russian playwright Sergei Tretyakov. The censors thought otherwise, refusing to grant a public license for the play. It was left to the Manchester Unnamed Society to stage Barbara Nixon's 1931 translation. *Roar China!* mirrors the transnational objectives of my broader project – written by a Russian, focusing on a real situation in China but, in Nixon's words, 'not directed against any one country so much as against imperialism in general'.[60] In the theatrical work and travel reflections included in *Migrating Modernist Performance*, Russia and Britain are often presented not in a duologue but in a more dynamic dialogue between multiple international contributors, as here in *Roar China!* The play's final lines spoken by the Student – 'Roar over the whole earth. Roar China in the ears of all the world'[61] – emphasise its transnational intentions. Indeed, its agitprop-style conclusion can be read in parallel to many performances mentioned in this book from Russia and Britain. In the Russian context Meyerhold's theatre produced this play in 1926 to mixed reviews; one of the most important British travellers to Russia, a figure mentioned often in this book, Basil Dean, witnessed *Roar China!* during his trip, referring to it as an 'absurd melodrama'.[62] American poet E.E. Cummings, whose semi-autobiographical avant-garde travel book *Eimi* describes his June 1931 trip to Russia, concluded likewise, describing *Roar China!* as 'a cheap melodrama, so cheap(alas) it isn't cheap enough' [sic].[63] Russian playwright and director Sergei Radlov seemed to agree with Dean and Cummings. He trained with Meyerhold and yet remained unimpressed by this performance as, while he thought the Chinese characters seemed heroic and sacrificial, the European characters were ridiculously overbearing and unnatural. 'If they were to speak their nastiness more casually and quietly,' said Radlov, 'without barking, screaming and hammering on every word (that is, a bit more like Englishmen!), they would be more terrifying and more convincing.'[64] Interestingly, for my purposes here, Radlov's reproof centres on the non-realistic presentation of Englishness.

With Gray unable to produce this play, the Unnamed Society's version of *Roar China!* took place in November 1931 at the Little Theatre, Lomax Street, Salford. This theatrical collective got round typical censorship laws by becoming a subscription-only society. Although established in Manchester, the Unnamed Society distinguished itself from the more famous Manchester

School of playwrights and Annie Horniman's Gaiety Theatre by directing 'its compass needle right away from that grey North which provided the magnetic satisfaction of its predecessor… Its aim is not to reveal Manchester, but to forget it'.[65] This conviction led to aesthetic decisions – the use of vibrant colour and fabric, for example – while also affecting play choice. The company's programme for *Roar China!* situates the production firmly in the context of Russian aesthetics. It mentions Meyerhold, Alexander Tairov and Lyubov Popova as leaders of the constructivist movement and describes constructivism as using a 'purely skeleton framework shorn of all ornament or realism'.[66] Clearly the Unnamed Society wanted to associate the performance with the play's original Russian aesthetic context. However, the programme also points to another recurring idea in this book: British audiences' lack of comprehension of Russian work. It concludes:

> For the benefit of those who may find the actual play strange or harsh in outline (and certainly the Russian idea of home life on board a gunboat is remarkable enough) it should be stated that the next production of the Society will be scenes from the life of Queen Victoria.[67]

The company's 1932 version of Laurence Housman's *Palace Plays* was the realisation of this promise. Fascinatingly, producer F. Sladen-Smith clearly pre-empted his British audience's reaction to *Roar China!*, suggesting that its Russian aesthetics and theme might prevent full understanding or might even put his supporters off future events. The choice of a distinctly British play to open the 1932 season was clearly not arbitrary.

Theatre became a key arena in which the relationship between Britain and Russia could be navigated. Theatrical responses to Russia varied from romanticised presentations of pre-Revolutionary Tsarism to direct condemnations of the rise of Bolshevism; from defences of British values against the terrifying 'spectre of communism' to celebrations of working-class emancipation inspired by the establishment of the Soviet state. Plays like Eden and Adelaide Phillpotts' *Yellow Sands* (1926), for example, set in a Devonshire fishing village, seemed far removed from the revolutionary fervour of Moscow or, indeed, the politicised urban centres of Britain; indeed, in many ways it is a 'pastoral romance'.[68] However, the 'spectre' is clear in the character of Joe, who propagates communistic ideological views much to the chagrin of his fellow villagers. Newspaper and magazine cartoons of Joe picture him as a brawny 'Bolshie', declaring his love in his work clothes and Russian-style cap (Fig. 1).

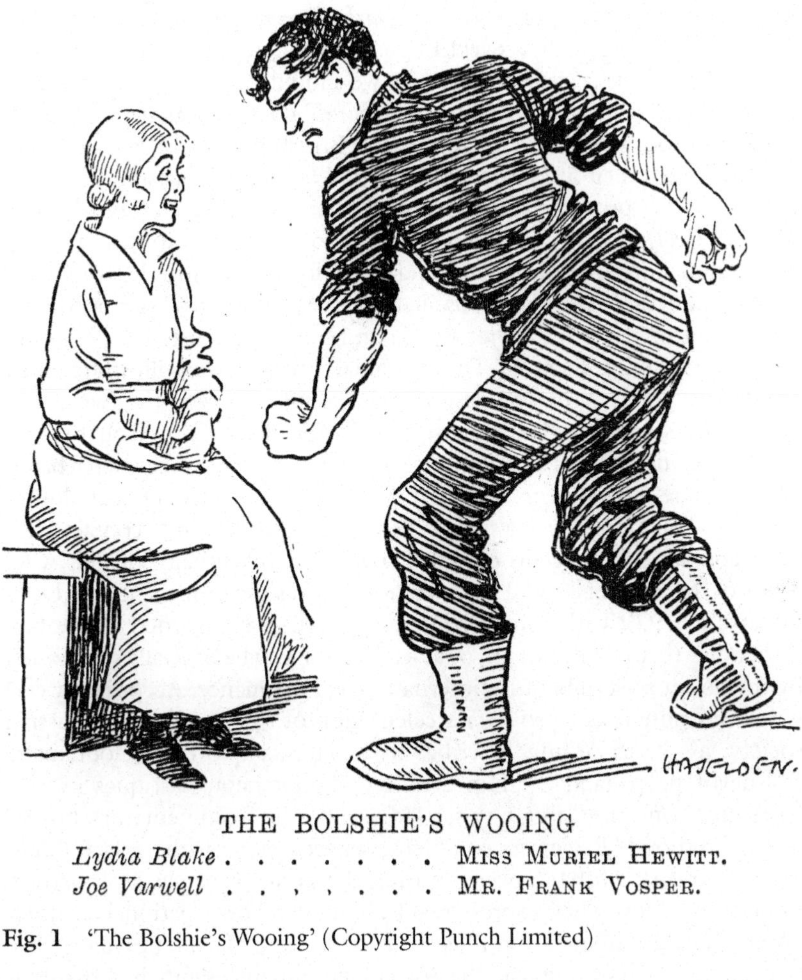


THE BOLSHIE'S WOOING

*Lydia Blake* . . . . . . . . MISS MURIEL HEWITT.
*Joe Varwell* . . . . . . . . MR. FRANK VOSPER.

**Fig. 1** 'The Bolshie's Wooing' (Copyright Punch Limited)

In the end Joe inherits, sets up a business under the auspices of helping the workers and resolutely turns away from his revolutionary plotting. Steve Nicholson confirms 'the refusal to take Joe seriously not only renders his ideas unimportant but also denies the need to be concerned about the power and threat of British radicals'.[69] This play can be seen as a direct repudiation of both Russian Bolshevik values and the fervent working-class activism that led to the General Strike in the same year. Reviewers, who seemed to unanimously praise *Yellow Sands*, also rejoiced in the play's celebration of national identity; the *Daily Mirror*, for example, confirms that 'throughout there is a sweet English flavour, and though we have had it all before, there is every reason why we should have it again. Long may it run!'[70] The reviewer revels in *Yellow Sands*' comfortingly familiar sense of nationhood; it is a far cry from many British reviews of Russian plays that denounce their linguistic, aesthetic and cultural exoticism.

Other plays provided a decidedly alternative perspective. Ted Willis's *The Jolly George* for Unity Theatre (1949), for example, narrates the story of London dockers refusing to load arms for use against Russia.[71] Still other productions seemed to oscillate between these two perspectives – celebrating or decrying Soviet Russia and/or communist theories – and rather confused audiences. These liminal performances illustrate most acutely the particularly troublesome relationship between the two countries. V.M. Kirchon and A.V. Ouspensky's *Red Rust* is a particular example. It tells the story of Constantine Teryokin (a fictitious character based on a real-life figure), a former Red Army hero who degenerates during the period of the New Economic Policy as he comes into contact with the trappings of bourgeois capitalist society. He eventually kills his wife. Adapted by Virginia and Frank Vernon, it was performed at the Little Theatre in 1929 with John Gielgud as Fedor. It is regarded as the first Soviet play to arrive in Britain, or at least the first to be officially sanctioned by the Soviet government for international performance. Accordingly one would imagine it as a pro-Soviet celebration of the new utopian Russian society: as Stuart Young describes it, as an example of 'melodramatic Bolshevist propaganda'.[72] However, contemporaneous critiques express particular confusion about this production with commentators unsure how to respond. Reviewers comment, for example, on the solace found in the National Anthem, played during the performance as a reassertion of British values. They express relief about their own national identity: 'Well, thank goodness I don't live in Moscow' and 'Thank heaven we live in England!'[73] They question the Soviet government's sanity in presenting this play as emblematic of contemporary Russian life: 'It is as if we sent out "Journey's End" as a sample of everyday conditions in England.'[74] The *Daily Telegraph* reviewer, unsure as to whether *Red Rust* was pro- or anti-Bolshevik, sums up the central issue as he sees it:

> The apparent paradox is simple enough. The play is not really propagandist at all, but a picture of a corner of modern Russian civilisation. That civilisation seems a fine thing to Comrades Kirchon and Ouspensky, who doubtless

> hope that we shall be persuaded to see it with their eyes. But we insist on looking at it with our own eyes, and so see it as a crude, lopsided Utopia which doesn't work.[75]

*Red Rust* proves a fascinating example of Russia-Britain theatrical exchange. It perfectly sums up some of the key communicative problems. While this play might have been understood as 'Bolshevist propaganda' in some circles, it is clear that through British eyes (or at least the *Daily Telegraph*'s British eyes), *Red Rust* presented a horrifying spectre. A discussion of the play in American leftist magazine *New Masses* casts further light. The author (H.W.L. Dana) cites the play as belonging to a particular period of Russian history (Lenin's New Economic Policy from 1921–1928) and as having 'died with the crisis that gave it birth' not long after.[76] Its resurrection, therefore, first in France, then in Britain and later in the US, took this play rather out of context. In addition, the translation process, says Dana, proved highly problematic: 'some of the passages in this double migration have suffered a sea change into something rich and strange.' Note that the Vernons 'adapted' rather than 'translated' this play. They seemed to have omitted Constantine's association with the Nepmen so that his demise could be falsely attributed to communist society rather than the lingering snares of the bourgeoisie. Dana cites particular examples of mistranslation – 'nucleus' is translated as 'cell' so that the communist students looked like they were incarcerated in a dingy prison rather than joining together in a receptive community; the respectable wedding celebration is transmuted into a 'sordid beer drinking party'.[77] Clearly the author of this article had his own admitted political leanings, but his analysis certainly sounds plausible given the British media's reaction to the play. *Red Rust* illustrates the problems inherent in the processes of translation and theatrical migration (of people, texts and techniques), problems this book engages with time and again.

At the start of my enquiry into the complex relationship between the Russian and British stages, this brief collection of examples illustrates a variety of foundational themes: the importance of translation, the cross-disciplinary nature of the work created, diversity of plays produced, responses of audiences (whether confused perplexity or excited appreciation) and political implications. These become key cornerstones for this book. British reception of these Russian plays remained fraught with misunderstandings. Indeed, the most popular plays seemed to be those that corresponded to or chimed with British traditions. Many of the other plays (*Roar China!* and *Theatre of the Soul* providing two cases in point) left British audiences largely perplexed, the plays proving 'baffling and alien' and acquiring the 'reputation of being emphatically highbrow'.[78] Other performances (like *Red Rust*) illustrated issues with translation, comprehension, political biases and migratory patterns.

The arrival of articles in little magazines and journals, the publication of new books and the ready availability of new playtexts engendered a fresh interest in Russian theatrical techniques. However, this coincided with a growing desire for 'embodied knowledge'. In a sense, my use of this term is guided by Pierre Bourdieu's notions of embodiment and habitus. However, it is more indebted to Diana Taylor's performance-based understanding of the term in *Archive and the Repertoire*. Taylor suggests understanding 'the repertoire of embodied practices as an important system of knowing and transmitting knowledge'.[79] The act of travel is, in itself, an embodied practice, of course. However, the way the travellers in this book engaged with theatre during their visits to Russia shows a particular corporeal approach: as audience members experiencing the visceral excitement of a performance, as set designers touching the materials and structures that made up the backdrops, as musicians physically feeling the resonance of a score ('affective hearing' as Adrian Curtin has it in *Avant-Garde Theatre Sound*),[80] or as actors grappling with the rigours of biomechanics or dancers attempting to emulate Nijinsky's remarkable leaps. Such corporeal interpretations are not reserved for performance studies; indeed, Tim Armstrong's work on the body (1998), Abbie Garrington's concept of 'haptic modernism' (2013) and Maud Ellman's studies of modernist body parts (2013),[81] among others, reveal the usefulness of embodied understandings for modernist studies more generally. Returning to Britain, these figures brought back – to again allude to Taylor's concepts – embodied memories[82] and attempted to reproduce them, or at least draw on them, in the course of their own theatre-making. If travel is a performative act in this embodied sense, then one could claim that going to the theatre is an act of travel; for many Britons, watching a Russian play in London was a way of travelling to a faraway land.

This migratory movement of cultural figures shifted both ways: British theatre-makers travelled to Russia (they provide the key focus of this book) but Russians also travelled to Britain. Some, like Theodore Komisarjevsky and Michael Chekhov, stayed in Britain for a considerable period, contributing significantly to the direction of British theatre history. Others, like Sergei Eisenstein and Sergei Diaghilev, visited for a short time yet impacted the British stage in interesting and diverse ways. All four will reappear at various points in this book. To borrow Inna Soloviova's words when describing Russian émigré experience, what 'they were abandoning and what cultural soil they carried away on their shoes'[83] is as important as their contributions to British theatre. Indeed, they all tread this Russian soil into the cultural landscape of Britain, creating a transnational amalgam where it becomes tricky (and unhelpful) to separate topsoil from subsoil.

This new breed of British traveller often wrote books detailing his/her experiences. The search for embodied knowledge, either in the very act of travelling and experiencing new cultures or by onstage embodiment of Russian theatre practices, drives many of these narratives. Commonly the authors were inspired to undertake (often uncomfortable) journeys spurred by a desire to uncover the truth: 'authenticity becomes the avowed purpose of both journey and narrative.'[84] Many of the travel books described in *Migrating Modernist Performance* claim authentic experience as a central objective, attempting to challenge the claims of other texts (namely mainstream newspapers) by making a case for actually visiting and describing a place. However, this textual commitment to making 'elusive experience concrete and ineffable meaning real'[85] is in no way straightforward. Blanton claims the travel narrative as a 'compelling and seductive form of storytelling' even as it searches after truthful description.[86] Robert Burden confirms this: 'travel has always generated stories, and narratives are structured like journeys.'[87] While this may appear paradoxical at first, such a balance between fact and fiction, truth and (borrowing Tim Youngs's term in his discussion of travel writing) 'embellishment'[88] defines the history of art, and particularly modernist art. This interweaving of truth and fiction also chimes with the history of Anglo-Russian interconnections more generally, the relationship tainted and augmented by political disagreements, social revolutions (or not), linguistic misunderstandings, cultural misreadings and artistic quarrels.

Travel writing often alludes to performance, even if the relationship between theatrical performance and travel writing is far less documented than that between literature and travel writing. Performance terminology haunts recent critical studies of travel writing as much as it does the original travel texts, with Stacy Burton, for example, describing travel writing as a 'complex performance'.[89] At once, writers are recollecting their everyday travel performances (and the performances of those around them) and then reperforming these events in written form. Youngs reflects on the troublesome chronological issues inherent in travel writing, stating that 'drawing attention to the time that has elapsed between the performance of travel and the writing of it invites reflection'.[90] Performance, in the Goffmanian and/or Butlerian sense, clearly informs travel writing scholarship.

In many ways the travel books discussed in this book (and perhaps this is true for travel writing more generally) are performance documents, often as fantastical and compelling as the best plays. Playwright Hubert Griffith, for example, wrote *Seeing Soviet Russia: An Informative Record of the Cheapest Trip in Europe* in 1932 following his visit. As well as describing the theatrical scene in detail, Griffith also comments on the architecture of the city. He writes a particularly striking description of Lenin's tomb:

> In the peculiar artificial glow of red lighting that fills the place, and that reminds one of the stage-effect when Hell opens to engulf Don Giovanni, even the living, filing in front of the crystal coffin, have the air of wax-works.[91]

There is notable theatricality in this description; it relies less on factual accuracy than on the trappings of the theatre – atmosphere, lighting, gothic scenography. Griffith also transforms his fellow visitors into theatrical presences, akin to Edward Gordon Craig's marionettes. This is only one example of the theatricality of travel writing, a characteristic of the genre that is particularly noticeable in narratives written by theatre-makers. However, it seems to be a defining characteristic of many twentieth-century travel narratives, in the broadest sense of this genre. One of the most well known is not by a British writer at all; American John Reed's *Ten Days That Shook the World* attempts to tell his English-speaking readership about the Russian Revolution, an event he witnessed in Petrograd. Lenin praised Reed's text, first published over this side of the Atlantic by the Communist Party of Great Britain in 1926. A.J.P. Taylor's introduction to the later British edition reveals the intrinsic theatricality of such narratives:

> Reed's book is not reliable in every detail. Its achievement is to recapture the spirit of those stirring days. As with most writers, Reed heightened the drama, and this drama sometimes took over from reality.[92]

Witnessing the events first-hand was no guarantee of factual accuracy; actually, as Taylor suggests, first-hand experience often meant writers were more subjectively involved in proceedings. Travel writing, in this context, becomes a mode of theatrical storytelling rather than a mimetic reconstruction of memory. Indeed, Sergei Eisenstein and Grigori Aleksandrov's film *October: Ten Days That Shook the World* (1928) translated Reed's narrative into film, and in 1967 the Maly Theatre theatricalised *Ten Days That Shook the World* in a play entitled *John Reed*. This interweaving of migration, subsequent travel narrative and theatrical art remains a key structural basis for *Migrating Modernist Performance*. The inclusion of Reed's narrative here provokes questions about the generic definition of 'travel writing'. When is a text a travel book and when is it a first-hand piece of historical writing? And, importantly for *Migrating Modernist Performance*, should it be classed as theatre studies scholarship or an experiential analysis of Russian culture? Certainly the books mentioned in the current project seem to slip between these categories. This is to be expected given the dramatic events that occurred in Russia during this period. American theatre critic, and traveller to Russia, Oliver Sayler puts it best as, in the midst of the Russian winter of 1917, he took cover in a Moscow station:

> Out on the street in front of the station the rattle of small arms rose and fell with all the realism of a well-staged western melodrama. Evidently I was to have my fill of drama in the raw and out-of-doors if not within the confines of Aristotle and the four walls of a theatre.[93]

While travel writing is certainly a highly performative mode, the reflections of those travellers caught up in the action-packed circumstances of 1910s/1920s Russia seem particularly theatrical.

In the introduction to *Russians in Britain*, Jonathan Pitches explains his aim as 'an alternative mapping of theatre traditions'.[94] In a sense, *Migrating Modernist Performance* follows this path, too, mapping (theoretically, performatively and geographically) new ways of understanding the relationship between British and Russian modernist cultures. In so doing, I focus on a range of disparate figures, united only by their interest in Russian theatre and their openness to travel to a country so often misrepresented in mainstream media and politics. Some of these figures have familial links with Russia (Marie Rambert, Alec Baron) but most do not. These figures include WTM leaders Charlie Mann and Tom Thomas; individuals associated with Unity Theatre such as André van Gyseghem, Herbert Marshall and Ivor Montagu; theatre impresarios like

Basil Dean; writers and journalists like Cicely Hamilton, Joseph Macleod, Marie Seton, Huntly Carter, Jane Harrison and Hubert Griffith; designers such as Edward Gordon Craig; choreographer/dancers Rupert Doone and (Irish) Ninette de Valois; famous playwrights like J.B. Priestley and (again recognising Irish ancestry) George Bernard Shaw; actors like Sybil Thorndike and Edith Evans. This project is by no means exhaustive, and does not claim to list every production of a Russian play in Britain or every figure with an interest in the Russian stage. Rather, these individuals exemplify the general narrative: the movement back and forth of theatre-makers and the subsequent assimilation/appropriation/repudiation of Russian techniques on the British stage.

Chapters are organised around aesthetic choices, and figures reappear time and again, reimagining their theatrical journeys and performative experiments through the relationship between British and Russian theatre. The opening chapter complicates the migratory relationship between Britain and Russia through focused study of three companies/collectives: Diaghilev's Ballets Russes, Alexander Tairov's Kamerny Theatre and the Jewish theatres. Chapter 2 takes a more overtly political stance, examining agitprop and the pageant, and claims a hybridised amalgam of the two that crosses national borders. The third chapter concentrates on contrasting forms of realism and constructivism, moving from Chekhov and the Moscow Art Theatre to Meyerhold's innovative physicalised playgrounds to the onset of socialist realism. Chapter 4 argues for the importance of Russian film for British theatre both as a technique on the stage and an influence over play structures. The Conclusion focuses on a single instance of migratory exchange in order to make some broader claims about the relationship between modernist studies and performance studies in the twenty-first century.

Ultimately this book navigates a troublesome relationship, one with few easy demarcations or characteristics. In his conclusion to *Russia in Britain*, Ken Hirschkop battles with unresolvable tensions, unable to identify a 'healthy and productive hybrid… for Russian culture may not have been the kind of material its host culture could adapt or amalgamate. Perhaps it was, in fact though not in intention, the critique of Britain's modernity, to be accepted or rejected.'[95] Following this, the reflections and theatrical experiments of the figures in this book negate easy description. Often they seem to say substantially more about British culture than Russian culture. They remain plagued by political agendas, accepted aesthetic traditions or language barriers. Yet they also enable a reconfiguration of the artistic migratory relationship between Britain and Russia, and, perhaps most importantly, situate performance at the centre of this burgeoning research area.

## Notes

1. H.G. Wells, *Russia in the Shadows* (New York: George H. Doran, 1921), 17.
2. Wells, *Russia in the Shadows*, 45.
3. Wells, *Russia in the Shadows*, 48.
4. Dance as a signifying concept is becoming a popular way of comprehending the turn to more expansively geographical ways of understanding modernism. In his chapter 'What Kind of Dance Partners?', for example, Thomas Faist presents the terms 'diaspora' and 'transnationalism' as 'awkward dance partners' (Rainer Baubock and Thomas Faist eds, *Diaspora and Transnationalism: Concepts, Theories and Methods* (Amsterdam UP, 2010, 9)).
5. Michel de Certeau, *The Practice of Everyday Life*, trans. Steven F. Rendell (Berkeley: California UP, 1988), 117.
6. Anon, 'Russia and Ourselves', *Daily Mail*, 22 February 1943, 2.
7. Sidney and Beatrice Webb, *The Truth About Soviet Russia* (London: Longmans, 1942), 19.
8. Taylor retained a leftist perspective throughout his career and propagated some controversial views, at least for the periods in which he was writing. His belief in the possibility of socialist economics and his opinion that Hitler was a political opportunist rather than evil Other, as well as his desire to popularise historical research, led to clashes with other historians.
9. A.J.P Taylor, *English History 1914–1945* (Oxford UP, 1965), 348.
10. Michael Whitworth ed., *Modernism* (Oxford: Blackwell, 2007), 3.
11. Erika Fischer-Lichte and Benjamin Wihstutz eds, *Performance and the Politics of Space: Theatre and Topology* (Abingdon: Routledge, 2013), 2.
12. Peter Nicholls, *Modernisms: A Literary Guide* (Basingstoke: Palgrave MacMillan, 2009).
13. Andreas Huyssen, 'Geographies of Modernism in a Globalizing World', in *Geographies of Modernism*, eds Peter Brooker and Andrew Thacker (Abingdon: Routledge, 2005), 6–18.
14. Susan Stanford Friedman, 'Planetarity: Musing Modernist Studies', *Modernism/modernity*, 17.3 (Sept 2010): 474.
15. Stephen Ross and Allana Lindgren eds, *The Modernist World* (London: Routledge, 2015), 3.
16. Simon Gikandi, 'Preface: Modernism in the World', *Modernism/modernity*, 13.3 (September 2006): 423.
17. Douglas Mao and Rebecca L. Walkowitz, 'The New Modernist Studies', *PMLA*, 123.3 (2008): 727.

18. Richard Schechner, "What is Performance Studies Anyway?" in *The Ends of Performance*, eds Peggy Phelan and Jill Lane (New York: New York UP, 1998), 357.
19. Brooker and Thacker, *Geographies of Modernism*, 3.
20. Richard Schechner, *Performance Studies: An Introduction* (Abingdon: Routledge, 2013), 30.
21. Paul Rae, 'Where Is the Cosmopolitan Stage?', *Contemporary Theatre Review*, 16.1 (2006).
22. Casey Blanton, *Travel Writing: The Self and the World* (New York: Routledge, 2002), 19.
23. Ford Madox Ford, *The Soul of London: A Survey of a Modern City* (London: Alston Rivers, 1905), 59.
24. Ibid.
25. Andrew Thacker, *Moving Through Modernity: Space and Geography in Modernism* (Manchester UP, 2003), 4.
26. Jessica Berman, 'Modernism's Possible Geographies' in *Geomodernisms: Race, Modernism, Modernity*, eds Laura Doyle and Laura Winkiel (Bloomington: Indiana UP, 2005), 282.
27. Susan Stanford Friedman, 'World Modernisms, World Literature and Comparativity' in *The Oxford Handbook of Global Modernisms*, ed. Mark Wollaeger (Oxford UP, 2012), 511.
28. Brooker and Thacker, *Geographies of Modernism*, 4.
29. Christopher Schedler, *Border Modernism* (New York: Routledge, 2002), 34.
30. De Certeau, *The Practice of Everyday Life*, 93.
31. Brigid Cohen, *Stefan Wolfe and the Avant-Garde Diaspora* (Cambridge UP, 2012), 15.
32. Emma Cox, *Theatre and Migration* (London: Palgrave MacMillan, 2014), 3.
33. Rebecca Walkowitz, *Cosmopolitan Style* (New York: Columbia UP, 2006), 6.
34. Schechner, *Performance Studies: An Introduction*, 37.
35. Although Britain's empiric authority was on the wane and Russia arguably had less world influence than its enormous land mass and population might have suggested, I argue that both retained a superpower status during this period.
36. Rebecca Beasley and Philip Ross Bullock eds, *Russia in Britain 1880–1940* (Oxford UP, 2013), 6.
37. Laura Doyle, 'Towards a Philosophy of Transnationalism' in *Locating Transnational Ideals*, eds Walter Goebel and Saskia Schabio (London: Routledge, 2010), 66.
38. WTM, *Red Stage* (January 1932), Working Class Movement Library Archives, Salford, 31000484/AG/TheatreBox1/A: 2.
39. WTM, *Red Stage* (November 1931), Working Class Movement Library Archives, Salford, 31000484/AG/TheatreBox1/A: 1.

40. WTM, *Red Stage* (April/May 1932), Working Class Movement Library Archives, Salford, 31000484/AG/TheatreBox1/A: 1.
41. WTM, *New Red Stage* (September 1932), Working Class Movement Library Archives, Salford, 31000484/AG/TheatreBox1/A: 2, 6.
42. *Soviet Travel* (1934: 1), qtd in *See USSR: Intourist Posters and the Marketing of the Soviet Union*, ed. Elena Sudakova (London: GRAD, 2013), 56.
43. Olga Ushakova, 'Russia and Russian Culture in *The Criterion*, 1922–1939' in *A People Passing Rude*, ed. Anthony Cross (London: Open Book, 2012), 232.
44. John Francis Hope, 'Drama', *The New Age* 15.8 (19 June 1919): 133.
45. M. Montagu-Nathan, 'Translations of Russian Fiction', *The Egoist* 2.9 (1 September 1915): 142.
46. Christina Lodder with Peter Hellyer, 'St Petersburg/Petrograd/Leningrad: From Aesthetes to Revolutionaries' in *The Oxford Critical and Cultural History of Modernist Magazines vol. III 1880–1940*, eds Peter Brooker, Sascha Bru, Andrew Thacker and Christian Weikop (Oxford UP, 2013), 1249.
47. Alexander Bakshy, *The Path of the Modern Russian Stage and Other Essays* (London: Cecil Palmer and Hayward, 1916).
48. Christopher Innes, *Edward Gordon Craig: A Vision of the Theatre* (Abingdon: Routledge, 2004), 311.
49. Rebecca Beasley, 'Modernism's Translations' in *Global Modernisms*, ed. Wollaeger, 558.
50. This is a contentious and much-debated point as discussed in detail by Silvia Bigliazzi, Peter Kofler and Paola Ambrosi in their introduction to *Theatre Translation in Performance* (Abingdon: Routledge, 2013).
51. Leonid Andreyev, *The Dear Departing* (London: Henderson's, 1916). With thanks to Naomi Paxton for introducing me to this play during a jolly conversation at TaPRA.
52. Stuart Young, 'Formless, Pretentious, Hideous and Revolting: Non-Chekhov Russian and Soviet Drama on the British Stage' in *Russia in Britain*, eds Beasley and Bullock, 98.
53. *Daily Graphic*, 22 February 1926, Cadbury Research Library, University of Birmingham, MS38/2427.
54. Ibid.
55. Nikolai Evreinov, *The Theatre of the Soul*, trans. Marie Potapenko and Christopher St John (London: Henderson's, 1915), 11.
56. Young, 'Formless, Pretentious, Hideous and Revolting' in *Russia in Britain*, eds Beasley and Bullock, 98.
57. 'Russia's Day', *The Times*, 19 November 1915, 11.
58. 'The Theatre of the Soul', *The Times*, 4 December 1915, 11.
59. Peter Cornwall, *Only by Failure: The Many Faces of the Impossible Life of Terence Gray* (Cambridge: Salt, 2004), 45.

60. Sergei Tretiakov, *Roar China!*, trans. F. Polianovska and Barbara Nixon (London: Martin Lawrence, 1931), 3.
61. Tretiakov, *Roar China!*, 50.
62. Basil Dean, *Seven Ages: An Autobiography 1888–1927* (London: Hutchinson, 1970), 293.
63. E.E. Cummings, *Eimi: A Journey Through Russia* (New York: Liveright, 2007), 59.
64. Sergei Radlov, 'Roar China!' (1929) in *The Soviet Theater: A Documentary History*, eds Laurence Senelick and Sergei Ostrovsky (Yale UP, 2014), 271.
65. The Unnamed Society, *The Unnamed Book* (Manchester: Sherratt and Hughes, 1924), Manchester Central Library Archive, TH792 094273Ma27, 3.
66. The Unnamed Society, 'Programme for *Roar China!*' (1931), Manchester Central Library Archive, TH792.094273UNI.
67. Ibid.
68. Charles Ferrall and Dougal McNeill, *Writing the 1926 General Strike: Literature, Culture, Politics* (Cambridge UP, 2015), 24.
69. Steve Nicholson, *British Theatre and the Red Peril: The Portrayal of Communism 1917–1945* (Exeter UP, 1999), 51.
70. *Daily Mirror*, 4 November 1926, Cadbury Research Library, University of Birmingham, MS38/5304.
71. Steve Nicholson, *The Censorship of British Drama 1900–1968: Volume 2* (Exeter UP, 2005), 357.
72. Young, 'Formless, Pretentious, Hideous and Revolting' in *Russia in Britain*, eds Beasley and Bullock, 104.
73. *Sporting and Dramatic News*, 16 March 1929, and *The Sketch*, 13 March 1929, Cadbury Research Library, University of Birmingham, MS38/235.
74. *Sunday Graphic and Sunday Herald*, 3 March 1929, Cadbury Research Library, University of Birmingham, MS38/235.
75. *Daily Telegraph*, 1 March 1929, Cadbury Research Library, University of Birmingham, MS38/235.
76. H.W.L. Dana, 'Yellow Rust: The History of a Crime', *New Masses: A Magazine of Workers' Art and Literature*, April 1930, 6.
77. Dana, 'Yellow Rust: The History of a Crime', 7.
78. Young, 'Formless, Pretentious, Hideous and Revolting' in *Russia in Britain* 1880–1940, eds Beasley and Bullock, 88–9.
79. Diana Taylor, *The Archive and the Repertoire* (Duke UP, 2005), 26.
80. Adrian Curtin, *Avant-Garde Theatre Sound: Staging Sonic Modernity* (New York: Palgrave MacMillan, 2014), 143.
81. Tim Armstrong, *Modernism, Technology and the Body* (Cambridge UP, 1998); Abbie Garrington, *Haptic Modernism: Touch and the Tactile in Modernist Writing* (Edinburgh UP, 2013); Maud Ellman, 'More Kicks Than Pricks: Modernist Body-Parts' in *A Handbook of Modernist Studies*, ed. Jean Michel-Rabaté (Boston: Wiley Blackwell, 2013), 255–80.

82. Taylor rightly and powerfully suggests 'it is impossible to think about cultural memory and identity as disembodied' (Taylor, *The Archive and the Repertoire*, 86).
83. Inna Soloviova, 'Emigration as a Cultural Problem' in *Wandering Stars: Russian Émigré Theatre, 1905–1940*, ed. Laurence Senelick (Iowa UP, 1992), 72.
84. Stacy Burton, *Travel Narrative and the Ends of Modernity* (Cambridge UP, 2014), 164.
85. Burton, *Travel Narrative*, 165.
86. Blanton, *Travel Writing: The Self and the World*, 2.
87. Robert Burden, *Travel, Modernism and Modernity* (Farnham: Ashgate, 2015), 8.
88. Tim Youngs, *The Cambridge Introduction to Travel Writing* (Cambridge UP, 2013), 7.
89. Burton, *Travel Narrative*, 167.
90. Youngs, *The Cambridge Introduction to Travel Writing*, 158.
91. Hubert Griffith, *Seeing Soviet Russia: An Informative Record of the Cheapest Trip in Europe* (London: John Lane, 1932), 102.
92. A.J.P. Taylor, 'Introduction' in *Ten Days That Shook the World*, John Reed (Harmondsworth: Penguin, 1977), ix.
93. Oliver Sayler, *The Russian Theatre Under the Revolution* (Boston: Little, Brown and Company, 1920), 1.
94. Jonathan Pitches ed., *Russians in Britain: British Theatre and the Tradition of Russian Actor Training* (London: Routledge, 2012), 5.
95. Ken Hirschkop, 'Afterword: A Time and a Place for Everything: On Russia, Britain and Being Modern' in *Russia in Britain*, eds Beasley and Bullock, 268.

CHAPTER 1

# Migratory Bafflement: Performing Russianness/Performing Britishness

In 1925 Virginia Woolf wrote the following words in an article entitled 'The Russian Point of View' in her collection *The Common Reader*:

> But the mind takes its bias from the place of its birth, and no doubt, when it strikes upon a literature so alien as the Russian, flies off at a tangent far from the truth.[1]

This concludes the article, a piece that questions whether 'for all their enthusiasm, the English can understand Russian literature' at all.[2] For Woolf (whose Russian translation work was often undertaken with Russian-born S.S. Koteliansky)[3] the problem lies in language; works stripped of their original contexts and linguistic utterances, and mediated through the mouths of scholars and artists who cannot speak the original language, exist in a confusing, disturbing, unfamiliar sea of multifarious meanings. As Woolf puts it, 'dashed to the crest of the waves, bumped and battered on the stones at the bottom, it is difficult for an English reader to feel at ease'.[4]

While Woolf focuses on the act of reading, the same could be said for performance. How can theatre productions, with linguistic and cultural idiosyncrasies, transcend geographical barriers and become intelligible for audiences many miles away? While this might seem a self-defeating question for a book predicated on transnational engagement, I am led to ask whether British audiences could/can understand Russian performance at all, and indeed what the verb 'understand' even means in this context.



C. Warden, *Migrating Modernist Performance*,
DOI 10.1057/978-1-137-38570-3_2

The Ballets Russes' performances were arguably the most influential and accessible for early twentieth-century British audiences, and so this chapter starts with Sergei Diaghilev's company in order to unpack the sort of cosmopolitan Russianness presented during its British travels. It is vital to remember that the troublesome question of transnational artistic engagement was as difficult for Russian audiences as for British, and in the work of Alexander Tairov, mediated through the travels of Basil Dean, we find the most prominent examples of British plays performed in the Soviet context. This book constantly reveals the intricacies and complexities of the relationship between British and Russian theatre, and the final part of this chapter illustrates this by discussing the intermingled, migratory tradition of Jewish theatre. All these examples complicate, to borrow Pitches's words, 'the linearity of transmission',[5] setting up an intricate framework of appropriation, repudiation, emulation and inspiration, fraught with political, linguistic and cultural tensions though prompted by a mutual desire to understand, that grounds the claims of the next three chapters.

## The Ballets Russes: Choreographic Internationalism

Susan Jones suggests that 'dramaturgy of the early twentieth century frequently developed in tandem with specific forms of choreography and movement practices', confirming the centrality of dance for modernist art in a general sense.[6] Dance performance influenced an enormous range of artists, not just dramatists, actors and directors, but also visual artists, poets and novelists. The gradual turning of modernist studies towards performance and *vice versa* is mirrored by a similar, more specific, exchange between modernism and dance studies. Carrie Preston contends that this choreographic expansion of modernist studies is vital, 'as dance highlights early twentieth-century preoccupations with varieties of movement: motions and rhythm in performance and other arts, bodies transported on stages and across national, racial, and ethnic borders'.[7] Preston's identification of modernist dance innovations with movement in art and in everyday life, particularly the migration of bodies through geographical spaces, matches the intentions of this book.

While the Ballets Russes' Russian heritage remains clearly embedded in the company's title and personnel, it was its transnational journeys that defined its location and ultimately led to its profound influence on the British scene. The Ballets Russes travelled to many countries and is associated less with Moscow or St Petersburg than Paris. Lynn Garafola even suggests that 'beginning with its name (French for "Russian Ballet"), the company was a creature of the West'.[8] Russian citizens were prominent members of Paris's foreign community.[9] Educated and wealthy Russians often spoke fluent French, and the number of Russian émigrés who found their way to Paris meant there was a ready community for newcomers. Due to the arrival of writers, artists and performers, Paris became less the capital city of France than a meeting space, a confluence of ideas and innovations. However, as often with migratory spaces, this engendered tension as well as creativity. Reviews of the Ballets Russes' groundbreaking *The Rite of Spring* (1913) often pointed to the company's perceived Jewishness, Otherness or homosexuality. One commentator complained of a 'so-called Parisian "audience" made up of people who are as foreign to France as they are to art'.[10] In addition, complicating its nationality still further, the Ballets Russes played with Eastern exoticism, a facet of its performance aesthetic that chimed with a general vogue on the London stage exemplified by the astonishing success of Oscar Asche's Arabian Nights-inspired spectacle *Chu Chin Chow*, which played for 2,235 performances between 1916 and 1921 while the Ballets Russes toured Britain.[11]

The Ballets Russes utilised the talents of artists from various countries so that, despite the clear national identification mark in its title, it did not have a particularly Russian complexion. Coupled with this diversity of contributors, the Ballets Russes looked to avant-garde experiment in Italy, Spain and France as well as Russia, engendering what Garafola refers to as 'a supranational character to company modernism'.[12] In a sense the Ballets Russes transcended national boundaries in terms of aesthetics and personnel, becoming the migratory modernist company *par excellence*. On the other hand, leader Diaghilev seemed eager to retain a distinctly Russian feel. He even gave mocked-up Russian names to some of the English dancers in the company; Hilda Mannings, for example, became Lydia Sokolova.[13]

The Ballets Russes significantly impacted the British cultural scene and references to the company's productions, particularly while resident in London, appear in the writings of many of the most prominent characters of British modernism, as well as in journals like *Rhythm* and *The New Age*. Osbert Sitwell, for example, recalls dining with Diaghilev and choreographer/dancer Léonide Massine on the evening of Armistice Day. He comments, 'the return of the Russian Ballet to London has constituted a private and sole omen of peace'.[14] Woolf notes likewise, associating the '"approach of peace" with the return of "the Russian dancers"'.[15]

It seems that the presence of the Ballets Russes in London felt like a political act, a direct comment on the changing nature of planetary transnational relations. Famed stage actor Ellen Terry casts further light on Britain's response to the Ballets Russes. Recognising that other European countries have their national ballets, she acknowledges 'English audiences, like children presented with a new toy, firstly shyly wondered at the novelty of the agile strangers, and then fell into transports of enthusiasm'.[16] Terry partially detaches the Ballets Russes from the shackles of nationalism, suggesting that the company worked predominantly with 'imagination which is neither the property of a nation nor the result of patriotism'.[17] For Terry the work of the Ballets Russes expounded a universal sense of creativity unencumbered by the restraints of national identity.

British opinions of the Ballets Russes varied, often falling into one of two camps: those who wanted to emulate Diaghilev's techniques and ideas in a British context, and those who regarded the Ballets Russes as ethically irresponsible, with its dreamlike, detached art.[18] That most contrary of modernist artists Wyndham Lewis, however, seemed in two minds about the Ballets Russes. He famously criticises the company as 'High-Bohemia' in *Time and the Western Man* (1927) but, years earlier, actually planned a ballet with William Walton and Sacheverell Sitwell to offer to Diaghilev.[19] The Ballets Russes' effect could be felt throughout modernist drama, particularly in the work of T.S. Eliot, who imagined the Russian ballet as 'the model for a potential new form of poetic drama that is simultaneously primitive and thoroughly avant-garde'.[20] Simultaneously, British designers also turned to the Ballets Russes for inspiration. Tom Osbourne Robinson, from the Northampton Royal Theatre, for example, watched the Ballets Russes' *The Sleeping Princess* at London's Alhambra Theatre in 1921 with his father, citing this event as a seminal moment in his career: 'I knew then that nothing would stop me from designing scenery and costumes.'[21] Oliver Messel's theatrical debut was designing the masks for the Ballets Russes' 1925 *Zephyr and Flore*.[22] He later went on to design for the Royal Ballet.

J.M. Barrie also regularly attended Ballets Russes performances and, in 1920, wrote *The Truth About the Russian Dancers* with music by Arnold Bax and design by surrealist painter Paul Nash. The Ballets Russes' Tamara Karsavina danced the principal role of Karissima in the opening 1920 production at the Coliseum.[23] Reviews, though not all complimentary, generally focused on the fusing of playtext and dance, or, as a critic of 16 March 1920 in *The Times* put it, 'Karsavina threading her way on the tips of her toes over a stage strewn with Barrieisms'.[24] Barrie set his play in Vere Castle, a stately home, and the characters and setting could not be more quintessentially English. In essence, *The Truth About the Russian Dancers* is a fairly conventional drawing-room play. However, Barrie described the setting as having 'a touch of the bizarre as in Russian ballet';[25] the addition of Karsavina, a real-life Ballets Russes dancer, further complicates the typical narrative. Despite the verbosity of the script, Karsavina (introduced as a family visitor) remains mute throughout, interpreting the various scenes (including a remarkable danced rendering of a golf shot) through her body. She recognised the challenges of her role in this production: 'before I could start producing my part choreographically I had to resolve a problem: how to tune the abstract language of speaking toes to the matter-of-fact lines of the actors.'[26] This image reappears again in the actual script when Lady Vere remarks, 'Roger told me none of the Russian ballet can speak – with their mouths I mean. He says they find it so much jollier to talk with their toes'.[27] By the end of the play, after Karissima has died in childbirth, the cast unites in dance with Lord and Lady Vere responding to Bax's upbeat final tunes by rising 'on their toes. It should be wildly gay'.[28] All the characters seem to have found it more appealing to 'talk with their toes'.

While Diaghilev's company significantly and inevitably impacted London, it also made some notable tours around Britain. Although in 1914 a cynical *Birmingham Daily Post* journalist confessed 'we are never likely to see the Russian Ballet in the provinces',[29] by 1919 the Ballets Russes had reached Manchester. By 1920 the company was performing in Nottingham, Sheffield, Leeds and Liverpool. A *Liverpool Daily Post and Mercury* journalist responds to the company's two-week residency in the latter city:

> Such beauty is heart-warming and inspiring. We came away from the sight of it regretfully and grateful. And when still thrilling from the call of it we find ourselves in the chill gloom of West Derby Road, with its black shiny pavements and the rank odour of the thronged 'fish and chip' shops, we realise what a queer thing civilisation is and how infinite in variety is man.[30]

The sharp contrast here is geographically situated on the streets of Liverpool, the Ballets Russes appearing pleasingly 'foreign' in this Northern industrial city. Notably, it is the unusual aesthetics rather than any particular allusions to Russianness *per se* that interests the journalist.[31]

Many British artists (or artists associated with the British art scene) came into contact with the Ballets Russes, but three particular figures worked directly with the company and their experiences transformed their future choreographic practice and/or their perspectives on ballet: Marie Rambert, Ninette de Valois and Rupert Doone. Polish-born and a Russian speaker, Rambert's contribution to the Ballets Russes began while under the tutelage of Émiles Jaques-Dalcroze, the founder of eurhythmics. Rambert visited Moscow in 1911 to participate in Dalcroze's lecture-demonstrations. Upon their return to Dalcroze's school in Hellerau, Germany, Diaghilev and Nijinsky visited to ask Dalcroze for choreographic assistance. Rambert subsequently took up a consulting role with the Ballets Russes as it prepared for *The Rite of Spring*. Her time with the company took her to London, which she described in less than glowing terms: 'we had arrived in the middle of a pea-soup fog. Even when it cleared, London made little impression on me.'[32] Despite this, Rambert later founded what eventually morphed into the Rambert Dance Company, a collective that continues to influence British dance. Although Rambert only remained with the Ballets Russes for a short time, the company's aesthetic techniques continued to shape her work. As her biographer suggests, 'no school or academy could have taught her the Diaghilev concept of ballet which shone like an illuminated flight path for her to follow on her own journey in presenting ballet as an art form'.[33] Through assisting with *The Rite of Spring* Rambert learned about the intricacies of ensemble work, developed her ability to discern musical rhythm and transmute it into physical action, and discovered a new appreciation of the value of intense rehearsal.[34] Her Ballets Russes experiences also significantly influenced her very choice of style, compelling her to move from Dalcrozian eurhythmics to ballet, although her former experiences at Hellerau continued to impact her work.

Ninette de Valois, like Rambert,[35] performed only briefly with the Ballets Russes but the experience remained a mainstay for her career. Her inclusion in this book is not to negate her Irish origin but, rather, to acknowledge the profound influence she had over British ballet. In fact, she maintained that her Irish background enabled her to better fit in with the company's ethos as 'my Celtic blood had far more in common with theirs than that of any other artist of a purer English strain'.[36] De Valois's first contact with Russian ballet came in 1921 when Diaghilev and Massine arrived in Covent Garden. While this first venture did not lead to a performance, de Valois joined the company officially in Paris in 1923. Despite later feeling restricted by the Ballets Russes' methods, de Valois remained effusive in her praise for Diaghilev:

> The main effect of Diaghilev on my dormant creative mind was to arouse an intense interest in the ballet in relation to the theatre... I had come to one conclusion: the same should happen, along the same line, and with just such an ultimate goal – in England.[37]

De Valois here appears to construct a direct lineage from her experience with Diaghilev to her later innovations in England. Even years later, when focused on creating a distinctly English ballet style, de Valois felt compelled to look back on the Ballets Russes' methods:

> We live in constant danger of losing all contact with those high standards set by Diaghilev concerning the perfect collaboration of choreography with décor and costume.[38]

The legacies of both Rambert and de Valois lay in setting up companies rather than choreography *per se*. These companies not only reflected the communality of the Ballets Russes but also arose partly because of the demise of the Russian company in the late 1920s. The vacuum left compelled them to set up their own collectives, responding, in a way, to the absence of the Ballets Russes.[39]

Oft overlooked in histories of British theatre, Rupert Doone's most abiding contribution lay in his founding of Group Theatre, a company that performed versions of plays by W.H. Auden, Christopher Isherwood, Louis MacNeice, T.S. Eliot and Stephen Spender, among others, reimagining poetic drama in visual and performative terms.[40] Doone performed with the Ballets Russes for a time in the late 1920s but it remains difficult to piece his career together. He certainly danced in the Ballets Russes' 1929 London season but unfortunately Diaghilev died that very year and Doone's connection with the company was subsequently cut short. However, like Rambert (in fact Doone performed for Marie Rambert's Ballet Club in 1931),[41] Doone remained indebted to his experiences with the Ballets Russes: in the Group's early days, 'Diaghilev's extravagant theatrical collages and the zealous purification of the theatre undertaken by Copeau were the great, contrary, inspirations'.[42] Mirroring Doone's career with the Ballets Russes, decoding Russian ballet's influence over Group Theatre's canon of work is tricky. Certainly the early productions contained a good deal of modernist dance experimentation alongside songs and sketches. Perhaps the company's 1934 version of Auden's *The Dance of Death* makes the connection a little clearer. In many ways *The Dance of Death*, thematically at least, tapped into the ideas of the workers' theatre, a tradition which found particular success in communist Russia. It theatricalises the potential death of the middle class, concluding with Karl Marx declaring it 'liquidated'.[43] However, aesthetically, it took influences from a number of Continental European and British theatrical methods, both historical and modern. As part of this piece, Doone asked Auden to include balletic elements that he could dance; in response Auden wrote the character of Death. Michael Sidnell suggests that Auden was influenced by two pieces by French avant-gardist Jean Cocteau: *Parade* and *Le Train Bleu*. Diaghilev produced both, in 1917 and 1924 respectively.[44] In *The Dance of Death*, Doone's character, Death, wore a sun mask designed by Henry Moore (who was incidentally married to a Ukrainian émigré), disguising his features in order to focus on the body, and danced a '*solo dance as* SUN GOD, *creator and destroyer*'.[45] A masked sun god made a previous theatrical appearance, of course, in *The Rite of Spring* as Yailo, the ancient Slavonic sun god.[46] One can only really speculate about direct connections between Doone, Group Theatre (and its playwrights) and the Ballets Russes. However, illustrating Marvin Carlson's recent historiographical claims that productions conjure ghosts of previous performances, one can say with certainty that Doone's early experiences with the Diaghilev company haunted his later productions.[47]

Despite the Ballets Russes' influence over British culture and the celebratory reviews which greeted them, some of the most influential figures in British theatre remained ambivalent about their practice. Designer and visionary Edward Gordon Craig, for example, seemed to oscillate between celebratory praise and perplexed criticism. Craig travelled to Russia three times: in 1908, 1910 and 1911. His theatrical project centred on simple, symbolist aesthetics, innovative light and sound and, most famously, puppetry and masking, which could be employed to overcome (what he considered to be) the intrinsic defectiveness of the human actor. I will reflect more thoroughly on his artistic experiences in Russia, and particularly his collaboration with Stanislavsky, later in the book. But it is worth exploring his trips here. In 1908 he was 'lodged in the vivid city of Moscow' writing a letter to John Semar (actually a pseudonym). Experiencing all the exciting theatrical innovations of that great city, Craig's subsequent epistolary reflections are rather odd:

> And I am perhaps more miserable than ever before in my life, because I realize the hopeless inactivity of England and its stage, the hopeless vanity and folly of its stage, the utter stupidity of every one connected with the Arts in

England, the death-like complaissancy [sic] with which London thinks it is active and intelligent about these matters, the idiocy of that section of the Press which calls every courageous attempt to revive life and art 'eccentric', that lack of comradeship in London, that lust for *twopence* at all costs.[48]

It might appear rather curious that, surrounded by the vibrancy and dynamism of Moscow, Craig's thoughts turned to London. However, travellers often say more about the world they leave behind than the world they travel to as, in Stanford Friedman's words, 'home comes into being most powerfully when it is gone, lost, left behind, desired and imagined'.[49] While this response becomes more acute when the loss is permanent (the forced eviction of communities from their homes, for example), nevertheless, the traveller can experience a similar palimpsestic layering of place as their home emerges through their current location.

Craig's changing opinion of the Ballets Russes is captured in articles for his journal *The Mask*. In 1911 he wrote 'Kleptomania, or the Russian Ballet' under the pseudonym John Balance. In it he is dismissive of the new Russian ballet, which he presumes to be 'the old French ballet warmed up': 'as a work of Art then the Russian Ballet is a myth, as a work of originality it is a fraud.'[50] By 1913 he appeared to have warmed to the company, seemingly because Nijinsky had applauded the work of American dancer (and Craig's lover) Isadora Duncan.[51] Later in the same year, he praised Nijinsky and Diaghilev as congenial people but remained underwhelmed by their innovations:

But, oh, you good people all of you, especially you dear Russians both of St Petersburg and Moscow… when the devil are we all going to wake up in the theatre? No seriously… WHEN ARE WE GOING TO WAKE UP.[52]

By 1929, just a few months before Diaghilev's death, Craig seemed to be a little more enthusiastic about the Russian's practice:

The success of M Diageliev's [sic] Paris performance was greater than ever… and indeed this is not hard to understand, for it is today the best ballet in the world.[53]

Interestingly, this revelation occurred in Paris, that important centre of modernist transnational exchange.

At first glance Craig and Diaghilev appeared to approach the stage in opposing ways. However, in the July 1912 edition of John Middleton

Murry's little magazine *Rhythm*, George Banks, reflecting on the Ballets Russes' version of *Petrouchka*, connects the two:

> Conveyed by puppets and visualized by the forms of the finest human material in the theatre to-day, it suggests to one that the idea of Mr Gordon Craig's Über-marionette is not a dream but a possibility of great meaning.[54]

Deciphering the practical consequences of Craig's ideas on the *Übermarionette* remains troublesome but, for Banks at least, the Ballets Russes inadvertently achieved Craig's objectives.

While Craig's response to the Ballets Russes oscillated between suspicion and admiration, classical scholar, influential academic and early feminist Jane Harrison professed high regard for the Russian ballet throughout her career. A polymathic Russian speaker, she visited the country only once in 1886. But in 1930 D.S. Mirsky (the Russian translator and academic who emigrated to Britain in 1921) recollected Harrison's abiding admiration of his homeland:

> She loved Russia, loved it like a human being. Her love could make you, if you were Russian, quite uncomfortable, so undeserved and unjustified did it seem.[55]

He even perceived what he understood as Harrison's particular Russian identity:

> This combination of a Radical intellect with Conservative tastes and manners cannot fail to remind one of these Russian revolutionaries born into aristocratic families who espoused and developed with the greatest sincerity the boldest revolutionary doctrines.[56]

Mirroring Woolf's conclusions in 'The Russian Point of View', Harrison described her strong attachment to Russia in terms of language:

> It was not these portentous things [the 'Slav soul' or even Russian literature] that laid a spell on me. It was just the Russian language... Language is as much an art and as sure a refuge as painting or music or literature. It reflects and interprets and makes bearable life; only it is a wider, because more subconscious, life.[57]

Harrison, along with her Cambridge Ritualist colleagues Gilbert Murray and Francis Cornford, placed theatre at the very centre of her Hellenist model. As Olga Taxidou suggests, Harrison remained largely concerned with ritual rather than myth, which moved away from 'narrative or text as the origin of aesthetic practice [and] posits theatre as the foundational art form'.[58] In light of this Harrison particularly admired the Russian folk tradition, namely *Vertep* theatre, a practice that began as a way of dramatising the Christian nativity using puppets and later became a more secular, slapstick form.[59] Her appreciation of the *Vertep* puppets in the Museum of the Imperial Sciences in St Petersburg seemed to rest on her understanding of them as 'objects of the living tradition she so cherished'.[60]

In *Reminiscences of a Student's Life* Harrison laments her lack of travel to Russia and her reflections chime with the impressions of many of the travellers mentioned in this book. She declared, 'but oh, what a fool, what an idiot I was to leave Russia without knowing it... never now shall I see Moscow and Kiev, cities of my dreams'.[61] Like others, Harrison placed considerable emphasis on experiential engagement with Russia, believing, despite her impressive scholarship and linguistic skills, that she could not fully 'know' Russia without being physically present in the space. This is a rather remarkable admission from such a celebrated linguist and academic. However, her admiration of Russian art remained; indeed, in *Ancient Art and Ritual* (1913) she mentions the preponderance of Russian ballet in England as confirmation of the growing artistic vibrancy of the English stage.[62]

This brief exploration of responses to the migratory Ballets Russes clearly reveals its profound effect on British culture and, specifically, its influence over practitioners who entered and interacted with the company's transnational network. De Valois described the process of rehearsing *The Wedding* (1923) as a 'mystical revelation of the soul of a country, a pagan ritual concerned with primeval joy and sorrow'[63] and ultimately it was this unique combination of the modern and the ancient, the spiritual and the personally emotive, that drew practitioners like her, Rambert and Doone to Diaghilev's company. For de Valois, as for many other Britons who came into contact with the Ballets Russes (as practitioners or audience members), Diaghilev's collective revealed something uniquely Russian and yet, simultaneously, provoked universal feelings like 'joy and sorrow'.

The careers and successes of de Valois, Rambert and Doone lie, to a greater or lesser extent, in their first-hand experiences of the Ballets Russes. This is an example of Diana Taylor's 'embodied practice', which 'offers a way of knowing'.[64] This is learning through doing rather than (or, more accurately, in addition to) just witnessing. It confirms the importance of physically engaging with practice and provides a transnational genealogy of embodied practice from the Ballets Russes to today's Rambert Dance

Company and the Royal Ballet. Negotiating the Ballets Russes' influence over British culture reveals the importance of understanding modernism in physicalised terms. Michelle Clayton's recent argument that to understand modernism is to understand 'the movement of modernist bodies-in-transit across a variety of spaces, whether geographical, scenographic, filmic, or textual' is upheld by this brief foray into the transnational history of the Ballets Russes.[65]

## Alexander Tairov and Anglophone Drama in a Russian Context: Basil Dean at the Kamerny

In 1932 the King and Queen arrived for a charity matinee performance at His Majesty's Theatre. Alongside an orchestra conducted by Sir Thomas Beecham and a sketch by Gerald du Maurier was a ballet from Anton Dolin and Alice Nikitina, the former a British principal Ballets Russes dancer, the latter a Russian who danced the part of Flore in the ballet Oliver Messel designed the masks for.[66] The event was organised by one of British theatre's most prolific producers: Basil Dean. Dean is generally categorised as a West End mainstream theatre impresario and later filmmaker. However, his canon of work was considerably more expansive, risky and innovative than his absence from British theatre histories would suggest. In 1923, for example, he produced the first British version of James Elroy Flecker's remarkable play *Hassan*, using dance choreography from Ballets Russes choreographer Michel Fokine and music by Frederick Delius. In the same year he produced Karel Čapek's *R. U.R.*, the play that introduced the word 'robot' into the English language. He also devised a particularly expressionistic rendering of J.B. Priestley's *Johnson Over Jordan* in 1939. He worked with stalwarts of the British stage, Laurence Olivier, Ralph Richardson, John Gielgud and Sybil Thorndike, and later became the head of ENSA, the Entertainments National Service Association, which, despite jokes about 'ENSA' standing for 'Every Night Something Awful', preceded the establishment of the National Theatre. Dean had admirable transnational ambitions for ENSA: 'the entertainment service I had in mind was radically different from anything known in Briton [sic] before: and it had no counterpart elsewhere indeed [...] other nations were to copy us in time.'[67]

Dean's interest in Russia seems to have begun over ten years before his eventual trip when he wrote to Michael Lykiardopulos, then secretary of the Moscow Art Theatre, seeking advice about producing theatre.[68] For his part Lykiardopulos expressed an interest in acquiring a book on the repertory movement in the English theatre.[69] Dean journeyed to Russia in 1926, setting up arrangements through Dmitri Bogomoloff, a diplomat from the Russian Embassy in London. In a letter of 7 January of that year, Dean explicitly mentions his proposed trip, a 'visit to Moscow that I desire to make to see the theatres there'.[70]

Dean journeyed to Moscow later that year with his wife, Lady Mercy Greville, and his designer, George Harris. His intentions chime with those of his fellow travellers:

> For some time now the English stage has been buzzing with exciting stories about happenings in the Russian theatre... I was anxious to see things for myself.[71]

Travel is again presented here as an act of authenticity, a way of uncovering experiential truth rather than relying on textual description or hearsay. He found the trip energising and inspiring, meeting with a range of important Russian theatre-makers, enjoying performances at the Moscow Art Theatre (to which he was apparently invited personally by Stanislavsky), and talking with Minister of Education Anatoly Lunacharsky. Reflecting on his trip, he wrote:

> The infinite variety of the productions, the astonishing range and power of performers, the bold designs, enthusiasm, experiment, passionate acceptance of the immature, equally passionate rejection of the obvious, the endless discussions and probings and heart searchings over endless cups of tea; the whole mad whirl of those astonishing days in Moscow left me with but one impression – vitality. When considering an art is there need to say more than that? Vitality![72]

Despite reservations, particularly about Meyerhold's innovations, Dean remained effusive in his praise. Rather comically, fuelling his adventures was the quintessentially English 'cup of tea', even if that tea was probably taken in the Russian style: with lemon rather than a splash of milk.

His trip to Russia was part of Dean's ongoing search for new theatrical techniques that would address some of the key issues of twentieth-century drama as he saw them. He was particularly concerned about the increasing absence of the actor; in an address to the Victoria and Albert Museum four years before his Russian travels, Dean stated that 'the thing we need more urgently than anything else is the return of the actor to the theatre'.[73] According to Dean, the actor had been eclipsed by the fashion for elaborate sets and spectacular *mise en scène*. This concern chimed with the reservations of his designer, George Harris, who accompanied Dean on his journey. Perhaps surprisingly given his scenographic focus, Harris was concerned that, on the contemporary stage, sumptuous stage design was far too prominent, obscuring the actor and the story. In his only published reflections on his practice, Harris finds blame and remedy for this in the techniques of the Ballets Russes. He suggests that the 'great appeal of the colour and movement of the Russian ballet suggested to the manager a means by which he could attract the playgoer'; mimicking the scenography of the Ballets Russes seemed, for Harris, to be a commercial decision by unscrupulous producers.[74] However, he simultaneously dismisses the 'realistic treatment of scenery' and suggests 'the Russian Ballet presented many examples of complete unity between decoration, dancing and music'.[75] Harris's reticence over British producers aping Ballets Russes' methods did not preclude his admiration for the company's brand of total theatre. Harris died in 1928 and therefore it is impossible to know how his experiences with Dean in Russia just two years earlier would have affected his theatrical output. However, his last design, for the 1929 *Beau Geste*, certainly seemed to nod to Russian influence, particularly in his poster, which appears remarkably like Russian constructivist images with its geometrical shapes and red and black colour palette.[76] Although the play is about three brothers joining the French Foreign Legion, there is certainly a Russian tinge to it; according to Dean some songs for the production came 'from the time of the Old Russian Imperial Army, forwarded via Riga, for fear of disturbing Soviet intelligence'.[77] Just three years after Dean and Harris visited, the former at least seems far more distrustful of Soviet officialdom and more inclined to look back to pre-Bolshevik imperialism.

Though Dean visited numerous theatres during his Russian trip he reserved his most fulsome praise for the Kamerny Theatre, established by Alexander Tairov in 1914 with his wife, the actress Alisa Koonen. The reputation of (and consequently support for) the Kamerny Theatre fluctuated depending on the aesthetic whims of the Soviet government. Celebrated, then marginalised, Tairov's reputation was cemented in 1932 when he was named a People's Artist of the USSR after his production of *The Optimistic Tragedy*, which, in an unusual move for Tairov who tended to keep explicit politics off the stage, he 'dedicated to the birth of the Red

Army as one of the first organizing and organized principles of the Great October'.[78] However, Tairov's legacy is largely based on his popularisation of plays from the USA and Britain, and it is perhaps this focus on the translated Anglophone canon that meant Tairov was one of the most popular of all Russian directors outside the Soviet Union. It was perhaps also the reason that Russian audiences (and officialdom) often regarded him with a degree of sceptism.

Tairov produced a range of British plays including, perhaps most famously, G.K. Chesterton's *The Man Who Was Thursday* (1923). An English writer and theologian, Chesterton showed a particular interest in Russia, reflecting, like so many of his compatriots, on British misunderstandings of Russian culture. In light of this interest he wrote an article entitled 'The English Blunder about Russia' in Winifred Stephens's 1916 collection *The Soul of Russia*, published 'in aid of the fund for Russian refugees administered by the general committee of the All-Russian Union of Zemstvos[79] under the presidency of Prince G.E. Lvov'.[80] This book attempts to reach across geographical divides and educate a British readership about Russia's vibrant cultural traditions. It is an act of transnational friendship and educative instruction. In its title it also confirms one of the central motifs British artists used to understand Russian culture: the Russian or Slavic 'soul'. This concept, so prevalent in discussions of (particularly late nineteenth/early twentieth-century) Russian writing, originated, to a point, in Russia. It was promoted by those who looked back to old Muscovite ways and the reign of Peter the Great. But, as Rebecca Beasley and Philip Bullock confirm, the anglicised concept of the 'Slavic Soul' appeared 'through a process of translation and reception across cultures'.[81] In Britain it acted as a remedy for Western industrialisation: a romanticised, historical image that counteracted the trappings of modernity. In other words, this version of the 'Slavic soul' was a foreign construct, a way of comprehending a complex culture of Otherness as well as providing an alternative to encroaching materialism in Britain. It also, as Caroline Maclean has illustrated, connects what she terms the 'vogue for Russia' with the 'vogue for the unseen', that is the early twentieth-century growth in spiritualism, the occult and various other theosophic or mystic practices.[82] Perhaps a helpful way to differentiate between the figures in this book would be to claim their responses to Russia as either 'unseen' or materialist, although I suggest that the two rather overlap for most of the travellers mentioned in these pages.

Chesterton's contribution to *The Soul of Russia* confronts the 'English blindness to Russia' caused by the English political party system that propagates misconceptions about Russia on both sides of the political divide.[83] Chesterton concludes in upbeat mood:

> It is to be hoped, and there is every reason for hoping, that in the better days after the War we shall approach the great Russian people with an open mind, if necessary as an entirely new people discovered on the other side of the moon… Then we shall see no more of this absurd cross purposes between Eastern and Western Europe.[84]

In this transformative year for world politics Chesterton hoped for transnational accord and understanding. It now stands as a flawed, naïve prophecy that, in the years to come, as many of the figures in this book testify, would prove sadly untrue.

Tairov presented Chesterton's allegorical thriller *The Man Who Was Thursday* in distinctly constructivist style with costumes and set designed by leading constructivist artist Alexander Vesnin. It clearly responded to Meyerhold's *Lake Lyul* of the same year, which moved the conception of set as a machine for acting to something rather more architectural.[85] The set for *Lake Lyul*, designed by Viktor Shestakov, represented an urban space, as did Vesnin's set for *The Man Who Was Thursday*.[86] In both there was a move to symbolically represent place rather than pure abstraction. On this stage Tairov's characters 'were turned into mannequins who spoke in standardised, monotonal fashion'.[87] Tairov's production epitomises a transnational aesthetic where British plays were reworked in a decidedly Russian avant-garde context.

Tairov also premiered J.B. Priestley's most enduring play *An Inspector Calls*. In 1945, unable to find a British home for his play, Priestley turned to the Russian stage. This represented a continuation of Priestley's interest in Russia. Indeed, around the same time as *An Inspector Calls* appeared at the Kamerny, Priestley was travelling to Russia with his wife as guests of VOKS (the Society for Cultural Relations with Foreign Countries). His reflections on his trip can be found in his 1946 book *Russian Journey*. At the beginning of this book Priestley acknowledges the inevitable accusations of bias that might be levelled at him as a socialist and a playwright whose work received considerable praise in Soviet Russia. However, he addresses this, saying, 'as I am supposed to be an experienced observer of ordinary men and women I made full use of this opportunity of using my eyes and ears and wits'.[88] Here are the pros and cons of travel: on the one hand one becomes emotionally invested in the places and people one meets; on the other this can lead to a rather one-sided perspective. Certainly travel, as many of the figures mentioned in this book illustrate, creates a subjective layering of experience. So, for Priestley, visiting Moscow for the first time, 'some parts of it looked like Manchester in November; other parts (notably the parks) like Blackpool; but there were always the green of gilded onion-shaped domes to suggest an Oriental fairy-tale'. Priestley here questions the easy demarcation of 'European'; Russia is less a Continental ally than a romanticised image of Asian folklore. He also, perhaps recollecting his 1934 *English Journey*, sees elements of the British landscape in the Russian capital.

Surprisingly, *Russian Journey* contains limited reflections on the theatre, despite Priestley's admission that he regularly attended theatrical events as he travelled around. In addition, his brief comments on the Russian stage are direct reproofs to his British readership rather than analyses of the performances as such:

> For the benefit of those who imagine that all Soviet plays are about Ivan the Terrible, cement factories or Guerrilla heroes, allow me to say here that I saw in Leningrad, among other excellent things, a very funny comedy of ordinary Soviet life, about a harassed fellow who keeps on taking other men's portfolios. And comedies of this kind should be promptly exploited, if only for the sake of those people who still think of the Bolsheviks as bearded monsters.[89]

Once again here is a challenge to British bias. However, Priestley also advocates the importing of Russian plays that might challenge preconceptions and entertain British audiences. He rejects a monolithic view of Russian culture, praising (problematically, it must be said) the championing of local and regional tradition: 'it deliberately encourages and fosters these traditional national cultures, and the wide Soviet land glitters and hums with their dance and song.'[90] For Priestley the landscape is a performative space, transformed by the artistic traditions of its inhabitants. Ultimately this is a travel narrative about friendship produced in response to unknowns. Unlike many of the travellers in this book whose Russian journeys occurred in the 1910s, 1920s or 1930s, Priestley visited Russia immediately after the Second World War. His book is inevitably littered with references to soldiers and wartime urban decay. However, Priestley looked past this temporary atrophy and imagined the inspiration Soviet

Russia could be to his readers back home. Rather than focus on materialist advancement, Priestley says, Russian authorities should promote the significant advancements made in other areas, 'the psychological and spiritual gains, on which they could issue a formidable challenge to the capitalist countries, with their masses of frustrated and often unhealthy-minded young people'.[91] In a sense, Priestley was harking back to the pre-First World War idea of the 'Slavic Soul' here, describing a culture that prided itself on atheistic materialism in almost transcendent terms.

*An Inspector Calls* appealed to Soviet audiences, disturbing established social orders through a combination of naturalistic dialogue and stock characters. The complex, almost supernatural figure of the Inspector acts as an unsettling presence in the Birling/Croft's capitalist-driven world. Many of his comments and accusations chime with the tenets of communist ideology:

> One Eva Smith has gone – but there are millions and millions and millions of Eva Smiths and John Smiths still left with us, with their lives, their hopes and fears, their suffering, and chance of happiness... And I tell you that the time will soon come when, if men will not learn that lesson, then they will be taught it in fire and blood and anguish.[92]

Tairov's version of this play, entitled *He Has Arrived*, premiered at the Kamerny in 1945. As Maggie Gale has identified, this play responds very directly to the British post-war context; while the war had disturbed the established hierarchies of British (perhaps specifically English) society, peace brought new challenges – 'as old distinctions and inequalities lay just beneath the surface it was the threat of their inevitable re-establishment in a post-war era which concerned Priestley.'[93] Tairov made distinct scenographic choices in order to further the political intensity of the play. So Inspector Goole was in 1940s dress in contrast to the Edwardian costumes of his fellow actors.[94] The stage area complemented the themes of the play:

> The manorial dining room of the Birlings is transformed under our gaze into a... court-room. The table standing in the middle of the room is almost an executioner's block and the four chairs arranged at the sides, the defendants' benches.[95]

Tairov's decisions transformed Priestley's well-made play structure (albeit a well-made play with shifts in time and reality/fiction) into a more symbolist image – what Tairov referred to as the 'theatre of neo-realism'.[96]

Like Dean, Tairov was committed to actor-centred theatres, believing that 'actors needed to be taught how to care for the material of their art – their own natures and their own bodies. The *corps de ballet* ought to have its theatrical counterpart in a *corps de drame*'.[97] In his 1923 *Das Entfesselte Theater*, Tairov placed great import on his actors 'ererbte plastische Schwerfälligkeit ankämpfen [fighting against their inherited plastic clumsiness]' and instead developing their physical bodies.[98] He remained convinced that modern actors in general used their bodies poorly, 'not as a Stradivarius but as a three-stringed balalaika'.[99] This does not lead him to the conclusion that the human actor is therefore rendered obsolete; indeed, while admiring Craig's enthusiasm and conviction, he frequently criticises him, claiming 'it is not the marionette but the living actor, the actor-creator, the actor-master' who needs to solve the contemporary theatrical problems.[100] Consequently, Tairov's training methods, which Dean witnessed, were highly rigorous. His choices regarding costume mirrored this dextrous turn. In performances such as Kalidasa's Hindu drama *Shakuntala* (1914), for example, Tairov experimented with using 'naked, painted bodies of the actors, moving in free rhythm'.[101] While such strikingly 'stripped down' costume choices did not appear in every Kamerny production, Tairov consistently focused on the needs of the three-dimensional acting body in a three-dimensional space. Costume, he reflects, 'is the actor's second skin, it is something inseparable from his essence, it is the visible mask of his scenic figure'.[102]

Tairov's physically liberated actors functioned on sets that partly responded to constructivist aesthetics so prevalent in Russia during the 1920s through the work of Meyerhold and Vakhtangov, among others, although there were clearly tensions between Tairov and his more politically minded compatriots. As Konstantin Rudnitsky suggests, Tairov embraced a 'balletic method of organizing space, where the centre of the stage is empty and the entire floor is clear'.[103] This meant his actors took a prominent role and (despite some exceptions to this rule, arguably, including *The Man Who Was Thursday*) refused to overshadow the human element of his plays with scenic spectacle. Given Tairov's interest in British playwriting and allegiance to actor-focused theatre, then, it is really no surprise that he got on well with Dean. The two spent a good deal of time together, indeed enough for the Russian to give him a photograph signed with 'Dear Mr Dean, you will be always heartily welcomed at the Kamerny Theater by your highly esteeming A. Tairoff'.[104]

Like Craig before him, Dean constructed clear connections between the vibrant Russian theatre scene and the rather moribund English stage, and saw potential benefits:

> The spectacle of a number of English actors being plastic in a Noel Coward drawing room is unlikely to do more than excite ridicule. On the other hand it is conceivable that the stage of Drury Lane filled with actors, trained in a new school of vigorous gymnastic movement, performing evolutions suggestive of the battle scenes in 'Henry V' might be an invigorating experience for even the most jaded West End playgoer.[105]

But how did Dean's experiences in Russia really affect his theatre? Such a question is difficult to answer as the vitality he witnessed in Russia seemed to largely contribute to his general distress over the state of British theatre, particularly in the economically motivated world of the West End, rather than encourage him to create new work responding to his Russian experiences. Just months after his return from Russia, Dean spoke on the radio about commerce as 'the root of all trouble… it cheats the people of the full joy in the theatre'.[106] No doubt such an opinion was partly engendered by his Russian travels. British travellers regularly (often erroneously) noted the contrast between funding systems in Russia and Britain. English writer, and Russian resident, Alexander Wicksteed describes the perceived difference:

> One thing must be insisted on – practically all the theatres are subsidized and are thus enabled to make the very interesting and varied experiments which I understand are beginning to influence even the commercialized Stage in England, at any rate that section of it that is managed by people who are striving after the highest standard of art obtainable without losing too much money.[107]

Wicksteed celebrates the subsidies given to Russian theatre groups, comparing the situation to the capitalist-driven theatres of Britain.

Wicksteed also suggests that theatrical innovations enabled by the Russian funding systems were beginning to affect the British stage. Dean did not always concur with this hopeful conviction. In his article 'Roast Beef and Cavaire [sic]: Reflections upon the Theatre in England and Russia', published by the *Soviet Union Monthly* in May 1926, Dean recognises the ebullience of the Russian stage and bemoans that 'the English theatre is just now in a state of dullness and lack of contact with progressive thought'.[108] Such despair over the condition of British theatre inspired Dean to turn towards film. It was not until the late 1930s, with the approaching war, that Dean regained an enthusiasm for the British stage. Indeed, in an interview with fellow playwright, critic and Russophile Hubert Griffith, Dean seems to have rediscovered the potential of British theatre:

> Mr Dean thinks the present time a good one for launching out boldly in the theatre: 'A time of serious national anxiety should be theatre's opportunity'.[109]

This is not to say that Dean did not continue making theatre during the later 1920s and early 1930s. And, fascinatingly, there are a number of allusions to his experiences in Russia. One of his most successful productions was *The Constant Nymph* (1926). Based on Margaret Kennedy's 1924 novel of the same name and written by Dean and Kennedy, *The Constant Nymph* moves from Austria to London to Brussels following the travails of composer Lewis Dodd and the 'nymph' Tessa. A brief look suggests little connection with Dean's Russian trip. However, in February 1927 Dean wrote to Russian actor trainer Madame Boleslavsky (wife of MAT actor Richard Boleslavsky and, later, co-founder of the American Laboratory Theater with her husband) suggesting *The Constant Nymph* for the Moscow Art Theatre.[110] He even proposed that 'if the play were to be given next Autumn I would come to Moscow to see the performance and should look forward to it with great pleasure'.[111] Perhaps it is a coincidence but the character of Trigorin, described in the prompt copy of *The Constant Nymph* as 'a large Russian, speaking abominable English'[112] is a choreographer who looks remarkably like Sergei Diaghilev (Fig. 1.1).

Kennedy continued to show interest in the Russian stage, translating/adapting (with Gregory Ratoff) Ilya Surguchev's *Autumn* for Dean's company in 1937 (touring to the Manchester Opera House in 1938). Reviews of this production played up its Russian connections. *Tatler*, for example, confirmed a particular Slavic feel as 'the introspective searchings of heart and soul by "Lady Catherine"... seem all very Russian' whereas *The Stage* reflected on the intensely 'Russian' atmosphere of the drawing room.[113] Not unusually for British reviewers of such plays, the Russian associations are noted but explained in rather vague, insubstantial ways as 'feelings' or 'atmospheres'.

**Fig. 1.1** 'The Constant Nymph'(Copyright of the University of Manchester)

While Dean did not bring Meyerholdian biomechanics back to the West End, intimations of his continued interest in Russian ideas can be seen throughout his canon. One of the most surprising appeared in his 1928 theatricalised version of Charles Dickens's *The Pickwick Papers*, *Mr Pickwick*. Ostensibly an adaptation of Dickens's first novel, the *Daily Express*'s review is most revealing. The journalist, named only Beachcomber, describes Dean's production as a 'Russian Pickwick' because the eponymous hero wears a Russian smock that Dean, apparently, picked up during his Moscow travels. The correspondent speculates about other potential Russian elements of the play:

> Maybe the public like their Dickens with a Russian tang. Perhaps Mr Pickwick will drink Russian tea instead of sherry, and Sam Weller contemplate suicide because, like the retainer in Chekov's [sic] play, the mice have been gnawing his livery.[114]

Two years after Dean's trip, journalists still alluded to the theatre-maker's Russian experiences. In an interesting transnational parallel, the MAT performed an adaptation of Dickens's novel, entitled *The Pickwick Club*, in 1934. Soviet theatre historian and director Nikolai Gorchakov (who worked with both Vakhtangov and Stanislavsky)[115] describes the set of this production as a return to the two-dimensional flats of earlier performances but, despite the interesting scenographic choices, he confirms the play was criticised for simply revealing 'the warmth of human hearts' rather than 'the "satiric and unmasking" aspect of Dickens who "lashed the mores of his period"'.[116]

In fact, Dickens's novels provided fruitful raw material for a number of Russian theatres, confirmed by British novelist Arthur Ransome's list of productions in his analysis of post-Revolutionary Russia, *Six Months in Russia in 1919*. Best known for his *Swallows and Amazons* book series, Ransome travelled first to Russia in 1913, later becoming a journalist correspondent, advocating the Bolshevik cause, marrying Trotsky's secretary, Evgenia Shvelpina, and attracting the unwanted attentions of MI5. His brief list in *Six Months in Russia* mentions *The Cricket on the Hearth* at the MAT, *A Christmas Carol* at the Komissarzhevskaya Theatre and *Little Dorrit* at the Theatre of Drama and Comedy.[117] It is rather perplexing to find so many references to a British nineteenth-century novelist in a list of Russian theatre outputs in 1919. Perhaps Dickens's political overtones found in the poverty of Tiny Tim and the greedy capitalism of Scrooge, or the critique of the debtors' prison in *Little Dorrit*, appealed to Russian theatre-makers aiming to engage with the politics of Civil War Russia.

If the innovative experiments of the Russian theatre-makers did not seem to dramatically affect Dean's methods, then perhaps his experiences impacted his choice of repertoire. Certainly there is evidence for this, particularly in his engagement with Tairov's work at the Kamerny Theatre.

Dean particularly appreciated Tairov's treatment of Eugene O'Neill's work and remained an admirer of the American stage for much of his life, making regular trips to the States. Indeed, America and Russia seem aesthetically connected in Dean's mind. Just before leaving for Russia he gave an address to the Nottinghamshire Playgoers Club:

> The most active work in the theatre is being done in the two countries at the opposite poles of circumstance so far as the great War is concerned, the one country almost untouched by it, the other dragged into the dust by Famine and Revolution: America and Russia. As I am just about to visit the latter country at the invitation of the theatrical artists there I feel I should say little about it but this I will say – on all sides I hear and from the premier of the Moscow Art Theatre Musical Studio which I heard recently in New York, I am convinced that work of great value is being done in the Russian Theatre and I am determined that such knowledge as I can glean over there shall be placed at the service of our theatre as soon as possible.[118]

Dean aligns the Russian and American stages, regarding them as the pinnacles of twentieth-century theatrical innovation.

Tairov attempted three Eugene O'Neill plays in the years surrounding Dean's visit: *The Hairy Ape* (January 1926, coinciding with Dean's trip), *Desire Under the Elms* (in the same year) and *All God's Chillun Got Wings* (1927).[119] Dean saw the former and was aware of the production of *Desire Under the Elms*, mentioned in a letter of October 1926 from Madame Boleslavsky.[120] Four years later Tairov and the Kamerny Theatre toured the O'Neill plays and the playwright himself saw the productions in Paris. O'Neill was welcomed backstage by the company and clearly enjoyed Tairov's rendering of his plays. In a *New York Herald* letter, he admitted not knowing what to expect, 'hence my amazement and gratitude when I saw your productions which in every way delighted me because they rang so true to the spirit of my work… a theatre of creative imagination has always been my ideal'.[121]

Tairov began his version of *The Hairy Ape* with a seven-minute pantomime. The unscripted scene saw the semi-naked stokers throwing mimed shovels of coal in the furnace to a soundtrack of shouts.[122] There was a profoundly visceral, almost bestial feel. Dean acknowledged the way the set and the actors worked in tandem, writing on the back of his photograph of scene V 'a very remarkable combination of vigorous realistic acting with impressionistic scenery'.[123] The photograph itself is of Yank's arrival in the city; the other characters in the scene are in (mostly) formal dress and wear masks. Yank's face is uncovered and his work clothes mark him out as an alien presence in this landscape. His posture, crouching, primed for action, contrasts with the elegant carriage of those around him. However, there is an addition in Tairov's scene: a circular construction suggesting a shop window or building with the words 'Ensors I.T.E. Limited' written upon it. This is absent from O'Neill's published play. Not only are the words written in Latin rather than Cyrillic script (marking this play out as distinctly Anglophone), it is also, I speculate, perhaps a nod to James Ensor and his well-known painting *The Intrigue* (1890) (or indeed any of his other mask paintings). There is no real evidence to support this but the parallel between Ensor's and Tairov's experiments in masking proves rather beguiling.

Later in 1926, in the same year as Tairov's version, Dean decided to produce *Desire Under the Elms*. The play focuses on the Cabot family, four farming men from New England. The arrival of young, vivacious Abbie Putnam, new wife to the elderly patriarch Ephraim, causes two of his sons, Simon and Peter, to leave the farm to try their luck in the California Gold Rush. Abbie and remaining brother Eben fall in love and have a child, passed off as Ephraim's, much to the nudge-nudge, wink-wink merriment of the local community. It ends in tragedy with Abbie killing her newborn child to prove her love for Eben, and grief-stricken Eben calling the sheriff before deciding that he will accept part responsibility and, presumably, take his place beside Abbie on the gallows. It is a play of ghostly apparitions and complex familial relationships where, in a Freudian sense, mother and lover seem to be one and the same thing.[124] After liaising with the Theatre Guild in New York, Dean earned the rights to produce the play if the Lord Chamberlain allowed it.[125] Later that year, in an article in *The Sphere*, Dean reflected on Tairov's treatment of O'Neill's work and confirmed 'I look forward greatly to the opportunity of producing this remarkable work [*Desire Under the Elms*] in England as soon as the British Censor has moderated his capers'.[126] Walter Benjamin's first-hand description of Tairov's *Desire Under the Elms* was extremely critical, yet his description gives some sense of the scenographic visuals:

> The outdoors seemed to stream in from every side. There were two more rooms on the second floor, reached by a stairway that was partitioned off from the audience's view by laths. It was fascinating to follow the characters making their way up and down the stairs behind the lattice.[127]

Despite his disappointment with the production, Benjamin praised the way bodies were compelled to move on this creative, constructivist-influenced stage.

By 1928–9 Dean had included the play (to be produced in conjunction with the Arts Theatre Club and designed by George Harris) in the programme for his autumn/winter season.[128] However (and given the brief synopsis above, unsurprisingly), the Lord Chamberlain continued to get in the way and banned any public performance. It was left to Peter Godfrey and the Gate Theatre to premiere *Desire Under the Elms* in Britain with, perhaps simply coincidentally, one of Dean's company's key actors, Flora Robson, as Abbie. Godfrey managed to escape the Lord Chamberlain's diktats because the Gate was, like a number of other collectives including the Arts Theatre Club, a private, subscription club. Theatre director Norman Marshall praised these sorts of groups, confirming that 'the English theatre was saved from stagnation and sterility by the small group of producers, players and playgoers who, supported by many of the dramatic critics, refused to accept the drab monotony imposed upon the theatre by the managers and by the Censor'.[129] Practitioners in Britain and Russia alike experienced the wrath of the theatre censor throughout the early twentieth century. In Russia, Tsarist institutions (coupled with the influence of the Orthodox Church) censored a great number of plays deemed unsuitable for public performance, including works by Pushkin and Lermontov, and foreign playwrights from Shakespeare to Ibsen. Despite many British traveller perceptions of Russian theatre as joyously free and experimental, censorship continued under the new Soviet regime, strengthening as Stalin's power increased.[130] While, in Britain, the Lord Chamberlain did not violently repress theatre-makers, censorship was the source of frustration to those pushing for freedom of speech. Dean certainly questioned the authority of the Lord Chamberlain; he expressed his consternation in a letter to Fenner Brockway (politician and leftist activist) in 1929:

> I believe that the Censorship of Art in any form whatever is an inimical thing… For those of us who are deeply concerned for the present condition of our Stage, this is a very serious matter. The English Theatre must re-establish confidence in the minds of the audience; it has got, somehow, to wake up and present life as it is lived, and not as the 'boulevardier' imagines it to be.[131]

Not until 1938, with a new Lord Chamberlain in post, was *Desire Under the Elms* resubmitted. It was eventually licensed in 1940 and performed professionally for the first time at the Westminster Theatre.[132]

## Theatricalising the Marginalised: Jewish Theatre in Moscow, London and Washington

Tairov's name reappears time and again in Dean's writing about Russia but the British theatre-maker also appreciated a range of other Russian performance styles, companies and practitioners, particularly innovative collectives such as the State Jewish Theatre (GOSET) directed by Alexei Granovsky. GOSET brought together a tremendous range of experimental artists including Marc Chagall and Isaak Rabinovitch. In his reflections on his trip Dean praises this enterprise where 'the most modern variants of age-old Jewish legends are performed upon frankly Constructivist principles. All actors appear to be gymnasts and pantomimists of no mean ability'.[133] Unfortunately, Dean and Granovsky never met due to the latter's illness. However, the Russian clearly felt an artistic affinity with Dean, writing in November 1926 to ask about the possibility of touring England.[134] Dean responded in early 1927:

> Allow me to tell you how deeply I admired the work which I witnessed in your theatre during my visit to Moscow last spring and I have made several references to it in various articles and lectures. With regard to your contemplated tour, I feel I must tell you that the theatrical world of Great Britain is passing through a period of great distress. Therefore I cannot give you a very optimistic account of your prospects in England.[135]

Once again, Dean's inspiring experiences in Russia did not compel him to emulate the styles he witnessed; instead he could only bemoan the lack of creatively experimental work in his own country.

Dean collected a number of photographs of GOSET, including one of *Night at the Old Market*, performed in the months leading up to his visit. On the back of this photograph is written 'The Jewish Kamerny Theatre under the direction of Granovsky has attracted great attention by its vigorous presentation of old Jewish stories in modern guise, usually with a strong note of grotesque satire running through the treatment'.[136] It is interesting that this commendation should be written on the back of a photograph from one of GOSET's most infamous and contentious productions. The photograph is rather disturbing: shadowy crooked shapes with a giant hand reaching through the roof. The characters are partly masked, their bodies jagged and almost otherworldly. While it clearly taps into Jewish folk tales (one of the central characters is the Badkhn, a Jewish jester figure)[137] it can also be read in parallel to the European modernist avant-garde, particularly symbolist plays by Maurice Maeterlinck and Stanislaw Wyspianski.[138]

The arrival of Russian Jews to British shores became a recurring motif of forced migration, whether in response to Tsar Alexander's pogroms in 1881 or Stalin's later purge of Jewish intellectuals. In 1883 the Russian government passed a law banning performances in Yiddish in the Russian Empire.[139] Consequently Jewish actors and dramatists left, travelling to Paris, London and New York. So, London (and other British cities, particularly Manchester) did not just attract a substantial number of Jewish migrants but *artistic* migrants. From this distinctly Russian origin grew a tradition of British Yiddish theatre, from the Hebrew Dramatic Club, set up in 1886, to the Grand Palais, a theatre that continued until the 1970s.[140] This entire lineage is embedded in the migration of thousands of refugees from Russia seeking better conditions for their art in Britain.

Arrivals included Israel Zangwill's parents, his father escaping as a 12-year-old to avoid conscription into the Tsarist army, his mother, also probably 12, as a refugee from the Polish pogroms.[141] Zangwill always associated himself with Yiddish culture and language, though he also mixed with a group of writers that included Thomas Hardy, Arthur Conan Doyle and J.M. Barrie, and, later, became friendly with Eleanor Marx and George Bernard Shaw, among others.[142] Zangwill was particularly excited about the potential of theatre, artistically and politically. Yet, like so many figures mentioned in *Migrating Modernist Performance*, he was also concerned about the health of British theatre, particularly in the commercially driven world: 'an aggravation of the economic factor at all times conspicuous as standing danger to art.'[143] At the end of his less than encouragingly titled 'The Doom of Drama' (1920: incidentally the same year as the seminal mass performance *The Storming of the Winter Palace*, which potentially counteracts his rather bleak perspective), Zangwill questions the future of Russian theatre, too:

> It is impossible to suppose that Bolshevism, with its presumption of a world made perfect at last, would be less asphyxiating to the breath of new life than

the existing censorship. Art cannot be produced under dictation, even 'The dictation of the proletariat'.[144]

For Zangwill neither financial catalysts nor political prescriptions could result in good art, a principle as true in communist Russia as capitalist Britain.

Zangwill's most famous play, entitled *The Melting Pot*, was first produced in Washington in 1908, arriving in London in January 1914. Dedicated (by permission) to Theodore Roosevelt, *The Melting Pot* is a celebration of the USA as a land of freedom and equality, a 'melting pot' of cultures, religions and ethnicities. Although this sounds utopian, its cheerful optimism is tempered by the play's horrific undertone. It follows the story of David Quixanos, a Jewish violinist and composer, living with his pianist uncle, Mendel, devout grandmother and stout-hearted Irish maid, Kathleen. David is captured by the American Dream: not its capitalist economics, which (in the person of brash Quincy Davenport Jnr) are generally portrayed as boorishly materialist, but its commitment to uniting diverse groups of European immigrants beneath the Stars and Stripes banner. David falls in love with Vera, an aristocrat with revolutionary tendencies, and, overcoming traditional prejudices about religion, it looks as if they will happily marry, enabled by wages from German conductor Herr Pappelmeister, who leaves Davenport's service in order to set up his own orchestra to play David's newly composed celebratory symphony of America. However, the straightforward narrative is constantly (and painfully) interrupted by events that occurred years before in a far-off land, namely Russia.

Europe is presented as a continent torn apart by historical hatred, prejudice and violence. David's condemnation of the fashionable audiences of New York sums it up: 'they look back on Europe as a pleasure ground, a palace of art – but I know it is sodden with blood, red with bestial massacres.'[145] David has first-hand experience of such things, escaping the Russian pogroms in his hometown of Kishineff as a child, an event which led to the violent death of his entire family. David's hatred of Russia is augmented by Vera's story; her revolutionary politics have led to her imprisonment in Siberia (from which she later escaped), much to the embarrassed anger of her reactionary Baron father and the new Baroness. But it is Russia's hatred of Jews that forms the central catalyst for the storyline. This is embodied in the character of the Baroness whose violently anti-Semitic opinions are encouraged by Davenport who refuses to have

Jews in his orchestra. In a cruel twist, it turns out that Vera's father, the Baron, was responsible for the murders of David's family. This trauma divides the lovers as David cannot purge the images from his mind. Russia here is a ghost, inescapably haunting David and Vera. The final scenes see Herr Pappelmeister's successful rendering of David's composition and the reuniting of the lovers as they decide that events in Russia will not separate them in America. Indeed, Europe is entirely rejected by David in his final speech: 'Ah Vera, what is the glory of Rome and Jerusalem where all nations and races come to worship and look back, compared with the glory of America, where all races and nations come to labour and look forward.'

Given the history of Zangwill's parents, the play can be understood biographically. But it becomes particularly disturbing when read alongside the appendices from the published edition. Appendix A provides statistics about the different people groups entering the USA in 1913. The variety of cultures and ethnicities taps into the positivity of David's melting-pot image. Appendix B interrupts this hopeful depiction of US nationhood by detailing the real events of the Russian pogroms. Confirming that the Kisheneff massacre actually occurred, it is an intensely graphic, first-hand account of the mutilations, rapes and executions of the Jewish population. The nurse telling this story affirms her intention: 'this story is told in the hope that Americans will appreciate the safety and freedom in which they live and that they will help others to gain that freedom.'[146] In addition, the appendices include the story of Daniel Melsa, a real-life violinist whose story mirrors David's, and a full description of the play's intention from Zangwill. In the latter, Zangwill refers to the English stage as 'sluggish and sensual', unwilling to engage with contemporary issues through theatre.[147] The decision to perform *The Melting Pot* first in Washington seemed to reflect as much on the moribund escapism of the British theatrical scene as on its relevance to an American audience.

Zangwill's play is predominantly naturalistic in design. However, there are interruptions to this narrative structure. First, the final scene seems almost symbolist with an effervescent sunset accompanying David's cry ('*prophetically exalted by the spectacle*'): 'it is the fires of God round His crucible'.[148] Second, while Mendel is trying to earnestly talk to David about his future in act 2, in another room his Grandmother and Kathleen are celebrating Purim by wearing '*grotesque false noses*'.[149] It is a metatheatrical ritual. At the start of the play the Grandmother's religion frustrates the Irish Catholic maid. However, as she puts on the Purim mask/nose,

Kathleen self-identifies with her Jewish family. In response to Davenport's question, 'why do you want a nose like that?' Kathleen replies, 'Bekaz we're Hebrews'.[150] This is not a mocking of religion, nor a troubling, insensitive appropriation of another's culture.[151] Rather Kathleen's move from aggressive anti-Semitism to willing engager with Jewish culture confirms Zangwill's utopian view of the melting pot. The literal 'putting on' of another's culture enables Kathleen to empathise with and relate to those she, until this scene, did not understand. This masking turns Kathleen and the Grandmother into characters who would not have looked out of place in GOSET's more experimental, folklore-inflected productions.

Dean was not alone in his admiration of GOSET. In 1933 director and producer André van Gyseghem arrived in the Soviet Union, repeating his journey four times during the 1930s, in the first instance as a member of the Workers' Theatre Movement delegation to the Moscow Olympiad and, during the final trip, staying for a year to work at the Realistic Theatre under Nikolai Okhlopkov. His 1943 book *Theatre in Soviet Russia* provides studies of Meyerhold, the MAT, the Kamerny, Vakhtangov, Oklopkhov and others. Van Gyseghem alludes to his first-hand experiences throughout the book but, towards the end, confirms the importance of his perspective:

> I do claim, however, to have given a picture of the Soviet theatre as seen in Moscow by a theatre worker from another country, and as such being a part which is fairly representative of the whole.[152]

Embedded in van Gyseghem's explanation of his role here is his acknowledgement of *Theatre in Soviet Russia* as an objective book, written by a figure outside the political and cultural biases inherent in 1940s Russia. By this time, many of the figures and ideas mentioned in his book had been censored or erased. This is also a wartime book, of course, and his final entreaty, 'it is to be hoped that, when victory is won, our two great countries will meet on the cultural as well as on the economic field', chimes with Priestley's conviction, and reveals his ongoing commitment to transnational artistic exchange as well as (reading between the lines) his leftist political leanings.[153]

Due to his diverse experiences and interests van Gyseghem reappears frequently in *Migrating Modernist Performance* as one of the primary conduits of Russian theatre techniques to 1930s/40s British theatre-makers. Van Gyseghem and Dean approached the theatre in fundamentally different ways, the former as part of what were distinctly workers' theatre traditions, the latter as a West End impresario. Yet both emanated from acting backgrounds and both enthusiastically turned to film as the century progressed. In fact, the two certainly knew one another with van Gyseghem acting in Dean's *The Constant Nymph* in the late 1920s.

Van Gyseghem's discussion of GOSET focuses on the same productions documented in Dean's archive. But he then moves the story on to the late 1920s and beyond to when Granovsky left the company and, further, to their 1935 version of *King Lear*, a production van Gyseghem almost certainly saw given the length and specificity of his description; he mentions both the 'great power' of S.M. Mikhoels as Lear and confesses 'for me the high spot of this production was the performance of V. Zouskine as the fool'.[154] In 1928 the company toured Western Europe to great acclaim. They played a number of cities in Germany (where their leader Granovsky defected) as well as Vienna and Paris.[155] Unfortunately, perhaps heeding Dean's warning, GOSET never made it to Britain. Benjamin Harshav sums up the reasons for their extraordinary popularity:

> For the left-leaning intellectuals, it represented the new culture created in the wake of the Russian Revolution as well as the miraculous rebirth of the Jews, the most oppressed nation in Russia.[156]

Evidently this theatre had inherent political attributes; it responded to the monumental political changes in Russia during the previous decade while also providing a voice for a voiceless people. In the next chapter we discover new ways traditionally marginalised people from Britain and Russia used theatre to incite political change.

## Notes

1. Virginia Woolf, 'The Russian Point of View' in *The Common Reader* (1925), Virginia Woolf, Chapter 16, accessed 25 August 2012, https://ebooks.adelaide.edu.au/w/woolf/virginia/w91c/chapter16.html.
2. Ibid.
3. See Clare Davison, *Translation as Collaboration: Virginia Woolf, Katherine Mansfield and S.S. Koteliansky* (Edinburgh UP, 2014), for a detailed examination of this fruitful alliance.
4. Woolf, 'The Russian Point of View', Chapter 16.
5. Pitches, *Russians in Britain*, 6.
6. Susan Jones, *Literature, Modernism and Dance* (Oxford UP, 2013), 307.

7. Carrie Preston, 'Introduction: Modernism and Dance' in *Modernist Cultures: Modernism and Dance*, 9.1 (2014): 1.
8. Lynn Garafola, *Diaghilev's Ballets Russes* (Oxford UP, 1993), vii.
9. Leonard Livak, *How It Was Done in Paris: Russian Émigré Literature and French Modernism* (Madison: Wisconsin UP, 2003), 42.
10. Juliet Bellow, *Modernism on Stage: The Ballets Russes and the Parisian Avant-Garde* (Farnham: Ashgate, 2013), 71.
11. William A. Everett, '*Chu Chin Chow* and Orientalist Musical Theatre in Britain during the First World War' in *Music and Orientalism in the British Empire, 1780s–1940s: Portrayal of the East*, eds Martin Clayton and Bennett Zon (Farnham: Ashgate, 2007), 277.
12. Garafola, *Diaghilev's Ballets Russes*, 96.
13. Nesta MacDonald, *Diaghilev Observed by Critics in England and the United States, 1911–1929* (New York: Dance Horizons, 1975), 255.
14. Osbert Sitwell, *Laughter in the Next Room* (London: MacMillan, 1949), 11.
15. Qtd in Jones, *Literature, Modernism and Dance*, 130.
16. Ellen Terry, *The Russian Ballet* (1913), accessed 24 April 2015, http://www.gutenberg.org/files/45299/45299-h/45299-h.htm.
17. Terry, *The Russian Ballet.*
18. Gareth Thomas, 'Modernism, Diaghilev and the Ballets Russes in London, 1911–1929' in *British Music and Modernism, 1895–1960*, ed. Matthew Riley (Farnham: Ashgate, 2010), 91.
19. Rebecca Beasley, 'Vortorussophilia' in *Vorticism: New Perspectives*, eds Mark Antiff and Scott W. Klein (Oxford UP, 2013), n16, 48. Beasley here makes a broader compelling argument about the parallels and connections between British vorticism and Russian art from El Lissitzky, Rodchenko and others. David Bomberg's 1919 book *The Russian Ballet*, a book which 'highlights the difference between Vorticism and the art associated with the Ballets Russes' is one case in point (Beasley in Antiff and Klein, *Vorticism*, 37).
20. David Chinitz, *T.S. Eliot and the Cultural Divide* (Chicago UP, 2003), 120.
21. Ctd in Richard Foulkes, *Repertory at the Royal* (Northampton: Northampton Repertory Players, 1992), 32.
22. Oliver Messel, *In the Theatre of Design*, ed. Thomas Messel (New York: Rizzoli, 2011), 58.
23. Garafola, *Diaghilev's Ballets Russes*, 216.
24. *The Times*, 16 March 1920, reprinted in *The Truth About the Russian Dancers*, J.M. Barrie (New York: Dance Perspectives, 1962), review section.
25. Barrie, *The Truth About the Russian Dancers*, 13.

26. Tamara Karsavina, 'Introduction' in *The Truth About the Russian Dancers*, Barrie, 7.
27. Barrie, *The Truth About the Russian Dancers*, 14.
28. Barrie, *The Truth About the Russian Dancers*, 28.
29. *Birmingham Daily Post*, 10 June 1914 in *Diaghilev Observed*, ed. MacDonald, 115.
30. *Liverpool Daily Post and Mercury*, 23 November 1920, in *Diaghilev Observed*, ed. MacDonald, 254.
31. Ramsay Burt suggests that British reviews of the Ballets Russes generally focused on the progressive aesthetics rather than Russian or Slavonic culture (Burt, '*Le Sacre du Printemps* in London: The Politics of Embodied Freedom in Early Modernist Dance and Suffragette Protest' in *Russia in Britain*, eds Beasley and Bullock, 131).
32. Marie Rambert, *Quicksilver* (London: MacMillan, 1972), 71.
33. Brigitte Kelly, '*Mim*': *A Personal Memoir of Marie Rambert* (Alton: Dance Books, 2009), 25.
34. Selma Landen Odom, 'The Dalcroze Method, Marie Rambert and *Le Sacre du printemps*', *Modernist Cultures*, 9.1 (2014): 13, 15.
35. De Valois and Rambert are regarded as the founders of English ballet. Perhaps understandably a great rivalry existed between them.
36. Ninette de Valois, *Come Dance With Me: A Memoir 1898–1956* (Dublin: Lilliput Press, 1992), 66.
37. De Valois, *Come Dance With Me*, 72.
38. De Valois, 'Some Problems of Ballet Today' (1955) in *An English Ballet*, ed. David Gayle (London: Oberon, 2011), 51.
39. Lynn Garafola, *Legacies of Twentieth-Century Dance* (Middletown: Wesleyan UP, 2005), 224.
40. Doone also choreographed de Valois in the 1932 *The Enchanted Grove*, which appeared at Sadler's Wells and the Savoy Theatre, London in 1932 with Scottish modernist Duncan Grant providing the scenery and costume (see 'Savoy Theatre', *The Times*, 8 June 1932, 12). Furthermore, performances of Auden and Isherwood's *Ascent of F6* and Eliot's *Murder in the Cathedral*, produced by Doone's Group Theatre, were presented at Ashley Duke's Mercury Theatre; Duke was Rambert's husband and the Mercury was the home of the Ballet Rambert (see Jones, *Literature, Modernism and Dance*, 352). Tangible connections between these former Ballets Russes members exist.
41. Michael Sidnell, *Dances of Death: The Group Theatre of London in the Thirties* (London: Faber and Faber, 1984), 44.
42. Sidnell, *Dances of Death*, 258.
43. W.H. Auden, 'The Dance of Death' in *Plays and Other Dramatic Writings 1928–1938*, W.H. Auden and Christopher Isherwood, ed. Edward Mendelson (Princeton UP, 1988), 107.

44. Sidnell, *Dances of Death*, 70.
45. Auden, 'The Dance of Death', 86.
46. Garafola, *Diaghilev's Ballets Russes*, 66.
47. Marvin Carlson, *The Haunted Stage: The Theatre as Memory Machine* (Michigan UP, 2003).
48. Edward Gordon Craig, *On the Art of the Theatre*, ed. Franc Chamberlain (London: Routledge, 2009), 70.
49. Susan Stanford Friedman, 'Bodies on the Move: A Poetics of Home and Diaspora', *Tulsa Studies in Women's Literature*, 23.2 (Fall 2004): 202.
50. John Balance, 'Kleptomania, or the Russian Ballet', *The Mask*, IV: 2 (October 1911) in *Craig on Movement and Dance*, Edward Gordon Craig, ed. Arnold Rood (London: Dance Books, 1977), 80, 84.
51. John Semov, 'The Russian Ballet, Nijinski's Acknowledgement', *The Mask*, V:3 (January 1913) in *Craig on Movement and Dance*, Craig, 90.
52. EC, 'Prelude', *The Mask*, VI:1 (July 1913) in *Craig on Movement and Dance*, Craig, 92.
53. Edward Gordon Craig, 'A Letter of Recent Travels through Europe', *The Mask*, XV:2 (April–May 1929) in *Craig on Movement and Dance*, Craig, 163.
54. George Banks, 'Petrouchka – the Russian Ballet', *Rhythm* 6 (July 1912): 58.
55. D.S. Mirsky, *Jane Harrison and Russia* (Cambridge: W. Heffer and Sons, 1930), 9.
56. Mirsky, *Jane Harrison*, 7.
57. Jane Harrison, *Reminiscences of a Student's Life* (London: Hogarth Press, 1925), 78–9.
58. Olga Taxidou, *Modernism and Performance: Jarry to Brecht* (Basingstoke: Palgrave MacMillan, 2007), 152.
59. Catriona Kelly, 'The Origins of the Russian Theatre' in *A History of Russian Theatre*, eds Robert Leach and Victor Borovsky (Cambridge UP, 1999), 34.
60. Alexandra Smith, 'Jane Harrison As an Interpreter of Russian Culture in the 1910s–1920s' in *A People Passing Rude*, ed. Cross, 178.
61. Harrison, *Reminiscences*, 77.
62. Jane Harrison, *Ancient Art and Ritual* (Oxford UP, 1948), 208.
63. De Valois, *Come Dance With Me*, 64.
64. Taylor, *The Archive and the Repertoire*, 3.
65. Michelle Clayton, 'Modernism's Moving Bodies', *Modernist Cultures*, 9.1 (2014): 29.
66. Basil Dean, *Mind's Eye: An Autobiography 1927–1932* (London: Hutchinson, 1973), 181.
67. Basil Dean, *The Theatre at War* (London: Harrap, 1956), 59.

68. Basil Dean, letter to Michael Lykiardopulos, March 1913, DEA 1/2/1125–6, Basil Dean Archive.
69. Michael Lykiardopulos, letter to Basil Dean, March 1913, DEA 1/1/2429–30, Basil Dean Archive.
70. Basil Dean, letter to Mr [Dmitri] Bogomoloff, January 1926, DEA 1/2/210, Basil Dean Archive.
71. Dean, *Seven Ages: An Autobiography 1888–1927*, 290.
72. Basil Dean, 'Roast Beef and Caviare [sic]: Reflections Upon the Theatre in England and Russia', *Soviet Union Monthly* (May 1926): 90–1, DEA 12/1/31, Basil Dean Archive. Dean's later description of his Russian trip in his 1970 autobiography *Seven Ages: 1888–1927* is far less positive and, while he still uses the word 'vitality', he tempers this by claiming that the Russian theatre he experienced 'failed to inspire any drama of international consequence' (297). This seems rather unfair and perhaps says more about Dean's late 1960s context than it does about his contemporaneous impressions of his Russian trip as documented in his archive.
73. Basil Dean, 'The Actor and His Workshop' (lecture presented at the Victoria and Albert Museum during the International Theatre Exhibition, July 1922), DEA 12/1/16, Basil Dean Archive.
74. George Harris, *George W. Harris* (London: Nisbet, 1930), 20.
75. Harris, *George W. Harris*, 21.
76. Harris, *George W. Harris*, plate 35.
77. Dean, *Mind's Eye*, 56.
78. Alexander Tairov, 'Speech to the Kamerny Theater Troupe', 2 October 1932 in *The Soviet Theater*, eds Senelick and Ostrovsky, 340.
79. Local government committees set up by the Tsar to initiate liberal reforms.
80. Winifred Stephens, ed., *The Soul of Russia* (London: MacMillan, 1916), frontispiece. Only a year after the publication of this book Prince Lvov became head of the Provisional Government, resigning just months later as first Alexander Kerensky and later the Bolsheviks took power.
81. Rebecca Beasley and Philip Ross Bullock, 'Introduction: The Illusion of Transparency', *Translation and Literature*, 20 (2011): 292.
82. Caroline Maclean, *The Vogue for Russia: Modernism and the Unseen in Britain, 1900–1930* (Edinburgh UP, 2015), 3.
83. G.K. Chesterton, 'The English Blunder about Russia' in *The Soul of Russia*, Stephens, 4.
84. Chesterton, 'The English Blunder about Russia', in *The Soul of Russia*, Stephens, 7.
85. Robert Leach, *Vsevolod Meyerhold* (Cambridge UP, 1999), 101.
86. Konstantin Rudnitsky, *Russian and Soviet Theatre: Tradition and the Avant-garde* (London: Thames and Hudson, 2000), 136, 154.
87. Nick Worrall, *Modernism to Realism on the Soviet Stage: Tairov, Vakhtangov, Okhlopkov* (Cambridge UP, 1989), 41.

88. J.B. Priestley, *Russian Journey* (London: Writers Group of the Society for Cultural Relations with the U.S.S.R., 1946), 3.
89. Priestley, *Russian Journey*, 32.
90. Priestley, *Russian Journey*, 19.
91. Priestley, *Russian Journey*, 36–7.
92. J.B. Priestley, 'An Inspector Calls' in *Time and the Conways and Other Plays*, J.B. Priestley (London: Penguin, 1987), 207.
93. Maggie Gale, '*An Inspector Calls* and Calls Again: Nation, Community and the Individual in J.B. Priestley's Play' in *Theatre and National Identity: Re-Imagining Conceptions of Nation*, ed. Nadine Holdsworth (London: Routledge, 2014), 103.
94. Maggie Gale, *J.B. Priestley* (London: Routledge, 2008), 145.
95. Y.A. Golovashenko, *Rezhissyorskoe iskusstvo Tairova* (Moscow: Iskusstvo, 1970), ctd in *J.B. Priestley*, Gale, 147.
96. Alexander Tairov, *Notes of a Director*, trans. William Kuhlke (Florida: Miami UP, 1969), 65.
97. Worrall, *Modernism to Realism on the Soviet Stage*, 35.
98. Alexander Tairov, *Das Entfesselte Theater* (Potsdam: Gustav Kiepenheuer Verlag, 1923), 50.
99. Tairov, *Notes of a Director*, 82.
100. Tairov, *Notes of a Director*, 76.
101. Tairov, *Notes of a Director*, 58.
102. Tairov, *Notes of a Director*, 124.
103. Rudnitsky, *Russian and Soviet Theatre*, 17.
104. Photograph of Alexander Tairov, DEA 9/3/57, Basil Dean Archive.
105. Basil Dean, 'The Machine Artists: Notes on a Recent Visit to the Russian Theatre', *The Sphere*, 28 August 1926, DEA 12/1/35, Basil Dean Archive, 3.
106. Basil Dean, 'My Aims in the Theatre', November 1928, DEA 12/1/45, Basil Dean Archive.
107. Alexander Wicksteed, *Life Under the Soviets* (London: John Lane, 1928), 123–4.
108. Dean, 'Roast Beef and Caviare'.
109. Basil Dean, 'Interview with Hubert Griffith', 25 October 1938, DEA 12/1/80, Basil Dean Archive.
110. I have not yet found any evidence that this suggestion was taken forward, even in the rehearsal studio.
111. Basil Dean, letter to Madame Boleslavsky, 15 February 1927, DEA 1/2/215, Basil Dean Archive.
112. Basil Dean and Margaret Kennedy, *The Constant Nymph*, prompt copy, DEA 6/8, Basil Dean Archive, 3.
113. *Tatler*, 10 November 1937; *The Stage*, 10 October 1937, Cadbury Research Library, University of Birmingham, MS38/594.
114. Beachcomber, 'Russian Pickwick', *Daily Express*, 17 December 1928, 10.

115. Laurence Senelick, *Historical Dictionary of Russian Theater* (Lanham: Scarecrow), 144.
116. Nikolai Gorchakov, *The Theater in Soviet Russia* (New York: Columbia UP, 1957), '338 The Second Decade', accessed 17 June 2015, https://archive.org/stream/theaterinsovietr002155mbp/theaterinsovietr002155mbp_djvu.txt.
117. Arthur Ransome, *Six Weeks in Russia in 1919* (London: George Allen and Unwin, 1919), 60. Thanks to Edward Braun for alerting me to Ransome's journeys and writings.
118. Basil Dean, 'Address to Nottinghamshire Playgoers Club', January 1926, DEA 12/1/28, Basil Dean Archive.
119. Rudnitsky, *Russian and Soviet Theatre: Tradition and the Avant-Garde*, 236–7.
120. Madame Boleslawskaia, letter to Basil Dean, 15 October 1926, DEA 1/1/327–335, Basil Dean Archive.
121. Eugene O'Neill, letter to *New York Herald*, 30 June 1930 in *The Unknown O'Neill: Unpublished or Unfamiliar Writings of Eugene O'Neill*, Eugene O'Neill (Yale UP, 1988), 418.
122. Katherine Weinstein, 'Towards a Theatre of Creative Imagination: Alexander Tairov's O'Neill Productions', *Eugene O'Neill Review*, 22.1/2 (Spring/Fall 1998): 161.
123. Photograph of *The Hairy Ape* (1926), Basil Dean Archive, 9/3/63.
124. Eugene O'Neill, *Ah Wilderness! and Other Plays* (Harmondsworth: Penguin, 1966).
125. Dean, *Seven Ages: 1888–1927*, 252–3.
126. Dean, 'The Machine Artists', 2.
127. Walter Benjamin, 'Moscow Diary [extract]', 30 December 1926, in *The Soviet Theater*, eds Senelick and Ostrovsky, 286.
128. Basil Dean, *Programmes*, DEA 10/6/119, Basil Dean Archive.
129. Norman Marshall, *The Other Theatre* (London: John Lehmann, 1947), 13.
130. Senelick, *Historical Dictionary of Russian Theater*, 66.
131. Basil Dean, letter to Fenner Brockway, 11 March 1929, Basil Dean Archive, 1/2/297–315.
132. Steve Nicholson, *The Censorship of British Drama 1900–1968, Volume 2 1933–1952* (Exeter UP, 2005), 90.
133. Dean, 'The Machine Artists', 3.
134. Alexei Granovsky, letter to Basil Dean, 13 November 1926, Basil Dean Archive, John Rylands Library, DEA 1/1/995–1036. As far as I can tell this tour never took place.
135. Basil Dean, letter to Alexei Granovsky, 10 January 1927, Basil Dean Archive, 1/2/738.
136. Photograph of *Night in the Old Market* (1925), Basil Dean Archive, 9/3/69.

137. Alexis Granovsky and Joseph Gordon, 'Night in the Old Market: A Mystery in Two Parts after I. L. Peretz', *The Drama Review*, 29.4 (Winter 1985): 98.
138. Mel Gordon, 'Granovsky's Tragic Carnival: Night in the Old Market', *The Drama Review*, 29.4 (Winter 1985): 93.
139. David Mazower, *Yiddish Theatre in London* (London: The Jewish Museum, 1987), 11.
140. 'Yiddish Theatre in London', Jewish Museum London, accessed 6 June 2015, http://exhibitions.europeana.eu/exhibits/show/yiddish-theatre-en/theatres/hebrew-dramatic-club.
141. Israel Zangwill and Edna Nahshon, *From the Ghetto to the Melting Pot: Israel Zangwill's Jewish Plays* (Detroit: Wayne State UP, 2006), 5.
142. Zangwill and Nahshon, *From the Ghetto to the Melting Pot*, 16, 18.
143. Israel Zangwill, 'The Doom of Drama', *Canadian Jewish Chronicle* (25 June 1920): 2.
144. Ibid.
145. Israel Zangwill, *The Melting-Pot*, act 2, accessed 17 June 2015, http://www.gutenberg.org/files/23893/23893-h/23893-h.htm.
146. Zangwill, *The Melting-Pot*, appendix B.
147. Zangwill, *The Melting-Pot*, appendix E.
148. Zangwill, *The Melting-Pot*, act 4.
149. Zangwill, *The Melting-Pot*, act 2.
150. Zangwill, *The Melting-Pot*, act 2.
151. For more on the non-Jewish playing Jews see Ted Merwin, 'Jew-Face: Non-Jews Playing Jews on the American Stage', *Cultural and Social History: The Journal of the Social History Society*, 4.2 (2007): 215–33.
152. André Van Gyseghem, *Theatre in Soviet Russia* (London: Faber and Faber, 1943), 210.
153. Ibid.
154. Van Gyseghem, *Theatre in Soviet Russia*, 176.
155. Benjamin Harshav, *The Moscow Yiddish Theater: Art of Stage in the Time of Revolution* (Yale UP, 2008), 34.
156. Harshav, *The Moscow Yiddish Theater*, 5.

CHAPTER 2

# Agitprop and Pageantry: Political Alliances and Cultural Tensions

21 February 1943. Royal Albert Hall, London. Only months after the Russian Army's decisive victory over Nazi Germany at the Battle of Stalingrad, the British government decided to organise a large-scale performance event as part of Red Army Day.[1] It honoured the Russian army and its victories (in the current conflict and at various historical junctures), encouraging British audiences and participators to support their Russian comrades. The performance met with general acclaim, with colourful socialite Edwina Mountbatten claiming 'it was a magnificent sight and all present were very thrilled and stirred'.[2] Despite some reticence over the plodding script, *The Times* was equally effusive, declaring that 'as a spectacle, *Salute to the Red Army* was a triumph'.[3] It was performed as part of the ENSA (Entertainments National Service Association) project nearly 20 years after its organiser, Basil Dean, had returned from his stimulating trip to Russia. In April 1939 Dean announced, 'we must dedicate the Theatre to the National Service without delay';[4] *Salute to the Red Army* was a vital part of this venture.

Using this under-researched performance as a tricky catalyst, this chapter claims a British tradition of Russian-influenced agitprop theatre, a form with distinctive objectives, both political and aesthetic. What proves particularly interesting is not the blind acceptance of Soviet agitprop techniques but, rather, the particular ways they were reimagined in a British context. Left-leaning practitioners and collectives, in particular, seemed to actively merge ideas and issues from overseas with local themes and traditions; sometimes these British performances were in keeping with official

 
C. Warden, *Migrating Modernist Performance*,
DOI 10.1057/978-1-137-38570-3_3

proclamations from the Soviet government; sometimes they seemed to counteract those sanctioned narratives. They existed within a loose worldwide alliance of agitprop companies, many of which looked to Russia for inspiration while flavouring their performances with national concerns and aesthetics. What transpires is not an agitprop duologue between Russia and Britain, but a transnational dialogue embedded in the movement of individuals and companies across geographical borders.

British responses to Russian agitprop in many ways reflected Susan Stanford Friedman's recent notion of circulatory global modernisms, where through a 'collision of differences [appears] resultant hybridization through processes of cultural mimesis'.[5] Friedman's theoretical construct permits us to uncover not only those instances where Russian agitprop appeared in Britain but, arguably more interestingly, moments of emerging hybridised, migratory models of agitprop experiment. Many of these composite performances contribute to the long history of British pageantry or British working-class entertainment as much as they do to the transnational growth of twentieth-century agitprop. This chapter argues that these innovative, exciting, though often aesthetically awkward, performances exemplified changing artistic fashions and the connections (and indeed disconnections) between British socialist theatre and post-Revolutionary Soviet dramatic experimentation. The history of Russian-influenced political theatre in Britain is a tale of artistic inspiration and methodological suspicion, of political wranglings, of small-scale workers' theatre groups and government-funded celebrations, of cross-disciplinary vibrancy and heartfelt sloganeering.

British responses to agitprop were bound up with broader, universal aesthetic questions: what is agitprop – is it a theatrical event or a political rally? engaging art or drab didacticism? innovative performance or, as E.E. Cummings described his experience of Proletcult productions during his 1931 trip to Russia, 'playless'?[6] Such concerns perturbed theatrical visitors to Russia as much as they did local audiences of British agitprop. Dean's response to the Soviet political theatre scene perfectly illustrates the equivocations of many of the other travellers. Looking at his own national theatre, Dean lamented, 'drama has been relegated to an inferior position amongst the minor amusements of the people'.[7] Yet, he was also concerned about what he saw as the degrading of artistic creativity in favour of polemics. In fact, his recollections about his 1926 trip exhibit both a joyous appreciation and a lingering anxiety about the new revolutionary Soviet theatre:

> Although it must be irksome to artists to find themselves turned into proselytes of a new faith, although they may protest that this is an arbitrary interference with their normal artistic life, yet there is something inspiriting in this call to the theatre to take up the responsibilities long since neglected or forgotten.[8]

Despite Dean's reticence, he remained an advocate of Soviet theatre, imagining it as a catalyst for worldwide theatrical renewal:

> Out of the call of Russia that her theatre shall be a living part of the national entity spring the progressive desire and present the vitality of her stage.[9]

The intersections of nationality, performance and revolutionary politics Dean alludes to form the complex bedrock of this chapter.

Other migratory figures were less complimentary about 'propagandist theatre' than Dean. One such was journalist, playwright, actress and prominent feminist Cicely Hamilton. Given her theatrical background, her book, *Modern Russia as Seen By an Englishwoman* (1934), written after her 1933 trip to the Soviet Union, unsurprisingly includes two full chapters entitled 'Matters Theatrical'. She travelled to Russia seven years after Dean, and the differences between their perceptions of the Soviet political stage reveal the dramatic change that occurred in Russian theatre in 1932/3, an event this chapter (and the next chapter) explores in detail:

> If the fanaticism of those days could have had its way, the theatre would soon have been reduced to the dimensions of a platform whereon the Revolution was lauded and its enemies denounced; but the theatre was stronger than fanaticism and came through the contest alive.[10]

She dismissed the egalitarian nature of agitprop as she felt the central communistic idea of total equality engendered poor art: 'when it comes to singing and dancing and acting, one man is not as good as another.'[11] Rather, as the popularity of agitprop in Russia significantly diminished, she celebrated the survival of theatre. Hamilton wrote notably politically engaged plays such as *How the Vote Was Won* and *A Pageant of Great Women* (both 1909) and was an ardent proponent of women's rights, a member of both the Actresses' Franchise League and the Women Writers' Suffrage League. So she clearly did not believe in art for art's sake; on the contrary she comprehended the benefits of using drama to further a political cause. Her objection to agitprop, then, seemed to lie in its aesthetics rather than its politics *per se*. But, as this chapter illustrates, not all British travellers agreed with Hamilton's assessment; in fact, many, particularly those who witnessed the phenomenon first-hand, regarded agitprop techniques as among the most vibrant, dynamic and transferable of the Russian theatrical experiments.

## The Workers' Theatre Movement in Context: Worldwide Agitprop and the Moscow Olympiad

'Agitprop' linguistically juxtaposes 'agitation' and 'propaganda' to create a form that seeks to galvanise its spectators and provide information: antagonise and educate. Desperate to engage politically with a partially illiterate population, participants in early to mid twentieth-century Russia understood that 'duty coincided with expedience in the spreading of news and political ideas'.[12] This sort of urgency is the defining factor of the experiments mentioned in this chapter. While the rise of agitprop responded to Bolshevik demands for a new type of theatre, it emerged (and continues to emerge) in countries around the world, some influenced by their Russian comrades, others simply responding to this feeling of political urgency.

Indeed, Russian and British agitprop did not exist in a vacuum; rather, of all the techniques, movements and theatrical ideas discussed in this book, agitprop (in a variety of guises) was arguably the most global. The success of the International Union of Workers' Theatres illustrated agitprop's popularity with 'committed memberships from Czechoslovakia, Belgium, Bulgaria, Poland, Japan and other countries'.[13] While the agitprop groups in most of these countries certainly looked to Russia, they remained remarkably local in their thematic concerns. A 1932 appeal from the Proletarian Theatre of Japan, for example, discussed the arrests of local comrades and organising bodies, while also crusading against international enemies: 'down with the intervention against the Soviet Union.'[14] This balance between local and international, focusing on specific proletariat conditions and potential global revolution, remained a vital characteristic of worldwide agitprop performance. Understanding the emergence of agitprop as an international movement rather than a centre-to-edge artistic hierarchy engenders a more fluid migratory network of workers' theatres. In a sense, the internationalism of the agitprop experiment confirms Stanford Friedman's conception of a 'transculturation of global modernisms [that] testifies to how local modernisms are not isolated, but come into being through a poetics of relation on a planetary landscape'.[15]

In Russia, the self-proclaimed Blue Blouse groups, so called because of their working-clothes 'costumes', led the post-Revolutionary turn to agitprop. Combining agitational sketches and local traditions of oral performance, the Blue Blouse troupes achieved significant success with their brand of gymnastic-infused, politically educational performances.[16] British theatre critic and author Huntly Carter witnessed the Russian Blue Blouse groups during his extensive travels throughout Russia in the 1920s and described them thus:

> Troupes of about twenty men and women, comprising actors and actresses who are also acrobats, athletes, dancers and musicians visit the factory and other theatrical clubs where they give performances free and without assistance from the Government. Their work is in intention social and political.[17]

Carter was struck by the skills of the performers, the accessibility of the performance and its partisan objectives.

Another British traveller, director and, later, academic Herbert Marshall, described the successes of another Russian agitprop collective, TRAM (the Theatre of Young Workers) in his 1977 *The Pictorial History of the Russian Theatre*:

> The drama was broken down into numerous episodes, constantly flowing and changing, using what is known in cinema as the 'mix'. They used numerous light changes, employing symbolic colors, and the actors would suddenly address the audience, thus enlisting its participation. The TRAM collective even tried to interpret the principles of dialectical materialism through the productions.[18]

To illustrate his account he included pictures of two TRAM productions: *The Days Are Smelting*, focusing on youth in industrialised Russia, and *Bell-Bottom Reverie*, dramatising the Five Year Plan (both 1929). The actors in the former exhibit agitprop's interest in gymnastics with figures throwing balls across a bare stage. In the background the two married young communists, trapped between their decision to have a family and their responsibilities to the Young Communist Collective, are cast in long, dark shadows. In the photograph of *Bell-Bottom Reverie*, performers dressed in typical working clothes pass metal machinery pieces around, drawing attention to agitprop's focus on the industrial.[19] Marshall's description of TRAM's project points to both the aesthetic qualities and particular political intentions of their theatre. It also details some of agitprop's most prominent characteristics: fragmented narrative, direct connection between 'actor' and audience, and the tackling of political issues that might not initially appear to provide particularly inspiring theatrical source material.

Concurrent with this growing network of global agitprop experimentation, a similar movement arose in Britain. British agitprop achieved particular success in the 1920s and early 1930s, buoyed by the successful establishment of the Soviet Union. Thematically it responded to wars (and the threat of wars), the rise of more reactionary or fascistic movements, and ongoing economic crises which, agitprop groups hoped, would cause the proletariat to question the tenets of society and its capitalist system of rich owners and poverty-stricken workers. Importantly, British agitprop groups did not simply jump on a transnational bandwagon; rather, 'British Movements sprang out of a long tradition of radical theatre'.[20] Indeed, one can see earlier incarnations of this politically engaged, slogan-based theatre in the dramatic work of the Luddites, Chartists and Clarion Clubs. While unpicking this genealogy is beyond the remits of *Migrating Modernist Performance*, it is vital to acknowledge that British agitprop was neither wholly dependent on overseas influences nor disconnected from its own national history.

With origins in an established, fruitful background of radical theatre practice, Britain's developing workers' theatre scene began in earnest with the establishment of the Workers' Theatre Movement (WTM), a collection of groups from across the British Isles. Throughout the early decades of the twentieth century, many left-leaning theatre groups appeared, with *Labour Leader* stating in 1922:

> There seems to be a great rush of organizations broadcasting their propaganda by means of plays and sketches and some branches of the ILP [Independent Labour Party] are enthusiastically entering into the production of socialist pieces. People come to witness a play when they would never dream of coming to listen to a speaker.[21]

By 1926, in the wake of the General Strike, Tom Thomas (stockbroker's clerk and committed communist) had set up the Hackney Labour Group (later the Hackney People's Players). Thomas's connection with the WTM began in 1927 when he watched a WTM show, which he dismissed as unsophisticated. However, he nevertheless affiliated his group to the movement in the hope that he could lead it in more profitable directions.[22] Over the next six years, the WTM became more intentional in its performances and more aware of the audience's requirements. Despite its agitprop-led aesthetic, the WTM's canon of work was more varied than might be imagined with plays by Eugene O'Neill and Henrik Ibsen jostling with more declamatory pieces. In fact, the WTM's most famous and influential production was arguably Thomas's remarkably successful (and predominantly realist) 1927 *The Ragged Trousered Philanthropists*, which played 30 times and spawned later productions.[23] However, agitprop rather than longer, scripted plays became the WTM's primary mode. Even in *The Ragged Trousered Philanthropists*, which, it must be remembered, is a theatrical reworking of that most traditionally naturalistic of forms, the novel, Thomas could not resist a nod to agitprop aesthetics, concluding the play with Philpot addressing the audience: 'Those in favour [of developing a union] – all of yer – shout "AYE" – let it go. One... Two... Three... (*And the curtain should quickly descend to a great shout of "AYE" from the audience*).'[24]

One of the most prominent and influential companies associated with the WTM (although the association was not always an amicable one) was the Salford Red Megaphones founded by Ewan MacColl (then Jimmie Miller) and later joined by Joan Littlewood among others. One can link Littlewood's enormously successful later company, Theatre Workshop, back to the rather rough-and-ready experiments of the Red Megaphones. Like many other WTM groups, the Red Megaphones took to agitprop on account of its immediacy and didacticism. Although his later plays experimented with expressionist poetry and innovative lighting and staging, at this early stage in his career MacColl placed far greater emphasis on politics than aesthetics. In a statement that would have made Cicely Hamilton shudder MacColl enthused, 'we are, we said, the propertyless theatre of the propertyless class so to hell with art, let's get on with the job'.[25] In his reminiscences (which often slip between fascinating historical biography and equally fascinating embellished stories) MacColl recalled meeting a representative from the Communist Youth League who had travelled from Russia to Manchester, the Red Megaphones' home city:

> I remember her telling me about these groups she'd seen in Germany and Czechoslovakia. She told me what they did, how they had megaphones and how they would appear on a street and do a very short political piece. This stuck in my mind as something absolutely marvellous.[26]

Later MacColl and Littlewood planned a trip to Russia to train at the Moscow School of Cinema and Theatre. Despite many eventful months waiting in London, the trip never occurred and the two went back to Manchester to bring a new group of actors together, nonetheless employing the techniques of Stanislavsky, Vakhtangov and Meyerhold.[27]

But Comrade Ludmilla's promotion of agitprop points to another vital aspect of British leftist theatre: despite the influence of the Soviet movement, British groups tended to look far more to Germany than to Russia. Certainly, in terms of playscripts, German writers, particularly Ernst Toller, appeared with regularity in workers' theatre seasons across the country. But it was similarly the case with agitprop experimentation. The 'Workers' Theatre Movement Monthly Bulletin' of December 1932 explains the high regard the British groups had for their German counterparts:

> The German comrades have had considerable [sic] more experience than the workers' theatre groups here, and it may therefore be worthwhile to see how they go about things… Besides songs, the German troupes use a lot of action in their short and snappy sketches.[28]

This article appeared just a year after Thomas and a London-based contingent travelled to Germany to watch the work of the workers' theatre groups. The trip had a far-reaching influence over WTM's aesthetic, as Thomas reflected:

> When we got back to England we decided to try it, building up a show from different items, and working to break down the barriers between players and audience… Instead of a theatre of illusion ours was to be a theatre of ideas, with people dressed up in ordinary working clothes. No costumes, no props, no special stage.[29]

Thomas here firmly connects his agitprop theatrical experiments with his trip to Germany. Performances emerged from migratory experiences, but in this case from Germany, not Russia.

Why did British agitprop practitioners look to Germany rather than Russia? I suggest that, for socialist Britons, Russia represented a utopian vision of the future, a longed-for conclusion to their struggles. Germany, by contrast, was similar (though by no means the same) as Britain. Despite the differing results of the First World War, the workers' theatres in these two countries struck an accord. Neither performed in the communist idyll they wanted. Britain had a constitutional monarchy inflected with capitalist (and indeed more ancient) hierarchical systems, while the German Kaiser had abdicated after the humiliation of First World War defeat, to be replaced by the shaky Weimar Republic. Despite Marx's belief that Britain and Germany provided the best conditions for communist revolution, the struggle had, so far, been fruitless. These political issues united the workers' theatres in these countries and meant that the WTM looked in more practical ways to Germany than Russia. Clearly Russia provided the model, but in political (and hence theatrical) terms German practitioners remained the WTM's closest allies.

In *The Workers' Theatre* (1930), future Labour MP Ness Edwards provided a manifesto document that chimed with proclamations made by Russian, German and British agitprop groups and practitioners. '*The Workers' Drama is an agitational force*,' he claimed. 'It is propaganda by a dramatization of facts; only the projected solutions are debatable or represent opinions'.[30] To substantiate his conclusion he investigated the difference between pre- and post-Revolutionary Russian theatre through a satirical sketch by Huntly Carter who, just a year earlier, had published *The New Spirit in Russian Theatre, 1917–1928*, a book that details the profound post-Revolutionary changes on the Russian stage. The sketch begins with the '*Playwrights of Gloom of the pre-war period in Russia*' crowded into a dreary farmhouse room with the weather crashing outside in overblown pathetic fallacy. During the scene each playwright commits suicide in a variety of imaginative ways: shooting, stabbing, taking poison, hanging and (finding the well dry) gassing in an oven. The second scene takes place on the deck of a Soviet boat where workers are singing, dancing and discussing politics: '*The scene ends with an assertion of vigorous life in contrast to the death-like atmosphere of the first scene.*'[31] Carter's sketch of contrasts, Edwards suggests, exemplifies the dramatic transformation in Russian theatre – from dismal bourgeois realism to vibrant working-class gaiety. Framed with Edwards's ardent advocacy of workers' theatre, the play suggests that a similar aesthetic change could be engendered on the British stage.

In *The New Spirit in European Theatre, 1914–1924*, written five years before his sketch, Carter laid out his vision for a workers' theatre. It reflected the Russian model, while also exhibiting an almost wistful utopian approach:

> As for me, I dream of a regenerated theatre that shall come new-born from the workers. If I say so it is because I feel that the workers do not need

> regeneration, but are the regenerators. I feel that their awakening to the importance of the theatre to cultural life means that we are faced by a new body of pioneers of a new dramatic motive, a new technique, and a new moral outlook. It is to the workers we must look for a pure theatre, for they have no corrupt traditions to get rid of.[32]

Carter's hope for theatrical change in Britain seemed to rest on a worker-led revolution akin to the political changes in Russia in 1918. He imagined a working class, untainted by economy-driven, empty, bourgeois entertainment, as the catalyst for artistic revolution alongside the predicted rise of communism. This is theatre embedded in the nation's people.

In 1933, with such hopeful utopian aspirations ringing in their ears, a delegation from the WTM travelled to Russia to participate in the Moscow Olympiad, a celebration of revolutionary theatres from across the world. The final sequence of Thomas's 1932 sketch *Their Theatre and Ours*, performed to raise funds for the trip, clarifies the group's intentions. In typical agitprop style, the end scene is simply a collection of numbered declamatory voices, directly addressing the spectators:

> 2nd: There we will learn from our brother organizations in these other countries
> 3rd: And see the victories of the Soviet working people in the building up of socialism
> 4th: And the development of working-class dramatic Art.[33]

By attending the Olympiad, Thomas intended to witness theatrical work from the global network of agitprop collectives, but also specifically study Soviet society. Here Thomas acknowledges the need to connect with worldwide workers' theatres while identifying the characteristics of Russian theatre and society as the ultimate goal. Such an approach is similarly clear in the reflections of figures such as Polish immigrant Fegel Firestein, who arrived in London in the late twenties and was instrumental in the Yiddish theatre groups explored in the previous chapter. She based her deliberations on her knowledge of the Russian stage and her belief in a workers' theatre that transcended national borders:

> Because the revolution was started already, and they wanted the people to get cultivated… to look after the revolution, and that's why you need workers' theatre and workers' movements.[34]

Such 'cultivation' of radical politics could be engendered, Firestein concluded, by an animated, dynamic global workers' theatre. The aim of events like the Moscow Olympiad was to generate such transnational awareness and cooperation.

The Red Players group from Lewisham won a national contest to attend the 1933 Moscow Olympiad. Eventually (presumably due to issues with finance and personnel) the group only took a few members, supplemented by others from the WTM; the diverse collective took on the name the Red Front Troupe.[35] On the boat were two leaders of British leftist theatre: Charlie Mann and André van Gyseghem. These two figures harboured quite different ideas about the effectiveness of workers' theatre techniques. The former focused on drill and regimented movement; he clarified his practices in his 1933 *How to Produce Meerut*, written to share the best production methods for a popular WTM sketch about Indian workers. At the end of the sketch Mann demanded, 'as the bars crash, stand up in a straight line shoulder to shoulder for two or three seconds before going off'.[36] Van Gyseghem, by contrast, aspired to a more artistically mature theatre, moving from polemic sketches and declamation to characterisation and storytelling. The presence of these two figures on the boat nodded to a growing aesthetic divide in the WTM, one that, as I will go on to show, reflected changes in Soviet dramatic methods and eventually tore the WTM apart. In addition, Thomas, who had travelled to Russia for the 1930 cultural Olympiad, also journeyed with the party. Back in 1930, Thomas had been extremely impressed with the Soviet theatre, which led the way in its use of agitprop and cabaret forms, and its promotion of street theatre.[37] Presumably, thinking back to his earlier impressions, Thomas imagined a similarly vibrant and inspirational 1933 event. As the company sailed over to Russia they turned the deck into a performance space, no doubt rehearsing their sketches with eager anticipation. Performance here became part of the migratory experience, the sea providing the backdrop, the deck a stage, the stairs the wings. Theatrical performance was directly interpolated into the travel experience; it was not just something to do upon arrival.[38]

The British delegation performed four agitprop pieces: *Class Against Class*, *Capitalist Rationalisation*, *Invergordan* and *Social Service*. The actors used slogans, disciplined movements, bare stages and simple working outfits, agitprop theatrical devices that had been so popular in Russia since the Revolution. However, the Soviet jury seemed unimpressed. Its report made the problems clear. The themes were interesting but 'nevertheless the artistic-political presentation of themes has very important mistakes':

> Of primary importance is the absence of any definite character, type, image, which means that people and events reach the eye and ear of the audience only schematically and superficially… The producers are not well acquainted with the means and technique of stage-expression and the actors themselves are neither schooled nor do they have the slightest technical training.[39]

After years of following the lead of the Soviet theatre scene, such a reproof must have come as something of a shock. Thomas's response was measured and perhaps a little idealistic. The problem, he suggested, was not the agitprop form itself but the quality of presentation. The Olympiad's committee advocated a more 'naturalistic' approach.[40] But this only seemed to revitalise Thomas's belief in agitprop; presentations, he proposed, would have to be more accomplished, retaining the open-platform setting while improving 'the quality and standard of performance'.[41] The four sketches the WTM took to the Olympiad probably did lack quality; however, the response of the jury suggested not only an absence of aesthetic craftsmanship, but also a profound misunderstanding of the most effective methods of creating political theatre. Subsequently the jury recommended four improvements for the British delegation: (1) 'organising of systematic political studies' in order to fill in the significant philosophical gaps; (2) 'organising of courses for political training' to move this theoretical material into tangible action; (3) 'organising of schools in order to raise the technical level and qualifications for actors' to address the poor quality of acting; and (4) the 'drawing in of professionals'.[42] In essence the Olympiad jury called for a total overhaul of British agitprop's foundations. Despite Thomas's unwavering commitment to agitprop, this migratory event marked a substantial change in the intentions and aesthetics of the WTM.

As fascism lurked in the world's shadowy corners, ready to pounce on unstable, broadly liberal governments, the focus for theatre changed. It was less about advocating communist revolution and intervening in the class struggle than uniting to fight against this new political threat.[43] Idealistic agitprop seemed strangely out of step with the terrifying growth of fascist dictatorship. But there was another aesthetic reason for the WTM's turn away from agitprop and eventual demise, hinted at in the jury's decision at the Olympiad. After a number of years of agitprop declamation, Russian theatre was rapidly changing, turning to a mode called socialist realism, a form that, at first sight, looked like nineteenth-century naturalism with developed characterisation and accurate, realistic set design. However, it significantly differed from naturalism in its focus on the heroic and its inclusion of consistently politically hopeful endings. The new aesthetic turn rejected avant-garde experimentation, regarded as bourgeois and decadent, and forcefully promoted, in the words of the organising secretary of the Union of Soviet Writers, Valery Kirportin, at the 1933 First Congress of Soviet Writers, themes of 'collective toil and the collective struggle for socialism'.[44]

This transformation in workers' theatre aesthetics in Soviet Russia affected significant transnational reorganisation. Accordingly, the Communist Party of Great Britain (CPGB) acknowledged the turn away from agitprop, and encouraged British groups to conform. However, this edict did not meet with universal acceptance in Britain. This was just another incident in an already tense relationship between the CPGB and the WTM. While it might be imagined that the intentions of the Party and the workers' theatre would coincide, the latter rarely garnered any real support from its political wing.[45] Certainly they received no financial assistance and rarely did the two camps discuss methods of connecting artistic agitation with party politics. On the one hand, WTM's tentative association with the CPGB implicated the British workers' theatres in the more general 'isolation and general ineffectiveness' of the former.[46] Dividing itself resolutely from the burgeoning Labour Party movement meant that the CPGB never achieved any real, long-lasting, working-class support in Britain. While some theatre groups nonetheless managed to produce influential work, many WTM societies seemed detached from their target audience. On the other hand, the CPGB's lack of consistent support for the WTM meant that the local divisions never had a real political mandate. Coupled with this was the growing independence of some WTM groups which the CPGB clearly saw as competitors rather than comrades.[47]

Unlike the far larger and more influential communist movement in Russia, the CPGB seemed unable to construct a comprehensible, coherent or well-developed artistic policy, and their advice to nationwide groups never made its aesthetic strategies clear. Initial readings of historical documents, however, certainly confirm the CPGB's commitment to creating a new revolutionary theatre:

> Theatre must become once more an integral part of the people, regarded not as a luxury or a business enterprise, but as something essential to the progress and well-being of the entire nation.[48]

Again, the CPGB's intentions parallelled the Russian focus on the relationship between actor and audience, on theatre that uniquely engages the 'people'. However, it never defined the character of this theatre. Partly this originated in a problem confronting all political theatre-makers: should political theatre educate or entertain, is it 'something to be enjoyed or endured'?[49] No doubt education and entertainment can coexist quite amiably, but many practitioners and groups struggled with this dualism. As Russia turned to socialist realism, in transnational solidarity the CPGB followed suit and began to crack down on more avant-garde experimentalism, displaying 'an active hostility towards the more creative spirits and protégés of the party's literary intelligentsia'.[50] While the CPGB remained a marginal institution, with some practitioners (the Red Megaphones as a case in point) defying its edicts, their acceptance of socialist realism points towards a broader issue: What should British political theatre look like and should it align with the Russian model?

While this turn was an artistic change, in Soviet Russia it had far-reaching consequences. In meeting Meyerhold, Dean experienced a prophetic sense of foreboding, wondering whether the Russian's commitment to constructivist ideas would eventually lead to clashes with those in power.[51] This proved true for all those who remained committed to more experimental theatrical techniques. Stalin's aesthetic decision prompted the ostracising of many theatrical methods that, until that point, had defined Soviet revolutionary theatre. Many of the agitprop groups died away, including TRAM, whose members, Marshall noted, were 'accused of formalism and of being partisans of the antipsychological theatre; that is, basically antirealistic'.[52]

It might initially be imagined that the onset of socialist realism (coupled with a new focus on the fascist threat rather than the prospect of imminent worldwide communist revolution) marked the end of Russian-influenced agitprop theatre in Britain. Certainly the WTM dwindled to be replaced (or at least succeeded) by Unity Theatre, a similarly multi-geographical grouping of companies that largely turned to a mixture of polemic pantomime and linear realism in their attempts to create contemporary political theatre. Actor, director and Russian traveller van Gyseghem provides some sense of genealogical continuity between the WTM and Unity. During the First National WTM Conference in 1932, the majority of groups decided that agitprop rather than naturalism afforded the most suitable form for politically engaged theatre.[53] Clearly, after the 1933 Olympiad, many groups revised this decision, but one year earlier van

Gyseghem's Rebel Players had been the only group that did not follow the agitprop line. Unity Theatre, founded in 1936, came directly out of this Rebel Players group.

Despite van Gyseghem's first-hand experience of the Soviet stage, critics Stourac and McCreery suggest 'he never really developed the sort of instrumental theoretical conceptions that were needed to "push the walls down"'.[54] However, van Gyseghem's perceived lack of revolutionary approach was a purposeful aesthetic decision. While the WTM understood theatre as an agitprop weapon in a class war, Unity focused on producing progressive drama, thematically, formally and politically. This did not, however, necessarily lead to the total rejection of Soviet aesthetics or, indeed, their Russian comrades. While Unity certainly focused on local political realism with plays like Bill Owen's *The Ragged Trousered Philanthropists* (1949, earlier produced by Thomas and WTM), Sean O'Casey's *Juno and the Paycock* (1945) and Miles Malleson's *Six Men of Dorset* (1948), it maintained a particular interest in Russia, producing a number of plays that showed support for Soviet communism. These included productions of Russian plays such as Konstantin Simonov's *The Russian Question* (1947), which placed the blame for the encroaching Cold War firmly with the West.[55] The Glasgow branch, particularly, continued to look to Russia, with plays like its 1945 *The Lower Depths* by Maxim Gorky.

Although he moved away from agitprop, van Gyseghem's commitment to theatre as a revolutionary force remained throughout his career. In the midst of the Second World War, in fact, the Russian-Today Society, a transnational solidarity group connected with the CPGB, published a short book entitled *The Theatre is Our Weapon.* It contains two plays – *Erna Kremer of Ebenstadt* by John Bishop and *According to Plan* by Geoffrey Parsons – preceded by an introduction from van Gyseghem. In it he reflected on the current situation and the potential impact of theatre:

> Now when the cry has gone out for tanks, tanks, and yet more tanks – when the planes stream out to help our Soviet Allies, and the ships are heavy with supplies of all descriptions – now more than ever before must the theatre throw off its apathy and race forward to keep pace with life.[56]

Both plays are actually about Germany but, after telling a story about German soldiers coming to the realisation they are fighting for the wrong side, *According to Plan* ends with an epilogue from a Soviet Red Army soldier. The Soldier, with a degree of perhaps unfounded optimism, says that such desertions happen regularly in the Nazi army and encourages the British audience to keep fighting on. He concludes:

> In Europe they [the Nazis] sowed death, destruction and despair. Here they are sowing death and destruction; but despair is a plant that doesn't flourish on Soviet soil... The end is certain; it is for the peoples of the world to make it swift. Comrades, let us get on with the job.[57]

Russian politics and aesthetics clearly still preoccupied van Gyseghem, even during the Second World War. He remained very willing to attach his name to the utopian visions of Britain's Soviet ally.

## Agitprop Solidarity and Celebratory Pageantry: The Case of *Salute to the Red Army*

No doubt, the transmission of documents about Russian revolutionary theatre in magazines/newsletters, the visits of people like Comrade Ludmilla and the migratory experiences of figures like Mann, Thomas and van Gyseghem (particularly during the 1933 Moscow Olympiad) influenced the British Workers' Theatre Movement, an agitprop collective that, though short-lived, enjoyed some success and acted as a foundational point for later companies like Theatre Workshop and Unity Theatre. However, one of the most interesting and under-researched agitprop-inflected performances in Britain actually occurred during the 1940s when such aesthetics had long been superseded by socialist realism in Russia. Entitled *Salute to the Red Army*, it was not a short sketch, nor was it performed on factory steps. It was not produced by Tom Thomas or Charlie Mann or Joan Littlewood. In fact, it took place at a centre of establishment entertainment: the Royal Albert Hall. It was not performed by unemployed workers desperate to share their convictions, but by Laurence Olivier, Sybil Thorndike, Ralph Richardson and John Gielgud, some of Britain's most eminent actors. And its director? Admirer of Tairov and Stanislavsky, Basil Dean. Despite Dean's earlier reticence about agitprop techniques, he created a piece (whether consciously or not) that can be read alongside the post-Revolutionary work of TRAM, the Blue Blouse groups and, on a grander scale, the agitprop-infused mass celebrations of the new Soviet state. Connecting *Salute to the Red Army* to recent conceptions of transnational and global modernisms enables a still more nuanced reading. Stanford Friedman's understanding of spatialised modernity functioning as 'the imitation of other's representational forms, with a *difference*'[58] indicates the workings of performances like *Salute to the Red Army*, as, while it might feel like an agitprop-infused spectacle, actually the influence of the local pageant form is just as vital. The transnational fluidity/multidirectionality produces a complex work that is both international and local in form and theme, familiarly indigenous yet identifiably global.

Like the early manifestations of Russian agitprop, *Salute to the Red Army* received support from the government, with the Ministry of Information commissioning and indeed paying for the event. The Ministry approached Dean in January 1943 (barely a month before the eventual production) with only vague ideas as to what the potential performance would look like.[59] Once Dean presented an initial plan, the government entrusted the whole event to him. The commissioning department seemed delighted with the eventual outcome; the Minister, Brendan Bracken, wrote to Dean, 'I hope you will accept my thanks on behalf of the Government for the admirable way in which you and your staff carried out this heavy assignment'.[60] The armed forces, too, appeared wholeheartedly supportive, with high-ranking officials writing to congratulate Dean:

> I realise what a short time you had in which to prepare and I think it was nothing short of miraculous that there should have been no hitch of any kind.[61]

However, as might be expected in response to an overt celebration of Soviet Russia, and by extension its communistic political system, many government officials and military figures had reservations about *Salute to the Red Army*. The Foreign Office in particular felt that the submitted script too strongly celebrated working-class support for their Soviet compatriots. The Office also worried about the 'near idolisation of the Soviet Union'.[62] Clearly the government wanted to prevent any suggestion that a similar political revolution might be welcome in Britain. While the lack of multiple scripted versions makes it difficult to discern the addendum, Dean certainly, albeit reluctantly, changed the script to meet the government's approval.[63] Some inflammatory elements did remain, however, including participants raising their fists in a communist salute. Dean recalled 'official personas present at the dress rehearsal were much alarmed to find their objections to this overruled'.[64] The context of *Salute to the Red Army* exemplifies the troublesome relationship between governmental politics and political art, and, subsequently, transnational alliances or tensions between nation states.

I claim *Salute to the Red Army* as an agitprop pageant, using declamation – or, as the playtext suggests, 'staccato commentary'[65] – as its primary method of dialogue. Dean later cited it as a 'premeditated happening'.[66] While not claiming any direct antecedent, it could be read alongside Russian revolutionary grand spectacles such as Nikolai Evreinov's *The Storming of the Winter Palace* (1920), which re-enacted the battle between the Reds and the Whites in Petrograd with a cast of many thousands. While the Russian piece was performed outside and on a considerably larger scale than *Salute to the Red Army*, both represented, borrowing James von Geldern's phrase, a 'reformation of recollection', that is a remembering and a re-enactment of previous events in order to encourage and embolden spectators in their current situation.[67] Like Evreinov's piece, *Salute to the Red Army* advocated solidarity and reassessed a particular (or a number of particular) moment(s) in history.

However, Dean's production can also be read in a genealogy of British pageantry beginning with the Medieval religious plays, on to the Elizabethan court pageants, the 1851 Great Exhibition and even the rather damp 2012 Thames flotilla celebration of Queen Elizabeth's Diamond Jubilee. In fact, when discussing the possibilities of a pageant for the 1951 Festival of Britain, Dean was presented as the potential director; a letter from Beverley Baxter (Conservative MP and theatre critic) to Herbert Morrison (Deputy Prime Minister in Clement Attlee's government) confirmed, 'you will remember his pageant at the Albert Hall "Salute to the Red Army" during the war. It was quite superbly done'.[68] Pageants celebrating local communities were extremely popular in Britain in the early decades of the twentieth century thanks, in part, to the work of Louis Napoleon Parker who presented a selection of pageants, based on the German *Festspiel*.[69] In fact, Sir Henry Beerbohm Tree produced Parker's pageant *Drake*, based on the life of Sir Francis Drake, in September 1912 at His Majesty's Theatre where, two years later, Dean began his theatre work.[70] Parker's conception of the pageant play most certainly chimes with *Salute to the Red Army* as illustrated by his introduction to his 1913 *Joseph and His Brethren: A Pageant Play*:

> As in my pageants I told the entire history of the town, so in these plays I attempt to tell the entire history of the man. The so-called unities of time and place are therefore of no consideration; but are replaced by a much more important unity: the unity of idea.[71]

Parker's technique of creating a multifaceted, expansive performance based around a single idea is reinterpreted in a more politically engaged way in *Salute to the Red Army*.

During the First World War Parker produced four pageants that navigated a similar trajectory as *Salute to the Red Army*: ways of understanding history and its relation to the present.[72] But politicised groups also took up the pageant form, eager to harness its strengths for particular causes. Despite Cicely Hamilton's later criticism of the Russian political stage, her 1909 *Pageant of Great Women* (produced at the Scala Theatre, London) works through a range of well-known historical women in an attempt to justify suffragist calls for equal gender rights. Eventually, based on this evidence, the figure of Justice decides that the Woman is indeed worthy and the Woman responds with hopeful intention: 'I have an equal, not a master, now./ I will go speak with him as peer with peer,/ Free woman with free man.'[73]

By the 1930s this pageant form, coupled with influences from American and Russian agitprop, had become one of the most prominent modes of British political theatre with performances like *We Are English* (1936), commissioned, despite their continued uncertainty about cultural forms, by the London District of the Communist Party and performed in Hyde Park with many thousands of participators and spectators.[74] The form gained particular prominence as the Popular Front, a rather tense coming together of leftist and centrist groupings, took on the might of encroaching fascism. Mick Wallis, in his comprehensive discussion of political pageantry (and rejection of Parker's more 'conservative' productions), connects the Popular Front's pageants firmly with 'mass spectacle… a major propaganda tool in the Soviet Union from the early years'.[75]

At this juncture, it is important to note that the techniques of political pageant did not simply travel one way from Russia to Britain. Platon Lebedev (Kerzhentsev) became a Bolshevik as early as 1904. Consequently, like Lenin, Trotsky and many others, he was exiled and took to travelling throughout Europe and America, experiencing a variety of theatrical performances. He particularly admired the pageants he saw in Britain, imagining that 'such "folk" or "democratic" performances, based on collective creativity, could provide the new form of theatre needed in the new society'.[76] While in London in July 1914 Kerzhentsev witnessed the summer pageant *St George and the Dragon* in Hampstead Garden Suburb, an area of London with a strong tradition of pageant performances. This particular event may have influenced Kerzhentsev in his conviction that pageants should have very few words, as he seemed to mishear or misunderstand some of the text of *St George and the Dragon*. He later suggested that narrative should be presented in dance, song and scene rather than intricate dialogue and there is a strong possibility that such an aesthetic decision came out of his London experiences.[77] But the pageant also influenced him in a more positive way; he was captivated by the idea that productions were organised and performed by local communities working together with a fusion of artistic methodologies.[78] While it is tricky to construct a lineage, Robert Russell concludes his 1986 *Theatre Notebook* article by saying 'it is likely that the Hampstead Garden Suburb pageant of 1914 exerted a direct influence on the Russian Revolutionary festivals of the Civil War era'.[79] Certainly Kerzhentsev mentioned *St George and the Dragon* in his 1923 book *Creative Theater*, using it to substantiate his conviction that 'the task of the proletarian theater is not to produce good professional actors who will successfully perform the plays of a socialist repertory, but to give an outlet to the creative artistic instinct of the broad masses'.[80] Kerzhentsev's beliefs in such democratic impulses (though these changed with the advent of Stalinism) can be partly traced back to the community pageants of the US and Britain.

*Salute to the Red Army* was by no means the only Second World War pageant advocating solidarity with Britain's Russian allies. Just a year earlier playwright (and later librettist for Benjamin Britten's *Peter Grimes*) Montagu Slater wrote the script for *An Agreement of the Peoples*, performed at Earl's Court, a piece that took influences from Russian clowning and for which Britten wrote the music. Three months after *Salute to the Red Army*, the National Council for British-Soviet Unity produced *Alliance for Victory*, another pageant piece that celebrated the Russian defence of Stalingrad.[81] However, for Steve Nicholson, *Salute to the Red Army* remains the 'most public and controversial pageant of all'.[82] I concur and suggest that *Salute to the Red Army*'s distinctiveness came about because of its positioning at the heart of London's theatre district, its complex and troublesome identification with the British government and, most of all, its apparent combination of agitprop mass performance techniques and the celebratory patriotism of the local pageant. It is a work, therefore, that sits uncomfortably on a number of generic, geographical and political fences. And orchestrating the entire extravaganza was a theatre-maker who had travelled to Russia in 1926 and directly experienced its culture, politics and aesthetics.

*Salute to the Red Army* lasted two hours without an interval 'so as not to interrupt the mounting climax'[83] and was planned by Dean, with the poet Louis MacNeice composing a special ode. It included in its cast, among others, Sybil Thorndike, Laurence Olivier and John Gielgud, and these three figures provide still more Russo-British connections. Laurence Olivier starred in a number of pro-Russian projects, including, in the same year as *Salute to the Red Army*, the film *The Demi-Paradise*, which dramatises the growing understanding between a Russian engineer and British industrialists, and advocates friendly (and fruitful) transnational comradeship. In 1965 Olivier travelled to Moscow to star in *Othello*. Sybil Thorndike journeyed to Russia in 1935. In fact, rumours that she and her theatrical husband, Lewis Casson, were 'followers of Russia' caused some tensions, particularly while travelling abroad.[84] Throughout her career she petitioned for stronger artistic bonds between Britain and Russia; even in 1958, during the Cold War, Thorndike maintained, 'we have sent our theatre to Russia, and our actors have been acclaimed there. I believe that if we use our theatre with other nations, we can get peace'.[85] Once again here is theatre understood as a political force for good. As for John Gielgud, he performed in *Red Rust* by V.M. Kirchov and A.V. Ouspensky, as well as taking a central role in Hubert Griffith's *Red Sunday*, a play we will return to in the next chapter.[86]

The music for *Salute to the Red Army*, with sections composed by Alan Rawsthorne, William Walton and Arnold Bax (the writer, as mentioned in the last chapter, who wrote *The Truth About the Russian Dancers* with J.M. Barrie), was provided by three well-established orchestras/choirs (the BBC Symphony, the London Philharmonic and the Royal Choral Society) and a collection of armed forces bands. Artist Denis Wreford designed the enormous backcloth covering the organ pipes, presenting a quasi-constructivist vision of 'Stalingrad or other modern Russian city'.[87] There were none of the colourful domes of Moscow, no impressive Winter Palace of St Petersburg. Here was a visual image of a city named after the current leader of the USSR, a site of heavy industry rather than historical beauty, a place at the very epicentre of the struggle against the Nazis. Just weeks before the performance, the Red Army won a decisive victory against the Nazi invaders in the Battle of Stalingrad. It proved to be one of the Allies' most important victories of the war, forcibly halting the German advance. Again, using suggestive images (combined with descriptive declamation) rather than mimetic sets, it recalled the plain, agitprop stages of the Blue Blouse groups, but also tapped into Parker's understanding of the pageant where 'the scenery in both plays [*Drake* and

*Joseph*] is of the simplest nature, or the play could not be represented. It happens, however, to be extraordinarily well painted' (Fig. 2.1).[88]

*Salute to the Red Army* began with an Announcer addressing the spectators:

> We are here to salute the Red Army. The Soviet Union and Britain today are allies… what concerns us is Today, but we will begin further back. Russia today is resisting the invader. She has beaten the invader before. She beat Napoleon in Eighteen-Twelve. She beat the Germans in the Middle Ages.[89]

From the opening speech, spoken in declamation style, the themes become clear: to tell a story with modern relevance, to assure the spectators of Russia's previous successes in resisting invaders and, most of all, to create a powerful sense of solidarity between the British and the Soviets. The rest of the pageant proceeded through Russian history up to the Nazi invasion. Although confident of victory, the Germans (symbolically

**Fig. 2.1** 'Salute to the Red Army' (Copyright of the University of Manchester)

represented throughout by the Nazi Figure character) gradually realised their predicament as the Soviet resistance held out against the onset of a bleak Russian winter.

On either side of the stage stood two plinths on which the two primary declamatory figures, the Spokesman and Spokeswoman with 'gold costumes and gilded faces',[90] described the change in fortunes until the Russian victory at Stalingrad when 'the light on the Nazi Figure is switched off suddenly, symbolising the extinction of the Sixth Army'.[91] The pageant concluded with MacNeice's ode, encouraging the British audience to support the Soviet army: 'our eyes look East/ To where our comrades fight/ Their Battle with the Beast/ That rages day and night.'[92] At the end of the performance, again legitimising this political pageant within governmental hierarchies, the Secretary of State for Foreign Affairs Anthony Eden (later to become the British Conservative Prime Minister) addressed the assembly. His final sentence appealed to the audience: 'I ask you all to stand and pay a silent tribute to the glorious dead of the Red Army.'[93] The performance concluded with a Red Army soldier appearing in front of a vast Hammer and Sickle flag and, in a slightly jarring musical juxtaposition, the singing of the 'Internationale' and then the British 'National Anthem', reminiscent of the WTM agitprop events which often included the former if not the latter.

Mirroring earlier agitprop experiments, solidarity provided a constant focus, in the arrangement of the auditorium (there were service personnel participating as well as illustrious guests as spectators) and in the performance itself. Take, for example, Sections 5, 6 and 7. This sequence began with the 'Volga Boat Song', a traditional Russian folk song, juxtaposed with Welsh factory workers singing their own local songs, 'All Through the Night' and 'David of the White Rock'. In between (Section 6), the Announcer reflected, 'We too can remember peace. English, Scots, Welsh and Northern Irish – not so long ago our way of life was peaceful. We worked the work of peace. We sang the songs of peace. The traditional songs of our people. Songs in English... in Gaelic... in Welsh'.[94] It was a request for international solidarity but also a demand for national unity – a purposeful and simplistic smudging of the barriers between the various areas of the British Isles. This idea was augmented by Eden's closing words, calling on the Allies to work towards a 'final victory that will be won together'.[95] Noticeably, however (and evoking the traditional pageant form), solidarity rests on pre-Revolutionary images from traditional folk songs. While *Salute to the Red Army* might have pronounced communistic statements of worldwide unity, the music was carefully chosen to allay the fears of the British government that the performance might too strongly advocate a political accord. It promoted cooperation with Russia rather than *Soviet* Russia. This was presumably the reason the play exhibited such an overwhelmingly historical focus; eventual victory was guaranteed not because of the vigour and discipline of the Soviet armies but because of the traditional character of the Russian forces, be they Tsarist or Bolshevik.

Despite the focus on pre-Bolshevism, Dean (in the extant script at least) remained committed to worker solidarity with the differences between the workers embraced rather than ignored. Over two thousand people took a direct role in the performance, 'representatives of every facet of the war effort'.[96] While the Spokeswoman addressed the 'working people of Britain', each individual labour area was mentioned by name from the fishermen to the post office workers, the national fire service to the 'distributors of food'.[97] Even more interestingly, women were deemed as important as men, not simply those who waited for their husbands but also those who worked in the land army or built aircraft or took on the roles of nurses. With the addition of Edward Elgar's 'To Women', a song associated primarily with the First World War, women retained a prominent role in this relationship of solidarity:

> Some of them [Women] fight like men as guerrillas, paratroops and pilots,
> But all have a fighting spirit;
> This is a woman's war and a man's! I therefore call upon all the women of Britain to greet their sisters, the women of Russia, and to greet their brothers in the Red Army.[98]

Music both created a sense of atmosphere and made a particular political comment. And Russian music appeared, too. When the Moscow Radio defiantly narrated the events of the Battle of Stalingrad – 'The Red Army defended it, / They beat you when you defended it. / Now the Red Army is attacking'[99] – the bands played the opening bars of Dmitri Shostakovich's *Leningrad Symphony*, a piece written as a dissenting voice against the Nazi invasion. In using symphonies so intertwined with national identity, the pageant once again maintained a certain sense of cultural difference while simultaneously advocating solidarity.

Just as music broke up the declamation, in typical agitprop style, participants also performed everyday dialogue. The most noticeable of these episodes was entrenched in the agitprop tradition through its use of the

Newsboy character, a recurrent figure in early twentieth-century agit-prop performance.[100] In this scene four British characters took copies of the newspaper and conversed about their Russian allies, expressing some doubt that they will achieve victory. The Spokesman's rebuke – 'Have you gone soft? The Red Army is not soft'[101] – of course, directly challenged any in the audience who may have doubted the abilities of their allies. But even in this almost naturalistic dialogue sequence, the play still employed visual, theatrical symbols. In this case the newspapers had swastikas on the back. Once the Spokesman caused the four Britons to reassess their opinion about the Red Army, they turned the papers around to reveal 'a large red star on a white background'.[102] The striking denotational imagery was an obvious agitprop technique.

While in Russia, Dean most appreciated theatres focusing on the human body of the actor and its movements, such as Tairov's marionette-styled actors or the pantomimic clowning of Granovsky. The movement of performers became a vital element in *Salute to the Red Army*, noted by Lieutenant RNVR Peacock in a letter sent the next day:

> It was a magnificent piece of production from every point of view and I was particularly impressed by the opening fanfares, the lighting and the ease with which great bodies of men and women were moved and grouped.[103]

The organisation of such a large body of people proved difficult. In fact, Dean described *Salute to the Red Army* as 'quite an undertaking in terms of movement'.[104] With representatives from every sector of war work walking into the arena, it was necessary to determine particular areas where the participants could stand and consider the process by which they reached these respective positions. And yet it all seemed to work beautifully, at least in the scenes shown in the existing British Pathé film. The final sequence, performed as the *Leningrad Symphony* continued, required all the groups to mass together in the arena area while Scottish pipers marched on followed by 'British, Dominion and Colonial flags which are grouped in a body in the centre'.[105] As with the earlier description of the British Isles, colonies were clearly implicated in this show of solidarity. The physical organisation of such a large body of people no doubt compelled Dean to reconsider movement on the stage, an issue he had been so fascinated by during that early trip to Russia. The surviving film shows the participants arriving on stage in lines, the movements as disciplined and unified as one would expect from military troops. But they also resemble the choreographed movements of (borrowing Dean's 1926 description of his experiences in Russia) the 'Machine Artists', particularly the gymnastic-influenced work of the early agitprop groups and the biomechanics of Meyerhold. Indeed, the prominence of disciplined marching is a reminder of Charlie Mann's exercises, rehearsed on the boat that took the WTM to the Moscow Olympiad back in 1933.

*Salute to the Red Army* represents a remarkable moment of cultural transmission; focusing on the wartime situation in Russia, it would not have looked out of place in 1926 Moscow. Indeed, *The Times*' reviewer made the connection between the Albert Hall performance and large-scale patriotic celebrations in Russia:

> The processions in Red Square of Moscow have proved often enough that the Russians themselves are experts in the art of wielding crowds and colour into effective patterns, and, although no Russians took an active part yesterday, M Maisky[106] and his compatriots in the audience must have felt that their country was being honoured in a way it could understand and appreciate.[107]

*The Times*' praise for *Salute to the Red Army* rested on a perceived 'collision', to return to Stanford Friedman's earlier quotation, between British and Russian forms. Maisky and his colleagues did not simply watch a British appreciation of the Soviet Army and its exploits, but were addressed in a familiar theatrical lexicon: a hybridisation of Russian parades and British pageantry that, perhaps inadvertently, resembled the agitprop of years previously.

Dean was wholly enthusiastic in his praise of the event: 'the audience sat spellbound for several seconds after it was all over. I sat in my control box completely overcome by the magic we'd created.'[108] However, his immediate response was tainted with a perceived sadness:

> The whole audience rises. Portly mayors and dignified civil servants clap and cheer and wave their programmes. The effect is overwhelming. Too bad that the general public had not been allowed to see it… As I drove away from the Albert Hall with my small daughter, the cheers of the audience still ringing in my ears, I felt like a child that had lost a precious toy.[109]

Dean was clearly mournful that his pageant experiment had come to an end (losing his 'precious toy') but his comment can also be directly read through his admiration for Russia during his 1926 visit:

> But the point which is desirable to make is that the Bolsheviks have instinctively recognized the need of providing some sort of outlet for the people. For all their repression of ideas, faiths and creeds that do not coincide with their own it has yet been found necessary to give the population places of general assembly where their minds and hearts can be lifted in a sort of warmth of emotion amidst all the hardships.[110]

In a different time of 'hardship' Dean again thought of a potential audience who could be challenged and entertained by the theatre. While *Salute to the Red Army* was aesthetically impressive and politically charged, it did not engage the people as agitprop performance in 1920s Russia had done – indeed, it could not, because the audience was made up of government-invited officials, British and Russian. The 'actors' in the arena did not speak directly to an immediate audience of their peers. Rather the 'working people of Britain' could only listen to the performance through BBC radio or witness snippets on film. The government isolated the performance still further by refusing to promote it; the Prime Minister went as far as to ban any publicity. Although it was announced on Moscow Radio (alongside the date and place of performance!), by and large this grand spectacular occurred with very little public fanfare.[111] Cloaked in worries about security, the government's reason for limiting the audience may have been more political. Nicholson even goes so far as to say 'the Government had also contrived to direct and limit the potential impact of the performance'.[112] A year later, the British celebrations of Red Army Day were far less grand with no direct political messages, instead presenting a selection of musical tributes and ministerial speeches.[113]

Despite its lack of impact either aesthetically or socio-politically, *Salute to the Red Army* retains an important position in my argument. Certainly it partly resembles the Russian agitprop experiments of decades earlier, both small-scale Blue Blouse performances and far larger mass spectacles. Yet it also imbibes the qualities of British pageantry, a form with a long, often reactionary, history. This means that it reflects not only a transnational fluidity, but also a chronological fluidity. Indeed, for all its proclamations about newness, innovation and experiment, modernist art established a complex, ambiguous relationship with the past, sometimes rejecting it as passé or traditionalist while, at others, cherry-picking suitable techniques, celebrating, to borrow Thomas Postlewait's term, its 'artistic heritage'.[114] Although *The Times* claimed *Salute to the Red Army* as exhibiting 'really a new art form',[115] its transnational historical precedents act as palimpsests emerging at various junctures throughout the performance.

*Salute to the Red Army* provides an apt case study for this book's broader claims: created by a migratory modernist, it can be interpreted as simultaneously a continuation of earlier revolutionary Russian agitprop techniques, a mirroring of Soviet spectacles and an extension of a well-established British pageantry form. Inspiring this fusion of transnational forms remained the sense of urgency engendered by a Second World War that hung perilously in the balance. Despite allying his work with a resolutely pro-Russian position, in 1943 Dean mourned the loss of the exciting, experimental theatre he enjoyed during his 1926 trip:

> The once virile and enlightened Theatres of Russia and Germany and other countries have gone out like doused candles. They have been savagely seized upon and used as the servants of Force and Unreason.[116]

*Salute to the Red Army* represents a transnational cultural collision displaying artistic techniques unacceptable (or at least largely superseded) in one of the countries; ultimately it played with a historical transnational dialogue rather than a concurrent one.

## Notes

1. Red Army Day was an annual celebration of the founding of the Soviet Red Army. In 1943, across Britain, cities held Red Army celebrations with rallies, marches and cultural celebrations. Often Russian dignitaries were invited to these events and joined local governmental and civil leaders in front of typical Hammer and Sickle insignia. For more visual representations of these events see *Salute to the Red Army*, British Pathé films, http://www.britishpathe.com/video/salute-to-the-red-army/query/01285200 (accessed 31 August 2012). This film documents events in Cardiff, Manchester and Sheffield before focusing on the Royal Albert Hall event. It remains the only extant recording of *Salute to the Red Army*.
2. Edwina Mountbatten, letter to Basil Dean, 24 February 1943, Basil Dean Archive, 5/3/8.
3. Anon, 'Salute to the Red Army: Impressive Pageantry', *The Times*, 22 February 1943, 2.
4. Basil Dean, *The Theatre of War* (London: George Harrap, 1956), 543.
5. Susan Stanford Friedman, 'World Modernisms, World Literature and Comparativity' in *Oxford Handbook of Global Modernisms*, ed. Mark Wollaeger (Oxford UP, 2012), 512.

6. Cummings, *Eimi*, 97.
7. Dean, 'Roast Beef and Caviare', 90.
8. Ibid.
9. Ibid.
10. Cicely Hamilton, *Modern Russia As Seen By an Englishwoman* (London: E.P. Dutton, 1934), 79.
11. Hamilton, *Modern Russia*, 80.
12. Robert Leach, 'Russian Theatre and Western Theatres' in *A History of Russian Theatre*, eds Leach and Borovsky, 410.
13. Leach, 'Russian Theatre and Western Theatres' in *A History of Russian Theatre*, eds Leach and Borovsky, 411.
14. Raphael Samuel, Ewan MacColl and Stuart Cosgrove eds, *Theatres of the Left, 1880–1935* (London: Routledge and Kegan Paul, 1985), 111.
15. Stanford Friedman, 'World Modernisms' in *The Oxford Handbook of Global Modernisms*, ed. Wollaeger, 513.
16. For more information about the Blue Blouse troupes see Olga Taxidou, *Modernism and Performance: Jarry to Brecht* (Basingstoke: Palgrave MacMillan, 2007), 193–201, and Robert Leach, *Revolutionary Theatre* (London: Routledge, 1994), 159–65.
17. Huntly Carter, *The New Spirit in the Russian Theatre, 1917–1928* (London: Arno, 1929), 261.
18. Herbert Marshall, *The Pictorial History of the Russian Theatre* (New York: Crown, 1977), 154.
19. Ibid.
20. Richard Stourac and Kathleen McCreery, *Theatre as a Weapon: Workers' Theatre in the Soviet Union, Germany and Britain, 1917–1934* (London: Routledge, 1986), 191.
21. Ctd in Stourac and McCreery, *Theatre as a Weapon*, 195.
22. Stourac and McCreery, *Theatre as a Weapon*, 198.
23. Colin Chambers, *The Story of Unity Theatre* (London: Lawrence and Wishart, 1989), 26–7.
24. Tom Thomas, *The Ragged Trousered Philanthropists* (London: Richards, 1936), 89.
25. Howard Goorney and Ewan MacColl eds, *Agit-prop to Theatre Workshop: Political Playscripts, 1930–50* (Manchester UP, 1986), xxvi.
26. Samuel, MacColl and Cosgrove eds, *Theatres of the Left*, 228.
27. Ewan MacColl, *Journeyman* (London: Sidgwick and Jackson, 1990), 228.
28. 'Workers' Theatre Movement Bulletin (December 1932)', Unity Theatre Archive, V&A theatre archive, THM 9/6/2/1, 6.
29. Samuel, MacColl and Cosgrove eds, *Theatres of the Left*, 89.
30. Ness Edwards, 'The Workers' Theatre (1930)' in *Theatres of the Left*, eds Samuel, MacColl and Cosgrove, 195.

31. Edwards, 'The Workers' Theatre' in *Theatres of the Left*, eds Samuel, MacColl and Cosgrove, 199.
32. Huntly Carter, *The New Spirit in the European Theatre, 1914–1924* (London: Benn, 1925), 278.
33. Tom Thomas, 'Their Theatre and Ours (1932)' in *Theatres of the Left*, eds Samuel, MacColl and Cosgrove, 146.
34. Ctd in Stourac and McCreery, *Theatre as a Weapon*, 255–6.
35. Stourac and McCreery, *Theatre as a Weapon*, 240.
36. Samuel, MacColl and Cosgrove eds, *Theatres of the Left*, 107.
37. Ian Saville, 'Ideas, Forms and Developments in the British Workers' Theatre, 1925–1935' (PhD diss., City University, 1990), accessed 5 April 2013, http://www.redmagic.co.uk/sites/default/files/documents/THESIS.pdf.
38. For a picture of onboard rehearsals see Chambers, *The Story of Unity Theatre*.
39. 'Workers' Theatre Movement Bulletin (March 1934)', Unity Theatre Archive, V&A theatre archive, THM 9/6/2/1, 5–6.
40. Samuel, MacColl and Cosgrove eds, *Theatres of the Left*, 171.
41. Samuel, MacColl and Cosgrove eds, *Theatres of the Left*, 172.
42. 'Workers' Theatre Movement Bulletin (March 1934)', 7.
43. Stourac and McCreery, *Theatre as a Weapon*, 246.
44. Valery Kirportin, 'Success of Soviet Drama (1934)' in *The Soviet Theater*, eds Senelick and Ostrovsky, 362.
45. Stourac and McCreery, *Theatre as a Weapon*, 266.
46. Saville, 'Ideas, Forms and Developments', 41.
47. Saville, 'Ideas, Forms and Developments', 57.
48. Anon, *A Communist Policy for Theatre* (London: Farleigh Press, 1948), 15.
49. Geoff Andrews, Nina Fishman and Kevin Morgan, *Opening the Books: Essays on the Social and Cultural History of British Communism* (London: Pluto, 1995), 91.
50. Kevin Morgan, *Against Fascism and War: Ruptures and Continuities in British Communist Politics, 1935–41* (Manchester UP, 1989), 207.
51. Basil Dean, *The Changing Theatre*, BBC Radio, The British Library csf. 846985 (17 December 1969), 3of4.
52. Marshall, *The Pictorial History*, 155.
53. Stourac and McCreery, *Theatre as a Weapon*, 233.
54. Stourac and McCreery, *Theatre as a Weapon*, 254.
55. Chambers, *The Story of Unity Theatre*, 299.
56. André van Gyseghem, *The Theatre is Our Weapon* (London: Russia-Today Society, u.d.), 2.
57. Geoffrey Parsons, 'According to Plan' in *The Theatre is Our Weapon*, van Gyseghem, 18.
58. Stanford Friedman, 'World Modernisms', 512.
59. Dean, *Theatre of War*, 304.

60. Brendan Bracken, letter to Basil Dean, 24 February 1943, Basil Dean Archive, 5/3/4.
61. Lt Col. Nugent, letter to Basil Dean, 22 February 1943, Basil Dean Archive, 5/3/9.
62. Nicholson, *British Theatre and the Red Peril: The Portrayal of Communism, 1917–1945*, 131.
63. Steve Nicholson, 'Theatrical Pageants of the Second World War', *Theatre Research International*, 18.3 (1993): 192.
64. Dean, *Mind's Eye*, 285.
65. Dean, *Salute*, 37.
66. Dean, *The Changing Theatre*, 4of4.
67. James von Geldern, *Bolshevik Festivals, 1917–1920* (California UP, 1993), 200.
68. 'Proposals for British Achievement (Festival of Britain)', Basil Dean Archive, 2/21/9–11.
69. Mick Wallis, 'Pageant' in *The Continuum Companion to Twentieth-century Theatre*, ed. Colin Chambers (London: Continuum, 2002), 580.
70. Louis Napoleon Parker, *Drake* (London: John Lane, 1912).
71. Louis Napoleon Parker, *Joseph and His Brethren: A Pageant Play* (London: John Lane, 1913), introduction.
72. For a stimulating reinterpretation of Parker's four productions see Meghan Lau's 'Performing History: The War-time Pageants of Louis Napoleon Parker', *Modern Drama*, 54.3 (Fall 2011): 265–86.
73. Cicely Hamilton, *A Pageant of Great Women* (The Suffrage Shop, 1910), 45.
74. Chambers, *The Story of Unity Theatre*, 88.
75. Mick Wallis, 'Pageantry and the Popular Front: Ideological Production in the Thirties', *New Theatre Quarterly*, 10.38 (May 1994): 134.
76. Leach, *Revolutionary Theatre*, 23.
77. Robert Russell, 'An English Influence on Russian Revolutionary Festivals', *Theatre Notebook*, 40.3 (1986): 118.
78. Russell, 'English Influence', 119.
79. Russell, 'English Influence', 121–2.
80. Von Geldern, *Bolshevik Festivals*, 28.
81. Nicholson, *British Theatre and the Red Peril*, 125–7.
82. Nicholson, *British Theatre and the Red Peril*, 128.
83. Dean, *The Changing Theatre*, 4of4.
84. Anon, *Sydney Morning Herald*, 26 October 1932.
85. Sybil Thorndike, 'Scrapbook', Sybil Thorndike/Lewis Casson archive, V&A, THM 33/1/5.
86. Jonathan Croall, *Gielgud: A Theatrical Life* (London: Continuum, 2001), 98, 101.
87. Dean, *Salute*, 1.
88. Parker, *Joseph*, introduction.

89. Dean, *Salute*, 2.
90. Dean, *The Changing Theatre*, 4of4.
91. Dean, *Salute*, 33.
92. Dean, *Salute*, 39.
93. Dean, *Salute*, 40.
94. Dean, *Salute*, 4.
95. *Salute to the Red Army*, Pathé film.
96. Dean, *The Changing Theatre*, 4of4.
97. Dean, *Salute*, 20–2.
98. Dean, *Salute*, 23.
99. Dean, *Salute*, 34.
100. The American Workers' Laboratory Theatre even produced a play entitled *Newsboy* that made its way across to Britain and was performed by Unity Theatre and Theatre Workshop. The playscript is included in MacColl and Goorney's *Agit-prop to Theatre Workshop*, 13–20.
101. Dean, *Salute*, 12&13.
102. Dean, *Salute*, 14&15.
103. Lieutenant RNVR Peacock, letter to Basil Dean, Basil Dean Archive, 5/3/10.
104. Dean, *Salute*, 37.
105. Dean, *Salute*, 37.
106. Ivan Maisky was the Soviet ambassador to London from 1932–43.
107. Anon, *The Times*, 2.
108. Dean, *The Changing Theatre*, 4of4.
109. Dean, *Theatre of War*, 309–10.
110. Basil Dean, 'Between the Public and Ourselves', Basil Dean Archive, 12/1/29.
111. Basil Dean, *Mind's Eye*, 284.
112. Nicholson, 'Theatrical Pageants', 194.
113. Nicholson, 'Theatrical Pageants', 195.
114. Thomas Postlewait, *The Cambridge Introduction to Theatre Historiography* (Cambridge UP, 2009), 14.
115. Anon, *The Times*, 2.
116. Basil Dean, 'The Theatre as a National Asset (1938)', Basil Dean Archive, 12/1/83.

CHAPTER 3

# Realism and Constructivism: From Revolutionary Experiment to Toeing the Party Line

*Salute to the Red Army* represented a composite of British pageantry and Russian mass performance, visually rendered using geometrical techniques reminiscent of Soviet painting and sculpture, amidst the quintessentially British atmosphere of the Royal Albert Hall. Dean mixed techniques and styles to form a new transnational, hybridised aesthetic. It theatrically represented a general, political, wartime consensus; despite ideological differences, Britain and Russia were now allies and should therefore accept and even celebrate each other's cultures. However, at first glance (and fallaciously, as this chapter illustrates), it would seem that British theatrical travellers to Russia, and indeed British audiences, felt a stronger affinity for one of two Russian approaches: realism or the more avant-garde experiments of the small agitprop groups and, emanating from a similar political impulse, the constructivists.

Realism, in this context, is a broad term, associated, not altogether straightforwardly, with Konstantin Stanislavsky and the Moscow Art Theatre on the one hand, Nikolai Okhlopkov's hyperrealism on the other (an innovation we will return to in Chapter 4) and, later, with the rise of socialist realism. The inclusivity (or, perhaps, fuzziness) of the term is recognised by J.M. Nikonov in a 1935 collection of articles arranged by C.G. Holme entitled *Art in the USSR*:

> Realism is a concept sufficiently broad to allow great variety in the methods of reproducing truth and reality.[1]



C. Warden, *Migrating Modernist Performance*,
DOI 10.1057/978-1-137-38570-3_4

Interestingly, in the introductory section of this book, A.Y. Arosev, president of the All-Union Society for Cultural Relations with Foreign Countries, expresses his desire that 'the collection will greatly contribute towards the establishment of a mutual understanding and a cultural *rapprochement* between the people of the Soviet Union and the English-speaking peoples, thereby serving the great cause of peace'.[2] Arosev's hope that an appreciation of art will lead to a friendly acceptance of Russian Soviet culture in a broader sense reflects the optimistic aspirations of many in this book. As this chapter illustrates, British experiences of Russian realism (in the very broadest sense of this term) provided a key artistic point of connectivity between the two countries.

'Constructivism' represents a decidedly less mimetic approach to the theatre, using geometrical shapes, physicalised gesture (from clowning to gymnastics) and the symbolic, mechanised (yet emancipatory) body. It built on the innovations of Russian workers' theatre, combining aesthetic experimentation with ardent leftist political messages. Despite constructivist pioneer Vsevolod Meyerhold's indebtedness to his teacher, Stanislavsky, these different ways of constructing theatre initially seem antithetical. British responses to the various facets of realism and the (sometimes perplexing) innovations of constructivism generally demonstrate a greater affinity with the former than the latter. Partly this was due to a strong British sense of realism which meant that Russian plays that slotted into that genealogy and 'corresponded to English tastes'[3] (or at least were performed in keeping with that genealogy) were more readily accepted. This chapter suggests that, while Russian realism garnered popular acclaim in Britain, British performances of Russian plays or adaptations of Russian methodologies generally revealed a tangible sense of British national and cultural identity rather than reflecting a distinctly Russianist aesthetic approach. This meant that many plays, particularly those by Anton Chekhov, probably the most popular Russian playwright in Britain and one who certainly sits awkwardly in narratives of realism, were often produced through the lens of British realist techniques. While most of the travellers preferred the MAT's performances to the bewildering work of constructivist Meyerhold, many met with the creator of biomechanics, and a number of British performances were clearly indebted to his innovations. Differentiating so conclusively between the two movements, however, overlooks a handful of British performances that juxtaposed (knowingly or otherwise) their techniques, characterisations and linguistic choices to create hybridised amalgams. The final section of this chapter focuses on some of these 'lost' plays. Ultimately this chapter is about transnational understanding, unearthing the way national identity affects production and reception of foreign works. It leaves us with a selection of performances that say as much about British culture as they do about Russian culture.

## Performing Chekhov: From the Moscow Arts Theatre to the London Stage Society

In 1928 and 1931 the Moscow Art Theatre Prague Group visited London, performing (at the Garrick and Kingsway theatres respectively) a selection of mostly pre-Revolutionary plays, including Chekhov's *The Cherry Orchard* and Maxim Gorky's *The Lower Depths*.[4] These tours were the first (and only) time the famed MAT performed in Britain. However, their presence in London attracted the ire of MAT co-founders Konstantin Stanislavsky and Vladimir Nemirovich-Danchenko who threatened to sue the touring company for the appropriation of the MAT name.[5] The contentious London performances were just the latest stage in a battle for the MAT brand that had begun when a group of performers left Moscow in the months after the Revolution. This collection of designers, performers and theatre-makers toured throughout Europe but became increasingly disconnected from their Russian compatriots. Olga Knipper, MAT actress, wife of Anton Chekhov and part of this breakaway coterie until she was called back to Moscow in 1922, reflected on the aims of this group:

> This connection in experience brings people in the West closer to us, through us they are introduced to the secret countenance, the soul of Russia.[6]

For Knipper, the group had a clear transnational intention: to act as a connective node between the West and Russian culture. Once again, Russia is understood in a British context through the intangible concept of the 'soul'.

However, as the years wore on, Stanislavsky felt increasingly uncomfortable about this touring community, imagining them as renegades creating their own aesthetic style disconnected from the original systems and techniques of the MAT. While in London, Maria Guermanova, one of the leading figures in the touring collective, felt compelled to confront the accusations levelled at her company in a letter to *The Times*. In keeping with the premises of this book, she attempts to address the migratory identity of her company, simultaneously connecting with and disassociating from its origin point:

> Those of our colleagues who have remained in Moscow are admirably carrying on the tradition… those of us who have stayed abroad are no less faithful to the tradition and are trying, sometimes in difficult circumstances, to interpret it to audiences in Western Europe.[7]

Her comment illuminates some of the central problems for émigré artists: the waning, though vital, connection to home, the justification of aesthetic choices and the troublesome problem of not simply *presenting* their indigenous theatre before a Western audience but 'interpreting' it.

This was not the only manifestation of the MAT to arrive in Britain during the 1920s. In 1921, theatre manager Charles B. Cochran sponsored the visit of Nikita Baliev's La Chauve-Souris (The Bat Theatre). Baliev had performed with the MAT until he decided that his natural 'merry countenance' could never fit into Stanislavsky's system.[8] He founded The Bat in 1908, committing to it fully in 1912, as the late-night offering of the MAT, presenting cabaret using Russian themes and traditions.[9] The company left Moscow after the Revolution, performing in Paris to great acclaim, before travelling to London and eventually to New York. In London The Bat performed at the Pavilion throughout August and September 1921, and in the November of that year transferred to the Coliseum until the end of December. The bill consisted of comedies and more serious vignettes, with music and impressive vibrant scenery, and included sections with titles like 'Russian Songs of Sentiment' and 'The Sudden Death of a Horse or the Greatness of the Russian Soul' (a short play by Anton Chekhov). The company transcended the usual class and social boundaries, including 'Russian workpeople's ditties' and 'The Three Huntsman: A Russian popular song' alongside the Chekhov playlet and 'Russian church themes after Rimsky-Korsakoff'.[10] The Bat returned to London in 1924/5 and was extremely popular, described by a newspaper reviewer as a 'perfect combination of taste with eccentricity'.[11] The 'Parade of Wooden Soldiers' proved particularly appealing for London audiences. Parallelling Craig's ideas (indeed, Craig saw The Bat in Moscow) this sketch used marionette acting styles[12] and was originally staged by Evgeny Vakhtangov, one of Russia's most innovative theatre-makers.[13] By 1924 British reviewers were trying to pinpoint the success and popularity of this Russian company:

> What seems to lift the performance above others is its appeal to the child that should still be in all of us. All the 'turns' seem to take us back to our childhood; or, at least, they seem to bring our childhood up-to-date for us... The scenery might have come out of a child's picture-book; the costumes from a child's imagination.[14]

This fantastical vibrancy clearly captured the imagination of London audiences. It also inspired new performances, namely A.P. Herbert's 1926 *Riverside Nights*, which played for 238 performances at Nigel Playfair's Lyric Theatre.[15] *Riverside Nights* is constructed in much the same manner as a Baliev show, with songs, poems and skits interspersed. One of these sketches shows a particular Russian influence: 'Love lies bleeding or Puss in Russian Boots.' It is framed by an introduction from John Smith, the rather grumpy narrator of the whole show. He suggests that the manuscript for the piece was discovered in Hammersmith, though written by a Russian playwright residing there. He concedes, 'either the characters in this play are quite mad, or I am. My daughter admits that they are not, perhaps, extravagantly normal, but she assures me, by degrees, every one of the audience will recognise in at least one of the characters a life-like portrait of himself'.[16] In essence this short sketch is a comedic pastiche of British reactions to Russian plays, particularly those of Chekhov. It includes characters like Henrietta Jolly who, according to stage directions, 'looks as if at any moment she might die, not from ill-health or age, but from concentrated melancholy'.[17] She is a parodic representation of a Chekhovian heroine. The sketch ends with a shooting but the tragedy is made ridiculous when the wrong man is shot. So in the middle of this variety show entertainment, clearly indebted to The Bat's structural innovations, is a short play that gently lampoons typical British reactions to more celebrated traditions of Russian theatre.

Even if not directly influenced by The Bat, other performances were imagined as building on the foundations set by Baliev's innovative company, whether successfully or not. One such production was the Barnes Theatre's version of Nikolai Gogol's classic *The Government Inspector* (1926), a play produced by Meyerhold in the same year in Moscow. Theodore Komisarjevsky produced the stage design for Arthur Sykes's classic translation; Komisarjevsky was, incidentally, named as 'Metteur en Scene' in The Bat's programme.[18] The *Observer's* reviewer describes the innovative set:

> Against a formalised panoramic background, and occupying most of the stage, stands a brightly-painted roundabout, with door and window frames where the horses and what not usually prance. This revolves to suit the action of the play, becoming indoors or out of doors in a twinkling, and thus permits swift continuity.[19]

Perhaps because of the contribution of Komisarjevsky, reviewers firmly connected this production to migratory Russian theatre seen in Britain during the preceding years. The parallels were not, however, particularly complimentary: 'for some reason or another, however, the Barnes production works out as something like a very bad cross between the methods of the Russian Ballet and the Chauve-Souris' and 'for once I did not like M. Komisarjevsky's production. It was too highly artificialized and looked like a bit of Chauve-Souris that had lost its way'.[20] For all the positive British responses to The Bat, these reviewers criticised *The Government Inspector* by comparing it unfavourably with Baliev's company (Fig. 3.1).

Of all the theatre companies and practitioners cited in this book, Stanislavsky and the MAT were arguably regarded most fondly by modernist British theatre-makers. The transmission of MAT ideas, however, is difficult to navigate; as David Shirley suggests, 'the passage of Stanislavsky's work into Britain is… erratic and piecemeal'.[21] Many of the theatrical travellers met Stanislavsky or witnessed his work while in Russia, and most unequivocally admired the director and his aesthetic systems. Basil Dean, who referred to Stanislavsky as 'the great father of modern Russian Theatre',[22] certainly visited the MAT during his 1926 stay in Moscow. André van Gyseghem described his attendance at the MAT in detail. He was primarily concerned with contextualising the theatre he witnessed during his travels and, therefore, attempted to uncover why the MAT still existed in a communist country so committed to revolutionising Russian culture in line with its new values. He suggested its survival was because 'the Communist Party aimed at preserving the highest expression of the old culture and giving it to the people as their right'.[23]

Stanislavsky's influence can be found in many different British theatrical contexts. French director and theatre trainer Michel Saint-Denis, who set up the London Theatre Studio in 1935, met the great Russian director in Paris

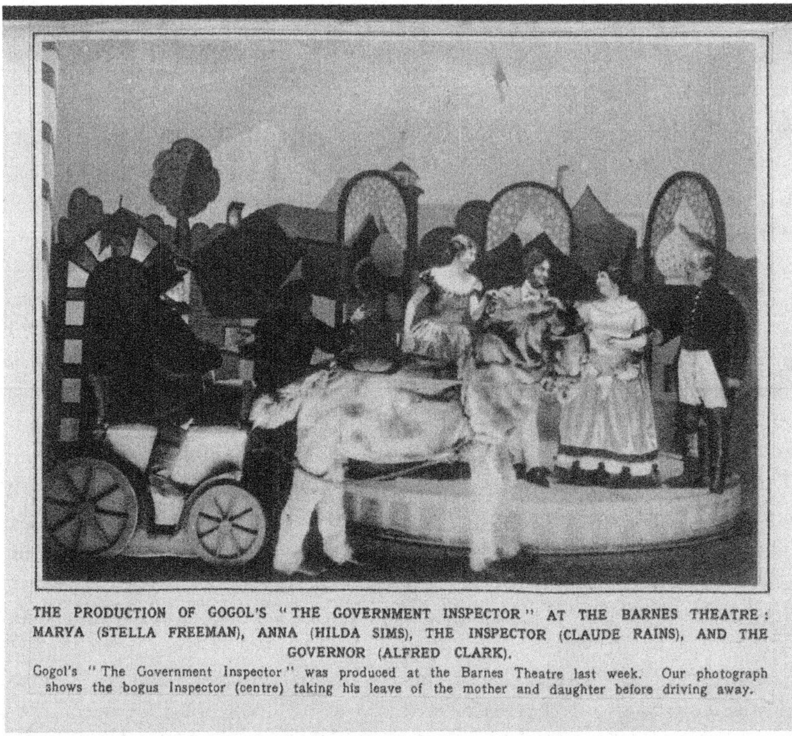


**Fig. 3.1** 'The Government Inspector' (Permissions given by Cadbury Research Library, University of Birmingham)

in 1922 and cited MAT's style as a dynamic catalyst for his own work.[24] And, of course, the arrival of Michael Chekhov imported Stanislavsky's methods (albeit shaped and changed) into a British context. But Stanislavsky's influence can also be found in the most surprising places. In Unity's newsletter of January 1939 appeared two letters from Stanislavsky reprinted from a 1933 edition of *International Literature*. These were first published, then, just as the WTM was disappointing the jury with its crude agitprop at the Moscow Olympiad. Stanislavsky's advice to theatre practitioners was a far cry from the foundations of the WTM:

The theatre has no right to lie – it must be intrinsically truthful. This imposes tremendous obligations upon the actor and makes equally tremendous

> demands upon his craftsmanship. Therefore, the attention of the theatre should be, at present, concentrated most of all on developing and raising the craftsmanship of the actor.[25]

Despite an attachment to political pantomime and documentary performance, Unity still approved of Stanislavsky's brand of realist acting. Indeed, as the 1930s progressed, the company swung away from declamation and sloganeering, partly influenced by the ideas of Stanislavsky.

Some of Stanislavsky's most famous and influential performances dramatised the works of Anton Chekhov. As van Gyseghem goes on to say, 'in the Moscow Art Theatre Tchekov found his spiritual home. Their interpretation and his genius were so closely bound up together that each grew and developed from contact with the other'.[26] I have no intention of detailing Chekhov's profound influence on British theatre, nor of providing a timeline of the many performances of Chekhov's plays in the first half of the twentieth century, nor, indeed, of detailing the various issues with translation and interpretation. Other scholars have already done these jobs admirably.[27] However, certain performances and figures further the central arguments of this book; accordingly, this all-too-brief discussion of Chekhov's works focuses entirely on particular interconnections with nationhood and travel.

During the early decades of the twentieth century Chekhov's plays appeared throughout the British theatre scene, from local workers' theatres to the plush auditoriums of the West End. At first critics and audience members alike did not seem to grasp the Russian's intentions or aesthetics. The general consensus was that Chekhov's plays were gloomy and melancholic, addressing issues and concerns unfamiliar to British sensibilities. *The Seagull* was the first to be performed in Britain, produced at the Glasgow Repertory Theatre in 1909; it met with some (relatively sympathetic) confusion. A scan through the reviews, as Patrick Miles undertakes in *Chekhov on the British Stage*, confirms that critics expected materialist naturalism but ended up with what the *Glasgow Herald* termed 'odd and elusive symbolism'.[28] *The Seagull* was translated by George Calderon, a figure Laurence Senelick describes as fortuitously (and unusually) 'both sympathetic and knowledgeable'.[29] Calderon's interest in Russia first appeared when at Oxford, choosing to study Russian as part of his degree. In 1895 he travelled to Russia and spent two years in St Petersburg, absorbing, according to his early biographer and friend Percy Lubbock, 'a profound and thorough experience of Russian ways'.[30] He seemed to use these first-hand observations in his translations of Chekhov's work. His versions challenge typical British presumptions about Chekhov's plays as naturalism; bringing the two strands of this chapter's argument together, he even consulted Meyerhold on current trends in Russian theatre.[31] Calderon maintained that Chekhov's plays are structured as a series of soliloquies rather than in any naturalistic manner. They are 'tragedies with the texture of comedy' he asserted, a point clearly missed by most British producers of the time.[32] Furthermore, he argued, 'the English method of acting is evidently ill-suited to Tchekof's [sic] work' as English actors tend to want to stand out rather than integrate into a united company.[33] Clearly, for Calderon at least, there were significant issues with the way Chekhov's work was translated, performed and received in a British context.

In addition to his ground-breaking translation work, Calderon wrote a single play with Russian themes: *The Little Stone House*. The Stage Society produced it alongside *The Cherry Orchard* in 1911. This one-act play is set in a small provincial town in Russia and narrates the story of mourning mother Praskovya, whose son Sasha died 20 years previously. In the intervening period she has transformed her university-educated son into a saint, spending many years saving up to commission the stone house of the title, a small tomb to house his grave. It turns out that Sasha is alive, an escaped convict from the Siberian silver mines, and that she has actually mistakenly buried his victim. In the final scene of the short play Praskovya calls for the police to take Sasha away for, as her lodger Asteryi confirms, 'what's man compared to an idea?'[34] She subsequently dies. Senelick reflects on this peculiar play: 'oddly enough, for someone whose analyses of Chekhov were subtle, insightful and poetic, Calderon's one play on a Russian theme perpetuates the melodrama tradition.'[35] Undoubtedly this is true; Calderon seems somewhat hamstrung by the short length of the piece (which means Sasha's entrance feels rather contrived, interrupting, seemingly by chance, a conversation about his death) and by a desire to break out of mimetic naturalism using symbolism: the icon containing pictures of saints and Sasha, and the ongoing patience card game which brings a feeling of chance and preordained fate to the narrative as well as mirroring the 'patience' of Praskovya as she saves her money. However, this play does give some sense of Calderon's perceptions of Russian society and politics. On the one hand, the narrative is driven by Praskovya's piety; this is an intensely religious society. On the other, Asteryi describes the revolutionary fervour breaking out, a movement that, as a young man, he would have joined.[36] The societal instability means that the Empress, who is passing through the town on her way to Smolensk, requires significant security.[37] *The Little Stone House* also attempts to ape Chekhovian methods in its 'atmosphere of silence, solitude, and Russian monotony'[38] although it certainly drifts into melodrama. Arguably, Russian traveller Calderon did more than any other figure to popularise and accurately present Chekhov's work. In fact, Miles suggests that 'with the exception of Calderon, there was no director sufficiently at ease with the material to recreate the dramatist's vision on stage'.[39]

In 1925 Calderon's translation of *The Cherry Orchard* appeared again, this time at the Lyric Theatre, Hammersmith under the direction of J.B. Fagan. Fagan invited Komisarjevsky to direct the production but he was producing his own version of the play in Paris.[40] Fagan was an Irish theatre impresario and playwright, and managed both the Oxford Playhouse and the Festival Theatre, Cambridge during the 1920s. The play, starring John Gielgud[41] as Trofimov, met with mixed reviews. American director Margaret Webster, for example, appreciated its 'charming laughter-and-tears quality' but proclaimed, 'it was probably more Irish than Russian'.[42] Quite what Webster meant it is difficult to tell, although in 1935 she joined a delegation from the British Drama League on a trip to the Theatre Festival in Moscow, witnessing works by Okhlopkov and Tairov, so no doubt she was able to formulate a stronger, first-hand opinion of Russian theatre.[43] Presumably her comment referred in some way to Fagan's nationality. Reviewers of Fagan's *The Cherry Orchard* attempted to pinpoint some of the key issues that prevented British audiences really engaging with Chekhov's work: 'It is a play of atmosphere and mood, of those vague feelings which we English are reluctant to express and hesitate to acknowledge even to ourselves.'[44] This version of *The Cherry Orchard*, then, seemed to engage with three distinct national identities: Russian, English and Irish. The result was a woven amalgam with a typically Chekhovian haunting atmosphere and sombre mood. The positive responses from reviewers and audiences confirmed, for James Loehlin, a 'deepened understanding of Chekhov'.[45] Fagan remained interested in Russian themes when he wrote his own plays, namely *The Greater Love*, performed at the Prince's Theatre in 1927 with Sybil Thorndike and Lewis Casson in lead roles. He based his play of revolutions and counter-revolutions in Vladimir, a provincial capital in Russia, in 1905. Magazine *Punch*'s reviewer makes a comical, direct connection between Fagan's new play and his direction at the Lyric:

> Mr Fagan, not disdaining to take a hint from his TCHEHOV [sic] productions, disposes about the stage various detached folk, some burbling (OFF or half-OFF) about general strikes, others staring gloomily into the samovar.[46]

Despite a growing appreciation of Chekhov's plays, such satirical descriptions were common and rested on the inactivity of their characters and general aimlessness of the narrative. Philip Godfrey, for example, in his 1933 celebration of peculiarities of the West End, *Back-Stage*, pillories theatre critics by citing a parody of a review of *The Cherry Orchard*:

> … a play about the sale of a cherry orchard, in which the characters wander on and off the stage during three acts for no particular reasons and in the end the cherry orchard is sold.[47]

For such a joke to occasion laughter, Godfrey must have been sure that this mock review was familiar to his readership. In a fortuitous turn back to the central concerns of this book, artist Pearl Binder, who, though born in Salford, was of Russian Jewish descent, provided the cartoonish images for *Back-Stage*. She would go on to travel to Russia and write several books including *Russian Families* (1942).

Calderon was not alone in his translation of Chekhov's work. Another migratory figure, Elisaveta Fen, for example, translated Chekhov's plays in the 1950s for Penguin. Fen was born in Russia and later published a number of compelling, nostalgic, sometimes tragic narratives of her childhood before the Revolution, including *A Russian Childhood* (1961) and *A Girl Grew Up in Russia* (1970).[48] Fen's introduction to her Chekhov translations reveals another perspective on transnational cultural exchange. She describes Chekhov's 'mood, characters, and dramatic technique' as 'profoundly Russian'.[49] However, she makes direct connections between late nineteenth-century Russia and the period between the wars in Britain, suggesting that both were characterised by unhappiness and frustration. Russians, she suggests, have a far greater capacity for sharing and dealing with such emotions. She concluded, therefore, that to 'watch Chekhov's plays may be to the sensitive Englishman a catharsis by proxy'.[50] As contemporary community theatre and theatre-in-education practitioners testify, watching theatrical performance can mean far more than just a jolly night out.

Maurice Baring, essayist and part of the Baring banking dynasty, also promoted Chekhov's work, though he seemed to differ from Calderon in his readings of the plays. Calderon heartily disagreed with Baring's focus on Chekhov's perceived realism:

> There is only one of his plays that does not end with a pistol-shot; they contain two suicides, a duel and an attempted murder. Surely Mr Baring must have been very unfortunate if he thinks that this is everyday Russian life![51]

Calderon's criticism is firmly based in notions of travel and empirical exposure to Russian culture. Surely, he comically seems to suggest, Baring fell in with the wrong crowd if his first-hand experience of Russia resembled the narrative of a Chekhov play.

While I acknowledge Calderon's criticism, Baring's travel writing and critical analyses did enable British readers to get a stronger sense of Russian culture in general, contextualising Chekhov's plays within broader socio-political structures. At the beginning of *An Outline of Russian Literature* (1914), Baring chimes with many of the travellers mentioned in these pages when he complains about his compatriots' lack of knowledge about Russia, saying 'this ignorance will always remain until English people go to Russia and learn to know the Russian people at first hand'.[52] Like van Gyseghem, Baring connected Chekhov's plays firmly with Stanislavsky's techniques:

> In order that the tints of Chekhov's delicate living and breathing photographs can be effective on the stage, very special acting is necessary, in order to convey the quality of atmosphere which is his special gift. Fortunately he met with exactly the right technique and appropriate treatment at the Art Theatre in Moscow.[53]

Reflecting on his Russian travels Baring wrote three separate analyses: *With the Russians in Manchuria*, *What I Saw in Russia 1905–1906* and *What I Saw in Russia 1907–1914*. They focus on the volatile political situation in Russia but also contain frequent references to the theatre, including a description of *Uncle Vanya* and an analysis of Maxim Gorky's *Children of the Sun*.[54] In his 1922 autobiography, *The Puppet Show of Memory*, Baring, like many of his contemporaries, claimed that in 1904 the MAT 'possessed the best all-round theatre in Russia, if not in Europe'.[55]

Like Calderon, Baring was also a playwright. In his *The Grey Stocking* (first produced in 1908 at the Royalty Theatre), Russia invades the English provincial setting of Surrey in the person of Count Peter Velichkovsky. The play begins with Lady Sybil Alston's confirmation of a Russian visitor.

Mrs Simpson's humorous response – 'How thrilling! Is he an anarchist?'[56] – points to British misapprehensions of Russia from the off. Velichkovsky is a prodigious traveller and linguist, dressing and speaking, say the stage directions, like an Englishman.[57] While Baring suggests that Britons harbour misconceptions about Russians, Velichkovsky acknowledges his own fallacies about England, errors only addressed by actually setting foot on British soil:

> All the things one is told about England beforehand are wrong. One is told that railway porters don't speak to you; and they are very polite. One is told that the shopmen are rude; and I find they pull the shop to pieces for you. One is told that it always rains in London; and I have been in London a week and I have never known such heat.[58]

The Count causes significant rupture in the household, proclaiming his devotion to Lady Sybil who admits to similar feelings. However, the play ends with Velichkovsky returning to Russia, leaving Lady Sybil with her husband. His inertia and gloominess seem to mirror the emotions of Chekhov's characters; in many ways Velichkovsky feels like a Chekhovian imposter in an English drawing-room drama.[59]

Baring's later play *The Double Game* (1912) moves to Moscow and is far more political. It contains characters on both sides of the political divide, and is a tale of spies and counter-revolutionaries. The play concludes with the most revolutionary character – aristocratic Marie Andreevna – committing suicide to avoid arrest. Alongside the predominantly Russian characters is London journalist Harold Jameson, whose reactionary, judgemental approach presumably reflected the opinions of many in the audience. Elizaveta Ivanovna comments on his change in character:

> It's St Petersburg that has changed him. He used to be quite Liberal. Now he says just the very same things all the Englishmen say when they come here to learn Russian, not understanding the situation, and judging everything from the English point of view.[60]

Interestingly, while I claim that travel enables an embodied experience of the truth about a country (or at least this is the perception of the traveller), Elizaveta Ivanovna's comment reveals that first-hand contact with a culture sometimes leads to a strengthening of prejudice. In many ways *The Double Game* can be read alongside Baring's own national theatrical traditions, although Senelick makes the suggestion that 'the unhappy ending is more common to Russian drama than to English melodrama'.[61] It was first produced at the Kingsway Theatre in 1912 and described by the critic from the *Playgoer and Society Illustrated* as 'a tragic little play, but hardly the sort of thing one would care to see on a hot afternoon'.[62] However, despite the reviewer's rebuff, there is an interesting twist here, discovered in the diaries of Russian director Evgeny Vakhtangov:

> March 5, 1912
> Suler[zhitsky] suggested going to London to direct Baring's *Double Game*. Honorarium: 60 rubles a day, and I would have to pay for my own travel.
> March 6, 1912
> Asked Nemirovich to let me go to London.
> March 9, 1912
> They did not let me go to London.[63]

Prevented from travelling to Britain, Vakhtangov never directed Baring's play but the thought of this English melodrama being produced by the Russian originator of fantastic realism is an intriguing one.

The works of Chekhov also influenced the writing of another Britain-Russia traveller – George Bernard Shaw – although, like Fagan, Shaw was actually Irish by birth. Baring firmly connects the two playwrights, concluding Chekhov was 'a softened, under-exposed Slavonic Bernard Shaw, not without humour, but with the wit warfare, and fantasy left out'.[64] Although I take issue with Baring's analysis here, it is clear that commentators recognised similarities between these two epoch-defining playwrights. In 1919 Shaw published *Heartbreak House*, a play he termed a 'fantasia in the Russian manner on English themes'.[65] 'Heartbreak House' is not only the play's title but represents a particular concept; Shaw confirms it is 'cultured, leisured Europe before the war'.[66] Chekhov's *The Cherry Orchard*, *Uncle Vanya* and *The Seagull*, Shaw claims, all examine this 'Heartbreak House' concept. In many ways *Heartbreak House* is a Shavian version of a Chekhov-style play. It is set in Sussex and does not mention Russia at all. However, Shaw confirms its distinctly Russian origins by beginning the published script with a prologue discussing Chekhov's plays and particularly their reception in England:

> We stared and said, 'How Russian!' They did not strike me in that way… these intensely Russian plays fitted all the country houses in Europe… The same nice people, the same utter futility.[67]

Contrary to the usual complaints that Russian theatre seems foreign and incomprehensible, Shaw here maintains that Chekhov's plays actually capture the Europe-wide pre-war condition. Shaw's tale of the eccentric Captain Shotover, captivating Ellie Dunn, socialite Hesione Hushabye, businessman Mangan and their families certainly encapsulates a pre-war naivety. In the final scene a bomb goes off, killing Mangan and the burglars. When this dramatic event is over the characters are less relieved than disappointed: 'how damnably dull the world has become again suddenly... what a glorious experience. I hope they'll come again tomorrow night.'[68] Ultimately this is a play about the First World War, where, from the Russian frontier to the Somme, bombs quickly lost their exciting appeal. Despite the clear contextual parallels in this final scene, it also provides another connection with Chekhov. The 'explosions', as they are referred to in the script, illustrate Shaw's interest in sound effects, a theatrical motif as vital to understanding Chekhov's plays: the breaking string in *The Cherry Orchard* is the most well-known example. In fact, Miriam Handley suggests 'the two dramatists are somehow united by sounds'.[69] Just as Chekhov's string denotes a multiplicity of meaning, so Shaw's 'explosions' (notably Shaw uses the term 'explosions' rather than 'bombs') are less straightforward than it might first appear. Hesione Hushabye responds to the sounds (which vary in intensity and tone) by saying 'the sound in the sky: it's splendid: it's like an orchestra: it's like Beethoven'.[70] Notably Hesione connects the sounds with a German composer. Handley convincingly maintains that 'the processes of interpretation set out in the play's dialogue suggest Shaw was hoping that the sound effects of his play would be interpreted as more than just falling bombs'.[71] Like Chekhov's string, there is potentially more to the explosions than first meets the eye.

While Shaw connected *Heartbreak House* with Chekhov, actually (and I am indebted to Angus Wrenn and Olga Soboleva's scholarship here) it seemed to better reflect the techniques of Maxim Gorky. The two playwrights became friends in 1907 at a party organised by Thomas Hardy and remained on good terms throughout their lives.[72] While Shaw firmly connects *Heartbreak House* with the works of Chekhov, its intention and thematic concerns resonate more deeply with plays like Gorky's *Summerfolk* (1904); both examine 'the notion of false pretence and the opposition of appearance versus reality'.[73] Gorky's plays captured the imagination of a number of British theatre-makers, with the Stage Society producing *The Lower Depths*, for example, in 1903, the same year as Max Reinhardt's company, and barely a year after its premiere at the MAT.[74] Over 40 years later Glasgow Unity performed *The Lower Depths* to celebrate its foundation as a professional company. This production became a vital moment in the history of Scottish theatre. First, it marked Unity's continued interest in Russia, which began in the 1930s with its precursor the WTM's visit to Moscow. However, this production of *The Lower Depths*, a play about lower-class urban experience, also acted as a direct comment on Scottish society. Glasgow Unity defined itself as a distinctly Scottish theatre collective, despite clear connections with the broader Unity movement. Accordingly, *The Lower Depths* 'was performed in the idiom of the actors without any attempt by them to become Russian'.[75] Translator Robert Mitchell describes this intentional linguistic decision in more detail:

> It started off by me doing a rough breakdown of it into the idiom – not so much the full dialect of Glasgow, not making it a Scottish play as such, but a changing of the idiom so it became easy to the tongues of the Glasgow Unity.[76]

Unity's promotion of distinctly Scottish linguistic structures began, then, in a Russian play. This became a company policy, throwing open the doors for future productions by Ena Lamont Stewart, Robert McLeish and George Munro. As Bill Findlay compellingly argues, choosing *The Lower Depths* as its first professional performance and deciding to use Scottish (specifically Glaswegian) lexicon proved a challenge to Sassenach linguistic dominance, promoted local (specifically working-class) idioms as perfectly acceptable theatrical dialogue and established Unity's (and more generally, I suggest, Scottish theatre's) international focus.[77]

Shaw understood the political potency of theatre and, immediately after the Revolution, turned his attention to the contemporary situation in Russia with his short, humorous sketch *Annajanska: the Bolshevik Empress* (1917), performed as part of a variety evening at the Coliseum in January 1918. The play is based in the fictional country of Beotia after a revolution. General Strammfest is concerned by the new, anti-hierarchical, anti-royalist state whereas his lieutenant, Schneidekind, is excited by the regime change. The Grand Duchess is brought before the General who struggles with how best to respond to her: his former sovereign brought low by a people's revolution. In the final sequence the Grand Duchess is revealed as a uniform-wearing supporter of the revolution and Strammfest nicknames her the 'Bolshevik Empress'.[78] While she is clearly embedded in Russian politics, the Grand Duchess can also be read alongside Shaw's other strong female characters of this period, figures like Vivie Warren in *Mrs Warren's Profession* (1902) and Barbara Undershaft in *Major Barbara* (1905). *Annajanska* is a rather odd take on Russian politics; it is far more ambivalent about the Revolution than one might initially expect from leftist Shaw. When Strammfest initially discovers that the Grand Duchess is a revolutionary, young and supposedly idealistic, Schneidekind says, 'We've all joined the Revolution. She doesn't mean it any more we do'.[79] In many ways, as Wrenn and Soboleva discussed at a recent Anglo-Russian Research Group event, the play embodies Shaw's rather ambivalent feeling about the October Revolution; unsure as to the merits or otherwise of the Bolshevik takeover, the usually verbose Shaw made no direct comment on the Revolution until two years after the event. However, he wrote *Annajanska* just two weeks after the Bolsheviks swept to power. So one could claim the play as a creative outworking of the playwright's own confused state of mind.[80] Shaw termed it a 'bravura piece', a theatrical trifle rather than a serious attempt to analyse Russian politics or reveal a transnational truth to his audience. However, typical for Shaw, this does not really do justice to the import of the play as a complex, multi-tonal attempt to theatrically respond, with haste, to the October Revolution.

Shaw visited Russia in 1931 with Lady Nancy Astor (the first female MP), many years after his Chekhovian experiment. During his stay he met with Stalin, though details of what they spoke about during their two-and-a-half-hour meeting remain sketchy. Suffice to say, Shaw proclaimed the Russian dictator as a 'giant… all in the West are pygmies'.[81] He also visited Gorky who was unable to leave his house due to illness, and was welcomed by flag-waving citizens and eminent theatre-makers (such as Tairov and Stanislavsky) alike.[82] However, this trip was (and remains) tinged with controversy. American journalist (and United Press's Russian correspondent) Eugene Lyons, at one time a committed communist and admirer of the October Revolution who became increasingly disturbed by the repressive Bolshevik government and troubled by the hardships endured by the populace, described Shaw's trip in a chapter of his 1937 collection *Assignment in Utopia*. He was highly critical of Shaw's attitude and behaviour, shocked by the playwright's perceived unthinking selfishness. Whether his account is accurate or not (it is certainly scathing) is immaterial, for it is his performance-led description of Shaw's visit that furthers the arguments of *Migrating Modernist Performance*. Lyons frequently refers to Shaw's 'clowning', assuming the role of benevolent and humorous entertainer, throwing tinned British food out of the train window in

Poland because he refused to believe the stories of rationing and deprivation in Russia. The fact that he ate tremendous meals at the Metropole Hotel, for Shaw, confirmed the abundance of food in the Soviet state and, for Lyons, upheld his opinion of Shaw as an ignorant egotist. Lyons associated Shaw's behaviour with his role as playwright:

> We wondered at the time that a playwright wise in the tricks of stage effect should be taken in so completely by his hosts and guides. Then we understood that he was not taken in, but himself collaborating in the deception, with the world at large as the common dupe.[83]

As a theatre-maker Lyons presumed Shaw would see through the trickery of his hosts. In fact, for Lyons, the playwright decided to construct his own version of Russia, one which was as imaginative as many of his plays. Lyons bemoaned the perpetuation of mistruths that Shaw's trip, and subsequent writing, engendered: 'Shaw wrote and spoke extensively on Russia after he got home. His every sentence carried the proof that he had seen nothing and learned nothing in his Soviet visit.'[84] Travel here does not generate a more accurate understanding of place as might be expected; instead the act of visiting a country merely gives more credence to myths. Shaw counteracted the accusation that he had been hoodwinked by a political hoax during his 1931 trip by providing his own theatricalised reading of the situation:

> When I say that I was completely taken in, it must be remembered that as a professional playwright of forty years' experience, I am an expert in theatrical illusion, and know all the tricks of the actor, scene-painter, property man, and producer inside and out. To have deceived me is a triumph of Soviet administration.[85]

Wherever the truth lies here, both the accusation from Lyons and the defence from Shaw are couched in an obvious theatrical lexicon; onstage performance and the performed act of travelling seem interchangeable.

Shaw's work certainly became extremely popular in the USSR, admired for its aesthetic and political qualities. Indeed, Shaw became one of the most popular foreign playwrights in Russia, although often referred to as English rather than Irish. The earliest production was *Arms and the Man* in 1905, and he was later championed at the Maly Theatre and by Meyerhold in versions of *You Never Can Tell* (1912) and *Pygmalion* (1915).[86] Just as British theatre-makers and audiences seemed to create distinctly anglicised versions of Chekhov's works, so Russian practitioners imbibed Shaw with an unmistakable Russian atmosphere. A reviewer of the 1914 Moscow Dramatic Theatre's version of *Pygmalion*, a production endorsed by Shaw, summed up the primary differences:

> From the English point of view Shaw is amoral, Russians accept him simply as a very remarkable writer, who provides the theater with excellently constructed, tastefully expressed, wittily executed plays. We repeat, in Russia Shaw is more looked at than listened to.[87]

The distinction here is an important one; for this pre-revolutionary Russian reviewer at least, Shaw in England is associated with troublesome ideas and socio-political analysis, whereas Shaw in Russia is assessed in far more artistic terms.

In 1924, Tairov, director at the Kamerny Theatre, produced another of Shaw's plays about independent women, *St Joan*, just a year after its world premiere in New York. American humorist Robert Benchley attended this production, paying particular attention to Tairov's satirical and rather arresting use of clowning:

> If Shaw really means to kid his countrymen, if the centuries and centuries of repetition of the same old historic formulas, the pomp and ceremony and majestic clash of arms, are to him the bunk that they seem to be, then he ought to adopt these Russians as his sons. If he is sore at what they have done, he doesn't understand his Shaw at all.[88]

Unfortunately, Shaw never saw Tairov's production. However, Benchley seemed convinced that the Russian had somehow realised a truer understanding of Shaw's intentions and convictions.

Watching a production of *The Cherry Orchard* or *The Seagull* was often a British audience member's first experience of the Russian stage. But other classic Russian plays made their way to the Britain, including *A Month in the Country* by Ivan Turgenev, a nineteenth-century tale of love and misunderstandings, performed by the MAT in 1909. It was produced at the Royalty Theatre in 1926 and famed critic James Agate's response says a great deal about British reactions to Russian theatre in general. He initially points to the differences between the two national theatrical traditions: 'the Russian realist, inviting subjection of the spectator's mood, consents that he shall still remain master of his intelligence; the English romancer insists upon surrender not only of mood, but of mind.'[89] It is a lament found regularly in the writings of the figures in this book. Certainly, Agate suggests, there are profound misunderstandings in the way British audiences comprehend Russian theatre. Watching *A Month in the Country*, he suggests, 'we are inclined to take this sadness a little more seriously than the Russians intended… that which we call a tragedy Turgenev calls a comedy, and we reflect that Tchehov intended *The Cherry Orchard* to be played as a farce'.[90] However, he concludes by confirming the possibility that such plays *could* be understood in a British context:

> All that is necessary is the absence of a star-actor and the refusal of the company, whenever the star opens his mouth, to suspend animation like a golf crowd watching Hagan drive off the last tee with a four for the championship.[91]

Agate uses the production of *A Month in the Country* to make a significant comment on British theatre in general and the way the influence of the Russian stage might rid it of its commercial, celebrity-focused philistinism.

## Migratory Collaborations: Craig, Duncan, Stanislavsky and the MAT *Hamlet*

One of the most well-documented examples of British-Russian modernist theatrical exchange occurred when American dancer Isadora Duncan introduced Stanislavsky to Edward Gordon Craig. Though American by birth, Duncan lived much of her life in Europe and her relationship with Russia was a long and fruitful one, with her first visit in 1904. While in St Petersburg she witnessed the dawn burial of those killed outside the Winter Palace as they presented their petition to the Tsar. Duncan claimed this travel experience as a seminal moment in her political consciousness:

> If I had never seen it, all my life would have been different. There, before this seemingly endless procession, this tragedy, I vowed myself and my forces to the service of the people and the down-trodden.[92]

Her travels in Russia both before the First World War and after transformed her socio-political outlook. However, Duncan's appearances in Russia also affected aesthetic change in St Petersburg and Moscow. She challenged Russia's longstanding love affair with the rigours and disciplines of ballet, and acted as an ally for practitioners seeking new ways of construing the performative body on the stage. Choreographers such as

Alexander Gorsky, Michel Fokine and Elena Rabenek built on the foundations of Duncan's free dance methods. Her appearances in Russia (particularly in the pre-war period) 'had the significance of an aesthetic program. She embodied a new mentality. Her appearance was an event of general interest, important not only to dance, but also to art and culture as a whole'.[93] Stanislavsky also admired Duncan's practice, particularly after the dancer gave a series of performances at the MAT in 1907. In a letter of January 1908 Stanislavsky effusively praised Duncan's work, clearly feeling a strong affinity with her:

> You are the first to tell me in a few simple and convincing words what is important and fundamental about the art I wished to create. That gave me a fresh burst of energy at a moment when I was about to give up my artistic career.[94]

In 1911 Stanislavsky and Craig, initially encouraged by Duncan, collaborated in a seminal production of *Hamlet* for the MAT. The details of this production are well known but it remains vital for this book as it draws attention to some of the perennial issues of transnational artistic exchange, particularly when there are substantial geographical distances and the process is reliant on occasional travel. Despite mutual admiration, Craig and Stanislavsky harboured very different ideas about theatrical process. Whereas Stanislavsky encouraged his actors to emotionally and intellectually invest in their characters, Craig's methods challenged this realist position. Published in his journal *The Mask* in May 1915, Craig's 'Hamlet in Moscow: notes for a short address to the actors of the Moscow Art Theatre' revisited his 1909 advice for the actors of the MAT:

> You must become ecstatic. You must lose yourself.
>
> It is impossible to believe that you can interpret so great a work without making use of your own greatness. You cannot do it by your reason, which is your littleness. You can only do it by the power of Imagination.[95]

It does not seem that he actually vocalised this advice,[96] but he clearly had particular ideas about an actor's approach to Shakespeare's canonical play, ideas reliant less on personal study of character than transcendental abandonment.

Perhaps he did not impart these comments because of the language barriers that plagued this production and, more generally, so often prevented the figures in this book from engaging fully with Russian culture.

Craig spoke neither Russian nor French, and Stanislavsky had no English, so it is certainly possible that the two never really understood the other's vision fully.[97] Craig's trips to Russia in the lead up to the performance certainly attempted to clarify his plans for the production. He arrived first in 1908 and, while he was not wholly uncritical of the MAT, his initial impressions of Stanislavsky's company were positive:

> The Art Theatre here (about which I write) is possessed of character and intelligence. Its director, Constantin Stanislawsky [sic], has achieved the impossible: he has successfully established a non-commercial theatre… Seriousness, character, these two qualities will guide the Moscow Art Theatre to unending success in Europe or elsewhere.[98]

Combining Stanislavsky's actor-focused, emotion-centred system and Craig's symbolist, non-mimetic suggestiveness was, as might have been expected, a combustible fusion. The disconnect can be seen in their understandings of Hamlet as protagonist. Reflecting on a sixteenth-century wood carving of Hamlet, Craig concludes that it is a more successful rendering than all the Hamlets he has seen onstage. This is a Hamlet as a constructed image, detached from the inaccuracies and personalities of the actor and, he gratifyingly notes, from the chatter and interruptions of all the other characters. Here, Craig suggests, 'dwells the soul of Hamlet with the part of Hamlet left out – and not found wanting'.[99] Stanislavsky perceived Hamlet in a very different way. In a later 1937 series of masterclasses, Stanislavsky focused on *Hamlet*'s protagonist, enabling his students to understand the character more fully. In sharp contrast to Craig, Stanislavsky asked his students to identify with the Danish prince, to ask questions about his feelings and emotions, to embody the character by fully empathising with his perspective, experiences and attitudes:

> You must clearly imagine your whole life from your childhood to the death of your father… once I have been given a role, say, Hamlet, thereafter there is no difference between Hamlet and me. I exist in Hamlet's situation. Take everything from your **Emotion Memory**.[100]

It is clear that Stanislavsky and Craig harboured profoundly different ideas about Hamlet the protagonist. The contrast between Craig's symbolic, representational approach and Stanislavsky's emotion memory reveals the broader disagreements that plagued this version of Shakespeare's play.

The eventual production, now regarded as a seminal modernist performance, was a flawed combination of the two styles. Reviews were mixed:

> First came the gimmicks of Gordon Craig, the screens and cubes. And only then the actor. Tacked on... Stanislavsky and Nemirovich are head and shoulders above this swell-headed Englishman. Let him learn from them, not they from him.[101]

This Russian reviewer focuses not only on the aesthetic problems of the play but on the transnational tensions. He seems to regard Craig's contribution as an imposition, an unwelcome dilution of the MAT's brand of actor-centred realism. For his part Craig concluded the project feeling rather dejected, but remained buoyant about the MAT:

> My enthusiasm for the Moscow Art Theatre is just what it was. There are one or two rats in the building, but they don't count... But the Art of the theatre still calls, and I, feeling refreshed after my late experience at Moscow, turn to the question of the Art with renewed pleasure and determination.[102]

Again, here is a British traveller finding rejuvenating inspiration from time spent in Russia. The production found longevity in Britain and Russia. It remained in the MAT canon for three seasons in Moscow and St Petersburg. At the same time, at the Leicester Galleries in London, Craig exhibited his *Hamlet* models.[103] The exhibition enabled visitors to interact with a production that had occurred (and indeed was still playing) many miles away. While reviews acknowledge the problem of taking these images away from their theatrical setting and placing them in an art gallery, there is also an appreciation of Craig's style:

> One is impressed anew by the variety of mood and atmosphere that Mr Craig can achieve by use of the simplest means.[104]

The simultaneous showing of the exhibition in Britain and playing of *Hamlet* in Russia reveals the undoubted transnational identity of this work.

This genial, collaborative relationship heated up when Stanislavsky's *My Life in Art* was translated into English in 1924. The Russian was actually extremely complimentary about Craig but he also mentioned the problem of the screens which 'wobbled and fell'.[105] Stanislavsky does not confirm whether this scenographic setback was caused by Craig's poor planning or errors from the MAT set builders. Either way, in the actual performances, the screens were weighted down, which meant they had little movement or vibrancy.[106] Stanislavsky charitably speculates 'and yet what wholeness and unity Craig's method of staging the sets would have given to the whole production'.[107] Despite this difficult collaborative experience, though, Stanislavsky remained supportive of the Englishman's artistic ambitions:

> He [Craig] protested on the one hand against the conventions which were redolent of normal theatre and, on the other, would not accept the humdrum naturalness and simplicity that took away poetry. Craig, like me, wanted perfection, an ideal i.e. a simple, profound, inspiring, artistic, beautiful expression of human feeling.[108]

Craig might have been cross that Stanislavsky drew attention to the failure of the screens but, had he looked further into *My Life in Art*, he would have seen that Stanislavsky never lost respect for his aesthetic objectives.

Years later, Craig's esteem for Stanislavsky remained despite disagreements about stage technique:

> Stanislavsky has always been a searcher. He does not seek to discover a simple truth, for the obvious does not appeal to him. He prefers, when looking for the highroad, to turn his back to it, to enter into the forest and grope in the very thickest of the undergrowth. If asked why he has left the highroad he will reply that everyone knows *that* highroad, and he prefers to look for others. Briefly his tendency is to avoid the ordinary, plain truth, and to search for more unusual truths in unlikely directions.[109]

Despite its perceived failure, the Moscow *Hamlet* remains a vital moment in modernist performance history. Senelick suggests it is 'not an isolated creative spasm, but a ganglion in which the nerves of some of the most important art movements of our time came together'.[110] Undoubtedly this is true for this production, revealing something of the vibrancy and diversity of modernist performance. However, I want to extend Senelick's comment and suggest that this formative moment acts as a linchpin for this current project: a specific example of theatrical experiment reliant (successfully or not) on transnational, migratory collaboration between Britain and Russia.

Thirteen years after the Craig/Stanislavsky *Hamlet*, Shakespeare's play appeared on the MAT stage again, this time at the Second Moscow Art Theatre under the direction of Anton Chekhov's nephew Michael.

In fact, Michael Chekhov had played a courtier and soldier in the 1911 production.[111] Years later Chekhov left Russia after being branded an anti-revolutionary and arrived in Britain in 1935, going on to set up the Chekhov Theatre School at Dartington Hall, Devon. Chekhov's commitment to creating 'harmony between the two, body and psychology'[112] attempted to solve issues that concerned Craig and Stanislavsky in different ways: how should the actor move onstage, and what is the relationship between the mind and the body? Partly influenced by Stanislavsky, Chekhov conceived of the psychological gesture, a single movement that would enable the actor to immediately grasp the fundamental spirit of the character: 'its task is to summarise the intricate psychology of a character in an easily surveyable form, to compress it into its essence.'[113] This seems to counteract Craig's *Übermarionette* concept. However, Franc Chamberlain connects Craig and Chekhov by saying that 'both were concerned that the actor's use of the face in their time was inartistic and that this had to be changed'.[114] So when Chekhov arrived in Britain he brought both the concerns of Craig and the aesthetics of Stanislavsky, and created his own theatrical methodology deep in the Devonshire countryside.

## Constructivist Fragments on the British Stage

Examining Craig's aesthetics, it is easy to identify discord between his ideas and Stanislavsky's system. In many ways a more successful British-Russian collaboration might have occurred between Craig and one of Russia's other leading directors, namely Vsevolod Meyerhold. 'Had Craig and Meyerhold cooperated in a production,' says Senelick, 'they would have spoken a common language and avoided the conflicts in which Craig and Stanislavsky invariably landed'.[115] The two were certainly aware of one another, and, although they never worked together, actually met in Moscow in 1935.[116] Despite the political differences, Meyerhold and Craig shared an appreciation for the symbolic and suggestive onstage, and for a breakaway from mimeticism.

Meyerhold's theatrical experiments tackled the very conventions Craig found so difficult to deal with at the MAT. He remained entirely in awe of Stanislavsky, his teacher and mentor and, even in 1921 when Meyerhold was producing the constructivist *Mystery Bouffe*, he maintained, 'in Moscow there is only one guardian of genuine traditions – the ever solitary Stanislavsky'.[117] He was careful to differentiate between Stanislavsky and the realist conventions of the MAT which he found so infuriating:

'Moscow Art Theatre is to blame for the passivity of the spectator whom it held in thrall for so long; at one time he was not even allowed to applaud when a surge of enthusiasm demanded applause. A theatrical performance should be a joyous event which rouses the public's emotions.'[118] While there are significant differences between Meyerhold and Craig – politics, use of clowning, centrality of the dextrous actor – they would certainly have concurred about the repressive nature of MAT techniques, even if they both retained an admiration for Stanislavsky.

While Craig and Meyerhold regrettably never worked together, other British travellers to Russia certainly met Meyerhold and a number were influenced by the ideas of constructivism that he posited. Opinions of the innovator varied. British journalist Launcelot Lawton's 1924 interview with Meyerhold sums up some of the British scepticism about the Russian's methods. He was unimpressed by the biomechanics he witnessed and confused about the workers' clothes worn as costumes on the stage. He concludes in rather cryptic terms, seemingly unable to really sum up Meyerhold's innovations:

> The symbol of this new society is the Machine. The Machine is sober, reliable, heroic, powerful and productive, and it is composed of many separate small parts, all of which possess these essentially proletarian qualities.[119]

Dean also met Meyerhold during his 1926 visit. He admired Meyerhold's passion but remained unconvinced by his theatrical methodology:

> Many things are being done under the guise of dramatic art that have nothing to do with art at all. For instance the theories of Meyerhold the great Communist producer are just so much sophistry. In an hour's conference with him we were enabled to reduce his position to so much chop logic.[120]

As so often in the reflections of the travellers, such experiences caused Dean to consider the state of British theatre. He reflected, 'there must be some middle course between the moribund drama and comfortable comedies of the English theatre and the bustling over-politicised plays of Russia'.[121]

At first glance, Meyerhold's work appeared to make little difference to the British theatrical scene. Partly this was because of Meyerhold's brand of clowning; politicised stylisation was anathema to the prevailing British realist tradition. However, Meyerhold's early death and subsequent erasure from Russian theatre history until his rehabilitation in the late 1950s also contributed to a lack of British performances influenced by his work. Husband of Marie Rambert and founder of the Mercury Theatre Ashley Dukes reflected on constructivism's fall from grace in 1942:

> In the early 1920s... the truly left-minded could accept as an article of faith (never having seen it) that the Russian stage was the only one even possibly worthwhile. Actually, out of all this Soviet architecture of ladders and platforms, out of all the clambering of actors in and out of windows and their marching up and down stairways, nothing of value to our current theatre seems to have survived.[122]

Two things about Dukes's comments are valuable to my project. First, Dukes notes that British practitioners imagined the vibrancy of the 1920s Soviet stage without actually witnessing it. He confirms 'it was difficult to visit Russia and see for oneself, and by the time the country was thrown open to "Intourists" there was less to be seen'.[123] Dukes, like so many, emphasised the value of travel as a mode of theatrical discovery. Second, by 1942, just two years after Meyerhold's death, it seemed constructivist techniques had entirely disappeared nationally due to enforced cultural norms, and internationally because of ignorance. While Dukes remained fascinated by Russian subjects – confirmed by his version of Alfred Neumann's *Der Patriot*, entitled *Such Men Are Dangerous*, performed to acclaim in Edinburgh and London in 1927/8, which told the story of Count Pahlen's conspiracy against the Tsar[124] – he never truly engaged practically with the ideas of Meyerhold.

But to leave it there would be to erase a small but vibrant British appropriation of Meyerholdian methods, centred around the work of a few notable theatrical travellers. Van Gyseghem devotes considerable space to Meyerhold in *Theatre in Soviet Russia*. His reflections emanate from witnessing Meyerhold's version of *The Forest* (1924, remaining in Meyerhold's repertoire until 1938[125]). Ostrovsky's comedic play was well known but Meyerhold transformed it because, in the words of Konstantin Rudnitsky, he 'was trying to overcome the distance separating "leftist art" from the wide, mass audience with one stroke'.[126] So Meyerhold took the bare, austere stage and transformed it with colour and vibrancy – bright costumes, clanging bells, slapstick comedy.[127] The extant images of Ivan Koval-Samborsky

(Petr) and Zinaida Raikh (Aksyusha) flinging themselves around the stage on swings confirm the playful excitement of Meyerhold's vision.[128]

A number of things stand out for van Gyseghem. First, he compares the audience demographic with his experience in Britain: 'compared to the wrinkled faces and white hair that predominate the stalls of an average English West End theatre, this audience is positively juvenile.'[129] Second, he notes the simple metatheatricality of Meyerhold's performance space, where 'hard glittering lights… reveal every corner of the stage-space in all its crudeness of brick and metal, paint and canvas'.[130] He plays this production off against his own expectations. Soviet revolutionary theatre, he anticipated, should include regimented actors, celebrations of militarisation and propaganda. *The Forest* counteracted these expectations: 'So our first reaction is one of bewilderment! And such, I imagine is the reaction of the majority of foreign visitors to Meyerhold's theatre.'[131] He also writes comprehensively about Meyerhold's version of *La Dame aux Camélias*, a play van Gyseghem saw, at least in rehearsal, alongside theatre-makers from Japan, Germany, Czechoslovakia and America.[132] Summing up Meyerhold's canon of work, van Gyseghem notes 'his ideas are like a pack of cards which he builds into a house only to sweep away and build again with hundreds of variations of form upon a single theme – the decay of bourgeois society'.[133]

Meyerhold's biomechanical methods – his intricate physicalised techniques which transformed the body into a playful, mechanised image of the Revolution – remained painfully under-researched (and subsequently under-used) in a British context until very recently. In fact, Amy Skinner suggests that van Gyseghem's description in *Theatre in Soviet Russia* was 'by far the most comprehensive' analysis of biomechanics to appear in Britain.[134] Van Gyseghem spends several pages describing Meyerhold's methods, particularly focusing on the étude 'Throwing the Stone'. He makes his way through each individual movement in the étude, carefully elucidating the actions of each part of the body. However, by his own admission, 'it is difficult to give a clear picture of such physical exercises with the written word'.[135] Indeed, as Skinner goes on to suggest, it was only many years later that reconstructions of Meyerholdian biomechanics made their way to Britain in any worthwhile embodied sense. Ultimately the lack of real body-to-body transmission ensured a limited British understanding of biomechanics.

But this restricted exposure did not entirely preclude British performances reflecting Meyerhold's unique ideas. One of Meyerhold's most important and influential productions was his 1922 *The Magnanimous Cuckold*. Van Gyseghem describes this production (which he terms '*The Magnificent Cuckold*') as showing 'the bare bones of bio-mechanics more clearly than any other' and that it 'spread the vogue for constructivist settings'.[136] Certainly with its gymnastic exuberance and playground-style staging, *The Magnanimous Cuckold* stands as a particularly impressive example of Meyerhold's work. In 1932, ten years after Meyerhold's production and as constructivism was on the wane in Soviet Russia, the Stage Society attempted a version of Ferdnand Crommelynck's play with an illustrious cast including Peggy Ashcroft and George Devine. Komisarjevsky designed the set and, while I am yet to find extant photos of this production, the *Daily Telegraph* reviewer describes the *mise en scène* in detail: 'a door, but no wall, a queerly straggling staircase, half a water-wheel, and a tower-like platform (on the height of which was a jazz band providing soft incidental music) all of rough wood.'[137] The style seemed to confuse reviewers entirely and they oscillated between describing it as a constructivist or expressionist production. Severely criticising the Stage Society's attempt, the *Sunday Times* gives some sense of how performers used the set:

> When M Crommelynck desires that somebody shall write, M Komisarjevsky first makes that scribe mount a pylon like the exalted contraption used for mending overhead tram-lines and then dip an outsize goose-feather into some monstrous, inky carboy, thereby endowing an everyday feat with Grock-like infeasibility.[138]

Such constructivist aesthetics troubled many of the reviewers, with a number reconnecting this performance to Russian theatre in their criticisms. The reviewer from the *National Graphic*, for instance, concedes, 'I was able to enjoy the Stage Society's production, in spite of the bleak art-crafty Moscow décor of bare boards... I did not think the Russian setting helped much.'[139] The *Observer*'s reviewer also condemns the constructivist set, 'a fad much favoured by the plodding anti-realists of the Soviet Theatre', sarcastically concluding, 'I wish I could understand the deep spiritual significance of putting up the furniture and then omitting the upholstery.'[140] Clearly many reviewers saw this production as decidedly Russian even though Crommelynck was Belgian and the cast was populated by British actors. I suggest the presence of Komisarjevky and the lingering spectre of Meyerhold's classic 1922 experiment haunted this British version.

Although one can create parallels between Meyerholdian constructivism and British theatre (bare stages, political motivations) it is profoundly difficult to make clear connections. The work of WTM member and poet Christina Walshe provides a case in point. Walshe certainly travelled to Paris in the early 1920s, falling in with a community of Russian émigrés. Given that this group had clearly detached themselves from the Bolshevik Soviet state, it might be surprising that, while in Paris, Walshe became a socialist and started to explore avant-garde aesthetics.[141] Returning to Britain she began to design for the theatre, writing articles for the *Daily Herald* and the *Sunday Worker*. In 1928 the Labour Publishing Company published Stephen Schofield's *The Judge of All the Earth*, a 'one-act expressionistic morality play'.[142] In performance (it was first produced at Ruskin College and, later, by the WTM) it used a platform set to represent the afterlife, designed by Walshe. The set is described as made of sugar boxes with splashes of colour: 'I have used cream, which looks like marble, and a carpet of gold up the steps, The back of the throne and the two pinnacles may also be of gold. A curtain of royal blue muslin looks very well, but black might be as good or better.'[143] The play is a highly political analysis of the afterlife in which a Guardsman is finally rewarded, a Bishop is exposed as a hypocrite and a Woman whom he excused of 'living in sin' is finally accepted into Heaven. While the connections between this and Meyerhold's work are sketchy, certainly the ideas for the set came out of Walshe's socialist convictions and cubist aesthetics that she found among the Russian émigré community of Paris. Comparing Walshe to the far better known Rebecca West, John Stokes acknowledges that her work with the WTM 'was to be deeply influenced by what they knew of Expressionism in Germany and constructivist exponents in Russia'.[144]

The lack of real constructivist experiments in Britain may be due partly to the inaccessibility of Meyerhold's productions. Whereas the Ballets Russes and the MAT's Prague Group toured Britain, and Tairov got as far as Continental Europe, Meyerhold's company was prevented from travelling outside Russia until 1930 when it finally journeyed to Germany and then to Paris.[145] The Soviet authorities denied the Meyerhold company permission to tour America[146] and it returned to Russia to face increasingly hostile artistic conditions. Unless practitioners travelled to Russia they were unable to experience Meyerhold's theatre first-hand, relying instead on written resources migrating over the English Channel.

The evidence here confirms the importance of Meyerhold's work in a British context, even if its effects were not keenly felt in the West End.

While the premises of constructivism and Stanislavskian naturalism might initially appear to be at odds, the two sprang from the same impetus and in some performances appeared together, if rather awkwardly. One particularly fascinating example of this appeared in 1932 when Nathan Zarkhi's *Joy Street* was produced at the Mayakovsky Theatre and Bolshoi Theatre.[147] It focused not on the successes of Bolshevism nor the heroics of the workers, but on the streets of London. Van Gyseghem confirms that the play contains 'two styles of acting; the realistic manner and the symbolic schematic manner'.[148] On the one hand there are the recognisable characters: the labour leader, his girlfriend, an Italian anarchist. On the other there are the marionette-like characters: the minister and the schoolteacher, among others, defined by their mechanisation and 'curious clipped speech'.[149] The clash seemed perplexing even to those familiar with Russian theatre such as P.A. Markov, drama critic and director of MAT's literary department, who commented on the performance of lead actor Judith Glizer, saying 'her eccentric method of interpretation ran counter to the entire production. I am not sure whether it was the fault of Glizer or of the production'.[150] It is difficult to fully comprehend the intentions here. Clearly the production tapped into both realist and constructivist acting styles; the most sympathetic, heroic characters utilise naturalistic methods while the representatives of bourgeois culture become puppets. Given the performance dates of this play, was this theatrical rendering of London a satirical mockery of the Meyerholdian stylisation that was about to be superseded by a turn to socialist realism, or a simple appropriation of methods? The extant photograph seems to suggest the latter. The set, designed by Ilya Shlepyanov, depicted the East End slum in realistic fashion. However, the action is framed by two staircases, reminiscent of Meyerholdian constructivism.[151] Whichever, the fact that this tension is enacted in a play about the East End of London is fascinating. It remained confusing for the British travellers in the audience, too. In the early 1930s British diplomat Reader Bullard was stationed in Leningrad. In May 1933 he went to see *Joy Street*, his diaries confirming 'we thought we ought to go and see a play about life in England'. He left unimpressed:

> We came out at half-time finding it more than our digestions could stand. The first two scenes were in a London slum. There was a strike with the trade union leader 'betraying the workers,' the police arrested the strike committee, a boy delivering washing is knocked down by a motor-car and discharged for soiling the washing, which included Lady Salisbury's lace

> knickers. A girl is raped. There is much hypocritical church-going. Bailiffs evict the washerwoman for being behind with the rent... We had had enough. The cloakroom attendant asked why we were leaving. 'England isn't like that'.[152]

Bullard seems to be offended by the national misunderstandings rather than the themes *per se*. However, Herbert Marshall, a migratory figure we will return to in more detail in Chapter 4, claimed to be a 'consultant for this production'.[153] While there is little definitive evidence for this, I have no reason to doubt him. Marshall was born in East Ham, London and so could claim the sort of first-hand experience sought by many of his sojourning compatriots. So often in this book the British travellers to Russia attempt to address false impressions about Soviet life. It is interesting to note, in the case of *Joy Street* at least, that misinterpretations, bias and subsequent incredulity from the local populace moved both ways.

## 'I KNOW NOTHING ABOUT AFINOGENEV BUT HE IS EVERYWHERE'[154]: THE RISE OF SOCIALIST REALISM

In 1944 Unity Theatre performed a version of the Sheynin Brothers' thriller *Comrade Detective*. The theatre's newsletter describes the play in glowing terms:

> As is usual with Soviet plays, the character-drawing is human and real. It shows how a Russian detective gets on the track of a ring of Gestapo spies and how he is aided in their capture by ordinary Soviet people.[155]

Unity, the group that emerged from the wreckage of the agitprop collective WTM, had clearly turned resolutely away from the sloganising declamation of their 1933 Moscow Olympiad performances. Instead, for this writer at least, Soviet theatre seemed defined by real characters, linear storylines and clear political messages about wartime victory and community collectivity.

In the last chapter I briefly noted the dramatic change in Russian workers' theatre aesthetics from agitprop to socialist realism. Platform stages, declamation and thrown-in songs were out, replaced by linear narratives, fictionalised characterisation and dialogue. This transformation affected the performances of the workers' theatres across the world as well as causing Meyerhold to fall from favour, regarded as dangerously and perplexingly avant-garde. His state-sanctioned murder in 1940 and subsequent 15-year neglect reveal the high stakes of producing such experimental work under dictatorship. P.A. Markov described socialist realism in *The Soviet Theatre*, a book that had made its way to Britain by 1934. Journalist John Hallett reviewed Markov's book in a 1934 article in the *Spectator*, recognising the accessibility of Markov's work and noting that it points to the 'two broad tendencies in Soviet theatrical production': realism beginning with the MAT and the 'bizarre, the conventional and the symbolical' Meyerhold.[156] Markov gives a potted history of post-Revolutionary Soviet theatre, moving from the MAT to Meyerhold, Vakhtangov, Tairov and other traditions such as the workers' theatre troupes and the Jewish theatre. His conclusion details the change towards socialist realism:

> Socialist realism, which means truth in the ideas and emotions directed towards the transformation of the world, is the essence and not merely the form of Soviet art. The theatre has long ceased to be an empiric chronicler of facts. It has long given up the photographic representation of reality. But to be truthful does not necessarily mean to give up all the romance of the Revolution. On the contrary, to be truthful means to look forward into the future.[157]

Markov's description of socialist realism, as with the form itself, is littered with contradictions. The aim is truth but the theatre does not chronicle facts; it seeks to transform the world in a direct, materialist way and yet is built on the 'romance of the Revolution'. This tense combination of realism and romanticism defined the socialist realist mode.

British theatre-makers responded to the challenge in a range of ways. One particular supporter of socialist realism was theatre producer, author, poet and journalist Joseph Macleod. In his 1952 *A Soviet Theatre Sketchbook*, an amalgam of travel narratives, short stories and factual reflections on Russian culture, Macleod included a chapter on a (fictional) Sir Stephen Walbrook who is undertaking an English Trade Mission to Moscow. His interpreter takes him to see *Pygmalion* but Sir Stephen initially rejects it due to poor costumes and errors in the *mise en scène*. His announcement, 'Outward things count you know. Especially in the theatre. People remember outward things', is met with his interpreter's seemingly far more thoughtful 'But it is the truth that matters'.[158] In the end Sir Stephen, mocked throughout as a thoroughly pompous and ignorant interloper, concedes 'perhaps there is something… to be said for this Socialist Realism of yours'.[159]

I suggest that Macleod's admiration for Russian socialist realist aesthetics can be traced back to his 1933–1935 directorship of the Festival Theatre, Cambridge. Macleod took over the Festival when Terence Gray stepped down. In a short time Gray had created one of Britain's premiere spaces for avant-garde experimentation in performance. As mentioned in the introduction, Gray was prevented from staging Tretyakov's *Roar China!* but he did succeed in transforming his playing space by getting rid of the proscenium and installing a revolving stage. In an active step away from the traditions of naturalism he sought a theatre that was far less reliant on language, instead looking to movement, believing that 'the human body is man's natural means of self-expression'.[160] The Festival Theatre developed a reputation for its similarities with the Continental European avant-garde stage, but when Macleod took over in 1933 the identity of the Festival changed. In an article in the *Cambridge Chronicle* Macleod, in a veiled criticism of his predecessor, said 'nothing will be done on the stage here which cannot be defended and supported… such art is decadent. We are ultra-modern… not "modernist"'.[161] Macleod produced an impressive selection of plays at the Festival, focusing on Shakespeare, realist classics by Ibsen and Chekhov and both parts of Goethe's *Faust*, no small undertaking for a chronically under-resourced theatre.[162] He stepped down in 1935, disappointed by the lack of support and saying, one might imagine with a degree of venom, 'I have not failed. My company has not failed… Cambridge has failed'.[163]

By 1937 he found himself in Russia, subsequently publishing his recollections in *The New Soviet Theatre* (1943), *Actors Cross the Volga* (1946) and *A Soviet Theatre Sketchbook* (1951). Macleod confirms that this compulsion to travel to Russia stemmed from his experiences in Cambridge:

> It was in 1935 that I first became aware of the Soviet Theatre with a more awakened consciousness than that of an unsuccessful experimental producer in a highbrow repertory theatre.[164]

It is unclear whether Macleod is criticising Gray here or whether this exclamation is self-parody. Either way, Macleod inextricably connects his experiences in Cambridge with his desire to explore Russia and its theatrical traditions.

His books on Russia are littered with references to his homeland; clearly, as for so many of the travellers mentioned in this book, Macleod's experiences in the Soviet Union taught him as much about Britain as Russia. Of particular note are the frequent allusions to Scotland, Macleod's country of origin. England (specifically London) is rarely mentioned except in a rather derogatory way. In his fictionalised, fact-based *A Soviet Theatre Sketchbook*, he compares the Moscow theatre scene and the West End:

> Nor did any London auditorium ever hold, night after night so large a proportion of teen-age spectators; nor did grey tabs of any London stage ever conceal so intimately glorious a show as those attend week by week.[165]

One can sense the disappointment of his perceived failures at the Festival in his condemnation of mainstream theatre in England.

But it is Scotland that reappears time and again in his writings. In Chapter 7 of *A Soviet Theatre Sketchbook*, entitled 'Describing Moscow', for example, the protagonist, Makovsky, goes to see *Truth Is Good, Happiness Is Better* at the Maly Theatre. The production is dated 1943 in this fictionalised rendering and, indeed, in real life. The play focuses on a poor man, Zybkin, and his grandmother who is described in this chapter as follows:

> By a small stretch of imagination, this figure might be sitting in Victorian Pollokshields and the shawl (for it is very like Paisley shawl) might have been the gift of some grateful dead employer in whose Blythswood Square household she had served.[166]

This sequence makes little sense unless you understand the history, geography and socio-political identity of Glasgow. Macleod imposes a distinctly Scottish image on a specifically Russian play. It also leaves a particular problem of narrative voice. While we experience the play through the eyes of Makovsky, actually he could not possibly make such a connection. Macleod as narrator appears here turning a fictional story into a traveller's experience.

These connections with Scotland continue through the books, from the comparison of the floral clock in Edinburgh and Kiev, to the juxtaposition of Moscow and Motherwell, to Ukrainian official Chebanyenko's incongruous use of Scottish idiom in his proclamation 'We're a wee bittie vexed'.[167] Macleod's constant allusions to Scotland appear to be politically motivated. This is clearer in *Actors Cross the Volga* in which he asks why there is a Ukrainian theatre but no Scottish theatre. Macleod suggests that, while both are in union with a bigger neighbour, the Ukraine has been able to keep its own language and culture, whereas in Great Britain, England is a dominant hegemonic force: 'There is an organic relation between [Russia and the Ukraine] on both sides of the footlights' whereas England and Scotland enjoy no such parity.[168] Macleod's reflections are certainly troublesome, but they reveal his convictions and suggest his trips to Russia did not merely inspire him theatrically but also politically; Macleod (rightly or wrongly) perceived a different, egalitarian manifestation of a union which caused him to consider the inequalities in his own national experience. Macleod's reflections reveal a little about the particularly close connections between Scotland and Russia during this period. The artistic Scottish Renaissance, with its socialist and nationalist overtones, increasingly looked to Russia for inspiration, understanding the Soviet experiment as an 'engine of cultural as well as political change'.[169]

Though Macleod admired Soviet theatre, he rejected the innovations of Meyerhold, suggesting that the Russian relied too much on formalist trickery: 'Meierhold was a Revolutionary. But he did not understand Socialism.'[170] He referred to avant-garde Russian performance as 'theatrical hangovers from the bored bourgeois world'[171] and instead turned to socialist realism as the most useful and striking of the Russian theatre forms. Macleod's conviction strengthened as the 1930s and 1940s progressed and, by the time he published *Actors Cross the Volga* in 1946, he was convinced that only socialist realism could really speak in a time of war: 'Socialist realism finds a new vindication in battle… no place for sentimentality or snivelling, sanctimoniousness nor sneers.'[172]

Macleod substantiates his claim for the efficacy of socialist realism by creating a genealogy of Russian realism that includes Chekhov and Stanislavsky. He saw *The Cherry Orchard* in 1937 at the MAT and, in *Actors Cross the Volga*, connects his experience of watching this play with the advent of socialist realist acting in Russian productions of Shakespeare plays. Macleod welcomes Russian audiences' responses to Shakespeare, accepting the playwright's 'creations as living people in actual situations of time and space'.[173] Reflecting back on *The Cherry Orchard*, Macleod recollects the marked sense of the real. He rejoices in the fact that, though in Britain Fiers was regarded as a 'silly, doddering old peasant manservant', in Russia he was understood as representative of a shared past: 'in that silence a proletarian audience was offering homage, almost expiation, to the sufferings of their fathers.'[174] By presenting *The Cherry Orchard* in this way, for Macleod at least, this version could speak directly to an audience.

Macleod never really imported his experiences in Russia; his impressive body of research into Russian theatre history seemed to hardly affect the British stage. Instead he became a BBC announcer and, under the pseudonym Adam Drinan, published a number of poems that can be read alongside the work of Hugh MacDiarmid, Naomi Mitchison and Edwin Muir, all of whom remained fascinated by Russian politics and art. While a prolific writer of theatre history, Macleod chose other cultural channels for his work. Again his discussions of Soviet theatre provide some rationale for his decision to leave the British theatre scene behind. In *Actors Cross the Volga* Macleod reflects on the theatrical life of Harkov, a business city in the Ukraine. Due to the nature of the city, audiences vary from uneducated merchants and foreigners who do not understand the language to the resident intelligentsia. He goes on: 'I don't doubt, from my own experience in Cambridge, that the two audiences would mix only to the call of a big name in the theatre world, about which both classes could be snobbish.'[175] The excitement of the Russian stage could not lure him back to a fault-finding British establishment theatre of pretence.

However, other figures did manage to bring socialist realism to the British stage. Plays by Alexander Afinogenov became particularly popular and in 1937 a new English-language production of Afinogenov's *Distant Point* (in reference to this production the playwright's name is often anglicised 'Afinogenev') appeared at the Gate Theatre Studio in London. Unity Theatre performed the play in 1940 before ceding it to a professional cast at the Westminster Theatre in 1941. Quite unusually, the Unity production received some national press coverage. The *Daily Telegraph* correspondent bemoaned the plodding dialogue but celebrated the characterisation of the play:

> Afinogenov happily is primarily a man of the theatre, not a mere propagandist, and the linesmen, switchmen, telegraph operators of an infinitely remote station on the Trans-Siberian railway who are charged with his propaganda are delightfully like Tchehovian [sic] characters switched in time from Imperial Russia to the Russia of Stalin.[176]

This reviewer constructs a similar genealogy of Russian realism (Chekhov to socialist realism) as Macleod.

Translated by Hubert Griffith (a figure whose work, writings and Russian travels I explore in more detail below), the latter performance at the Westminster Theatre was produced by van Gyseghem. *Distant Point* therefore brings together two central players in this book. The play reflects the conventions of socialist realism – it is situated in a nondescript railway station and, in the course of the play, this rather marginal, transitory space is revealed as home to heroic workers for the Revolution. The arrival of Red Army officer Matvei Ilyich causes each character to reflect on their role and responsibility in the new communist society. Before leaving, Matvei exclaims to idealistic Glasha that, even though they have only known each other 24 hours, they have already become friends: 'It's because we've the same aims and interests. And it's because of that, my friends, that we're strong and unconquerable.'[177] In this society, high-ranking army officials and lowly, obscure railway workers are 'friends', seemingly working together for the good of society. After attending the 1941 production Basil Wright in the *Spectator* praised Griffith's script but criticised poor direction, noting that 'dramatic tension is seldom, if ever, achieved; and each episode straggles across our consciousness with an aimlessness which ill accords with the directness of plot and dialogue'.[178] It seems, as with British productions of Chekhov plays, that British producers and directors struggled to bring a sense of vibrancy and dynamism to Afinogenov's work. No doubt this was partly a case of context. *Distant Point* is based in the unfamiliar landscape of rural Russia, Red Army officers are admired unequivocally and the other characters are (largely) working together for the benefit of Russian society as a communist concept. All these elements sat rather oddly in British society. Perhaps more than any other theatrical method, socialist realism was the one connected most entirely with Russian context.

This did not prevent British companies taking on the challenge of these plays, however. In addition to plays by Afinogenov, Unity Theatre also attempted Konstantin Simonov's *The Russian Question* in 1947, the same year as its Russian premiere. The play was produced by Unity stalwart Bill Owen (Rowbottom) (later better known as *Last of the Summer Wine*'s lovable scruff, Compo) and focuses on an American journalist, Harry Smith, who wants to travel to Russia and write a book that could provide an accurate description of a country so misunderstood and misrepresented in the US press. He is overruled by his boss who refuses to allow (what he deems to be) pro-Soviet propaganda to be published in his paper. Gradually Smith's life unravels, and he loses his job and wife. The *Daily Worker*'s review pinpoints the central aim of the play: 'it is the newspaper politicians, whose scaremongering and warmongering cannot be exaggerated that the Soviet playwright pillories.'[179] Smith's aim clearly chimes with the objectives of many of the figures in this book. *Illustrated* magazine's praise for this production reveals something more:

> By the time American characters, drawn by a Russian, had got into the hands of the English, Irish, Scots and Welsh amateur players, a crude charade might have ensued. But it does not. The play has an air of possibility.[180]

The journalist understands the perils of such geographically complex works. What she quite means by 'an air of possibility' isn't totally clear but, suffice to say, the production did not lapse into caricature; instead, it spoke directly to the audience. *Illustrated*'s article is surrounded by a collection of production images taken by Czech photographer Erich Auerbach (not to be confused with the author of *Mimesis*, although, given the dynamic realism of this play, the parallel is an interesting one). The disintegration of Smith's life is parallelled in the scenographic changes, moving from cosy living room to an almost entirely bare space, reminiscent of one of Meyerhold's sparse stages. Five years later, in 1952, Unity organised a conference to address the difficulties facing the company. As so often with politically engaged theatres, Unity was in severe financial crisis and the conference sought to discuss the best way forward. One of the attenders was Konstantin Simonov.[181] Unfortunately there is no clear evidence as to what Simonov said. But his contribution marks this as another migratory relationship between British and Russian practitioners.

## Realism? *Red Sunday*, *The People's Court* and *Comrade Enemy*

Two clear paths emerged then: realist and constructivist, fighting for pre-eminence in Soviet aesthetics. The two initially appear diametrically opposed, the former concerned with presenting accurate images of people, places and events, the latter focused on formal experimentation, popular performance and direct political challenge. However, two British theatre-makers with Russian connections seemed to actively question the solidity of realism by augmenting their plays with other, far more formalist, techniques. In doing so they created fascinating theatrical renderings of Russian politics.

Playwright, author and, later, flight lieutenant Hubert Griffith travelled extensively around Russia in the 1930s. His reflection on his inaugural trip, *Seeing Soviet Russia: An Informative Record of the Cheapest Trip in*

*Europe* (1932), edited collection on Russian culture, *Playtime in Russia* (1935), and later description of his lectures on Russian society given to British airmen, *This Is Russia* (1943), all reveal a particular fascination with the Soviet Union. The act of travelling remained vitally important for Griffith. His travel books are not merely for academic interest; in the preface to *Seeing Soviet Russia* he confirms his central intention:

> If I have induced any group of persons to visit the most interesting country in the world at the moment – to see for themselves rather than to sit at home and read libels about it – the purpose of the book will have been carried out.[182]

Once again, here is a playwright who places considerable emphasis on the travel experience, especially as a method for discerning the real conditions of society, for 'what one knows before one goes to Russia is not worth knowing. In Russia one learns a new truth a minute'.[183] As Stacy Burton suggests, the expectation that 'travel provides a distinctive form of access to truth' has a long history.[184] Griffith, and many of his fellow travellers, imagined they could uncover truths about places, truths that had become rather warped by mainstream narratives.

Unsurprisingly for a playwright, Griffith visited a number of theatres during his time in Russia. On his first trip, for example, he went to see Reinhold Glière's political ballet *Red Poppy* (a piece he rejected as dull and propaganda-driven), a circus where, he drolly comments, 'two thousand slaves of Communism were roaring with laughter at clowns falling off bicycles' and a 'disappointing' comedy, *Our Youth*.[185] At this latter production he was joined by Maurice Hindus. A Russian by birth, Hindus and his family later moved to the US. He wrote a good number of books on Russia for the Western audience, contributing significantly to a transnational understanding of Russian culture. Though these books examine Russian society, politics and culture in a broader sense, Hindus recognises the importance of the stage in the concept of the nation:

> The theatre has played no small part in the education and edification of Russians... It has been an outstanding source of public entertainment and social festiveness.[186]

While Hindus is interested in the socio-political situation in Russia and, particularly in 1940s books like *Russia Fights On* (1942) and *Mother*

*Russia* (1943), in constructing an encouraging image of a wartime ally, he still acknowledges the importance of theatre.

While advocating a truthful representation of Russian life, Griffith concludes his *Seeing Soviet Russia* by saying that 'the bare, spare life of modern Russia – with all its thoughts and all its aims bent so drivingly upon the future – is life in a romantic land'.[187] By 1943, giving lectures to the RAF on Russian politics and society (and after returning to Russia in 1941 for military reasons), he is less 'romantic' about Soviet society, acknowledging 'the extreme of misrepresentation *from all sides* that Soviet Russia has suffered from at the hands of the British Press'.[188] Yet simultaneously, as in Dean's *Salute to the Red Army*, there is a new romanticism based on the military strength of Britain's ally. He states, for example, that 'the defence of [Stalingrad]... by the Russians will not rank amongst the classic defences of all time, but as *THE* classic defence of all time'.[189] Inevitably the changing socio-political landscape engendered a connected change in the way individuals perceived other nations.

Two years before Griffith's first trip, however, he revealed his interest in exploring Russian history by writing *Red Sunday*, a play about Lenin's rise to power, from his early meetings with Trotsky, exile, the (eventual) death of Rasputin, the overthrow of the Tsar, and the transference of governance to the Bolshevik party through to the attempted assassinations in the 1920s. The rationale for *Red Sunday* chimed with Griffith's later intentions in travelling to Russia: he wanted to expose the truth about Russian society to a British audience. Griffith's commitment to negotiating such recent Russian history on the London stage caught the attention of the Lord Chamberlain, *The Times* and even the Royal Family who requested that the play not be granted a licence.[190] The criticisms of all three, which eventually led to the former rejecting Griffith's calls for *Red Sunday* to be produced in the West End, focused on three elements: the problem of presenting such recent history on the stage, concerns about incorporating real people into the performance (especially the Tsar) and the perceived pain that such a performance might cause to exiled Russians in London. Griffith hit back, first with a letter to *The Times* in which he maintains that 'these are legitimate matters for the freest possible public discussion',[191] and second, with a scathing prologue to the published version of the play.

In order to create the effect of a 'detached observer', Griffith took on the persona of a resident of fictional place Ping-Pang-Bong. This, unfortunately, infuses the prologue with a troubling air of colonial imperialism. However, for the purposes of this book, it is an interesting device.

Travellers are deemed to be more independent, able to sum up situations in other countries from a dispassionate, objective perspective. In addition, this device 'makes strange' British culture as a Brechtian *Verfremdungs-Effekt* might do in the theatre. It enables the reader to see the idiocy of British censorship laws by focusing on the incredulity and bewilderment of a character markedly removed geographically and culturally. This prologue character cannot comprehend the decision of the Lord Chamberlain and sarcastically exposes the Censor's intentions:

> Most important of all, the British public must be maintained in its delusions, like a lunatic beyond hope of recovery, and shut away from its possibility of arriving one step nearer the truth.[192]

Like Griffith's journeys and travel writing, *Red Sunday* is an attempt to expose the truth, to bridge the events of Russian history and a British audience that remained largely ignorant about such matters. He later reiterated his Ping-Pang-Bong citizen's vexation, stating in *Seeing Soviet Russia* that *Red Sunday* 'had come up against a certain side of British susceptibility. The truth – or even part of the truth – must not be told on stage'.[193]

In an attempt to uncover and reveal the truth about twentieth-century Russian history, *Red Sunday* presents it in three acts: pre-war (1906–1914), the events of 1916, and during and after the Revolution. Like its playwright, it travels geographically; it begins in Odessa before journeying to Siberia and St Petersburg. Act II divides its time between Prince Yussoupov's house in St Petersburg and Geneva where Lenin and Trotsky are in exile. The final act returns to the Palace and runs from the 1917 Revolution up to a failed assassination attempt on Lenin. Unlike the unwaveringly hopeful finales of the workers' theatre performances mentioned in the previous chapter or the disingenuously optimistic conclusions of socialist realism, the end of *Red Sunday* reflects the bleakness so often found in naturalist plays: Lenin is injured and Trotsky laments, 'who is going to save our revolution now?'[194]

Indeed, in many ways *Red Sunday* is rather trapped by its allegiance to naturalism. As I've mentioned in previous scholarship, the play's Russian history 'might well have sat better (aesthetically if not with the critics who were confused enough by his stylistic experiments) in a more radical format'.[195] While its dialogue, characterisation and chronology might be in keeping with the conventions of naturalism, *Red Sunday* simultaneously (and arguably unworkably) plays with elements of montage, 'the intercutting [of] short scenes'.[196] A number of these scenes challenge the tenets of naturalism. Act III, scene 2, for example, is set at a post-Revolution celebration in the Marie Theatre, St Petersburg where Vera Figner is giving a speech:

> When thousands of people, separated, spread over many years, all drive independently towards the same idea – then it's a madness that looks too much like common-sense.[197]

Figner, like Lenin and Trotsky, is a real historical figure. Her case is described by fellow traveller James Purves-Stewart, a British doctor who journeyed to Russia in the same year as Griffith. He describes her 24-year imprisonment, her release in 1905 and her return to Russia in 1915. 'She is still alive in Moscow,' Purves-Stewart says, 'a very old woman'.[198] Figner's speech is not only one of the most overtly political moments of a play that contains a surprising lack of direct political comment, it is also highly metatheatrical: a stage upon a stage:

> *The stage is as the stage of a theatre usually is for rehearsal, quite bare, with stacks of scenery leaning against the back and side walls.*[199]

It is reminiscent of Meyerhold's *The Government Inspector* (1926) in which the final scene is played on a stripped-back stage, emptied of all props and furniture. Jonathan Pitches suggests that this clearing of the stage to reveal usually hidden structures underneath represented 'the emptiness of Tsarist Russia underlined in a deft theatrical coup'.[200] I have not uncovered any specific connection between these two performances, but nevertheless, the theatrical device (intentionally or otherwise) seems to enact the same political comment in Griffith's play.

Other scenes also challenge the linear illusions of naturalism. In act II the action flits between the grand palaces of St Petersburg, and Lenin and Trotsky languishing in exile on the banks of Lake Geneva. Lenin and Trotsky enjoy none of the grand props of the Palace; instead '*the scene can be played quite simply in front of curtains, the two figures only being illuminated*'.[201] This aesthetic decision connects this play to the stripped-back stages of Meyerhold and the blank, illuminated spaces of Craig. In addition, the juxtaposed action in the Palace further suspends naturalistic rules, staged as a gothic horror with the amoral, predatory 'Mad Monk'

Rasputin at its centre. The poisoning, the image of Rasputin as he '*seizes a candlestick, and brandishes it wildly above his head*',[202] and the horror of his seeming immortality turns this scene into a terrifying revenge tragedy. In fact, the reviewer for *The Stage* praised it as 'almost fit for Grand Guignol in its realism and melodrama'.[203]

*Red Sunday*'s challenge to the conventions of naturalism was augmented by its director: Komisarjevsky. In 1929, the same year as he produced *Red Sunday*, Komisarjevsky wrote:

> An imaginative actor needs no naturalistic copies of the environment of his personal life to help him to act, as he is able to transform any object before him into anything he chooses to make it... Nothing on the stage can be called 'natural', because the Theatre is a form of art, and is therefore inventive.[204]

So while the photograph of the production illustrates the play's commitment to visual accuracy with uncanny impersonations of Trotsky, Lenin and Trotsky's Wife sitting around a table, Komisarjevsky would presumably have been far more concerned with theatrical art than mimetic naturalism.[205] Indeed, *The Stage* inadvertently picked up on this, seeing a disconnect between the realist script and its production:

> There is little we can congratulate M. Komisarjevsky on in the production. For example, he makes a surely unpardonable mistake in these advanced days – putting a red 'spot' on Lenin on his first entrance in scene 1. There was nothing in that cellar that could possibly have flung that halo of light on the wall of a steep staircase, nothing to switch it off immediately the character began to speak.[206]

The reviewer seems to have rather misread the genre of the play here, criticising Komisarjevky's production for being unrealistic: 'where was the light switch?' he asks with irritation. The Russian's symbolist response to the narrative, clearly illustrated in his lighting choices here, confuses the reviewer who evidently reads the narrative as a naturalist realist exposition of Russian politics. From such a perspective Komisarjevsky's direction seems strangely incongruous. However, questioning the solidity of *Red Sunday*'s generic definition, as I have done here, Komisarjevsky's imaginative direction supports the play's aesthetic ambiguity. This exposition of Russian history was produced at the Arts Theatre in June 1929 with John Gielgud as Trotsky. Gielgud praised the Komisarjevsky-directed performance as a celebration of 'continuous life and movement on the stage'.[207] It represents a clear illustration of the central tenets of this book: a play about Russian history for a British audience, the discomfort of the British establishment about Russian politics, and the collaboration of a British playwright who later travelled to Russia and a Russian émigré director.

Despite the fact that *Red Sunday* never made it to the West End, the story has a fascinating migratory coda. Two years later, during a European tour (1931), Griffith visited the Turkish island of Prinkipo where, coincidently, Trotsky lived in exile. Griffith decided to meet the influential figure of Bolshevism, turning up on his doorstep only to be prevented from entering by Trotsky's secretary. Griffith directly connects his desire to meet Trotsky with *Red Sunday*:

> I have been an interested student of the life of Trotsky. I have read much about him from all sides. I made him one of the leading characters in a play of mine in London, which was denounced by a leading article in *The Times*, and was censored by the Censor.[208]

Upon arrival the secretary quizzed Griffith as to his intentions: 'I answer a volley of questions, and am made to recount the entire plot, in detail, of 'Red Sunday', my censored masterpiece.'[209] He never met Trotsky but it is rather striking that years after the original brouhaha surrounding this play, *Red Sunday* should be interpolated into Griffith's European travels in such a dramatic way. Griffith's protestation that he made Trotsky 'one of the leading characters' in *Red Sunday* blurs the boundaries between acting and actual historical figures, between theatrical construction and real travel experiences.

Later, Griffith wrote a new play, *The People's Court* (produced at the Embassy Theatre in 1933). The play focuses on a Judge in a Soviet People's Court, attempting to find out who is the father of a baby. The mother of the baby and her mother sit before the Judge and her assistants. The accused, a Communist Party member and worker named Remisov, denies that he is the father. Perceptively seeing through his lies, the Judge makes a powerful speech challenging Remisov about the importance of a communist's word of honour. He relents and admits liability. There are a few noticeable things about this play. First, the Judge, who uses her powers of reasoning, deduction and persuasion, not only issues from the upper peasant class but is also a woman. This dual challenge to expectations of class and gender must have struck 1930s audiences. Many British travellers to Russia admired the gradual erosion of gender binaries (as they perceived them) in Soviet society. Scottish poet Naomi Mitchison, for example, travelled to Russia in 1932 and, while critical of other aspects of Soviet society, celebrated this transformation of typical gender roles, saying 'I feel they have solved, or nearly solved, the sex question which has preoccupied us for so many years, simply by giving women complete economic freedom and equality'.[210] Whatever the accuracy (or not) of this assumption, the role of women in Soviet society certainly became a model for some to emulate. The Judge points to the differences between British and Russian society in this regard relating events at a Workers' club some nights previously when the members had entertained a delegation from England:

> They were charming people, those English, so friendly, so interested – and so naïf! One of them got up and said 'Tell me, Comrades, is it literally true that in Russia *all* the women get exactly the same pay as the men, if they are doing the same work?'... there was a shout of laughter at the idea that a woman should *not* get the same pay as a man.[211]

Like Macleod, Griffith incorporates specific reference to Britain in an otherwise entirely Russia-based story, presumably as a direct challenge to the local audience.

Second, *The People's Court*, like *Red Sunday*, straddles generic and artistic categories. On the one hand it feels like a naturalistic narrative with fleshed-out characters, linear structure and dialogue. However, Griffith's 'author's note' casts some doubt on this easy demarcation:

> Except in small details, the following play is at least as much a literal transliteration as a work of imagination... the woman Judge is drawn from the Author's own observation; and in actual case, both in its broad outlines and the particular effect that the Judge's reference to a Communist's word of honour had on a witness, is an authentic one.

Like *Red Sunday*, the naturalistic structure is interrupted by other theatrical techniques. In this case, *The People's Court* seems to be an early example of verbatim theatre, based in the author's reminiscences about Russia.

However, that said, *The People's Court* remains rather tricky. While it could be classed as verbatim and clearly relies on the real-time experiences and memories of the playwright, it also seems that Griffith overlooked (willingly or through ignorance) the problems of the Soviet judicial system. Steve Nicholson suggests that, despite the obvious attempt at realistic verbatim, 'there is surely a tragic naïvity or disingenuousness in the playwright choosing a court-room as a setting in which to demonstrate the supposed justice and superiority of the Soviet society'.[212] Here is an example of the 'romantic land' image Griffith would later question in his lectures to the airmen.

Eleven years later, Unity Theatre (Leeds) premiered Alec Baron and Kate Plenty's *Comrade Enemy*. Though born in Leeds, Baron's parents were immigrants from Lithuania and spoke Russian, Hebrew and Yiddish.[213] He developed an insatiable appetite for theatre and film at a young age, attending a performance by Baliev's The Bat as a child. He remembered an almost deserted auditorium and Baliev entering the stage to give a speech:

> He looked around at the rows and rows of empty seats, then he made a little speech. 'Ladies and Gentlemen', he said, 'I don't want you to think that because there are so few of you here this afternoon we are going to give a performance that is anything short of our best. In fact, we are going to give you the best performance we have ever given in our lives'. And they did. And the applause from the dozen or so of us was deafening for we tried hard to compensate for our lack of numbers. I have never forgotten the lesson he taught us that afternoon.[214]

Written so many years after The Bat's performance, Baliev's generous, upbeat speech clearly made quite an impression on the young Baron. Instrumental in setting up the Leeds Film Society, which imported the best of Russian and German cinema into the Northern industrial city, and a key player in Leeds Unity, which presented a range of challenging plays, including many with Russian connections (living newspapers about the Finnish War and, interestingly, Griffith's translation of *Distant Point* and *The People's Court*), Baron, like so many talented, industrious figures of the WTM/Unity Theatre movement has been criminally overlooked by theatre history.

Like Griffith's *Red Sunday* and *The People's Court*, *Comrade Enemy* is grounded in real experiences, based on 'actual incidents during the Nazi invasion of the U.S.S.R. in the Summer of 1941'.[215] Baron elucidates further in his unpublished autobiography: 'when the Soviet Union was invaded by Germany, the two of us embarked on writing a full length play which we called "Comrade Enemy".'[216] This declaration of legitimacy is explicit in all three plays. Like Griffith's plays, *Comrade Enemy* contains distinct characters and is constructed through realistic dialogue. It narrates the fates of Soviet soldiers and their families left at home, a German soldier and his émigré German wife, and the left-wing political community in England. The play flits between these different locations and experiences until, in the end, it concludes in England with German wife Elsa hearing about the death of her patriotic but socialist husband, Hans, over the radio from Russian broadcaster (and reluctant killer of Hans) Igor. Igor's final broadcast confirms the aim of the play:

> Our enemies are the same you know. And we will not fail. When we crush these black Nazis, it is your enemies that we crush, and you German people can take your liberty… And we'll pay tribute to a fine soldier, to a comrade and in him to all comrades everywhere for solidarity with us the guardians of Socialism.[217]

The final scene sees Elsa and the female members of Igor's Russian family stand together on the barricades. Ultimately, this play suggests, there are freedom-loving comrades in every army and the Soviet soldiers will lead the way in crushing the reactionary forces and reuniting the individuals who currently fight on opposing sides. While much of this reads like naturalist realism, the finale confirms the persistence of symbolic gesture in order to present the political message in the clearest way.

The characters certainly have a more developed sense of identity than those in the sketches of the WTM or the early plays of the Unity movement. However, occupying such a didactic, polemic piece of work, they seem to shift between styles and genres. Miles Tomalin, playwright and veteran of the Spanish Civil War, wrote positively about this play on behalf of London Unity but had reservations over characterisation:

> The characters are replete with political morality save the one or two who are permitted to deviate in order to lay greater emphasis on the line. For this reason they do not seem to me alive. If they are to be treated frankly as morality types (the Soviet Comrade, the German Comrade, the Old Bolshevik etc) they should be given a more stylised dialogue, without any attempt at realism. Otherwise the types, as such, should be more neatly concealed, and emerge only by implication.[218]

Are these characters simply stock figures to emphasise theme or empathetic sufferers of a horrendous world war? *Comrade Enemy* seems to use both methods of characterisation simultaneously.

Furthermore, the transitions between the scenes challenge any sense of mimetic realism. In the opening scene this means that, although it begins on the frontline with Igor, the narrative flips back to him leaving his farm and his family, thereby disrupting linear chronology. Later in Elsa's retelling of the story of how she met Hans, the audience is suddenly transported from an English wartime flat to a misty mountain in Germany. The stage directions clarify the way the actors should approach this challenge: 'he [Hans] speaks this out of memory, and gradually his voice becomes more natural and conversational.'[219] These transitions between spaces and time periods clearly compel the actors to employ a distinctly theatrical device, despite Baron and Plenty's protestations that the play is firmly based in the real. In keeping with the major arguments of this book, the structure of *Comrade Enemy* is strikingly transnational in design. Not only can characters clearly travel between countries, they can communicate across great geographical distances with few concerns for the rigidity of realism.

The Lord Chamberlain's notes cast further light on the transnational character of this play. The requested deletions focus specifically on the way the English are portrayed in this play so, in act II, scenes 2 and 3, the Lord Chamberlain requests that all reference to England not sending enough help to Russia, and the suggestion that powerful people stand in the way of such help being sent, had to be deleted.[220] While the play retains a distinctly transnational identity, it is national concerns that drive the Lord Chamberlain's decision.

Despite troubling themes and awkward aesthetics, these three plays fascinatingly respond theatrically to the situation in Russia, aiming for factual accuracy and realism even if the theatricality (intentional or coincidental) and the unfounded assumptions of the playwrights get in the way. They certainly reflect a deeper impulse described by Griffith on his return from his first trip to Russia in 1931:

> I came back from Russia with three ideas uppermost in my mind. The first of them was that our English Press had been telling lies about Russia profusely, scandalously and ceaselessly. The second was that the general condition of Russia was not nearly as bad as most of our newspapers pretend. The third was that we, as English people and therefore presumably with a patriotic regard for the welfare of our country in the next decade or so to come, would have seriously to consider if Russia could not teach us a lesson or two worth learning.[221]

These plays use an augmented realism in order to directly address the three concerns Griffith brought back from his travels.

This chapter has attempted to negotiate the contrasting aesthetic practices of constructivism and realism in all their myriad guises. It concludes with three works that appear to create a dialogue between them. What is particularly interesting, of course, is that by 1942, the year of *Comrade Enemy*, both the *joie de vivre* of Meyerhold's constructivism and the character-led realism of Stanislavsky had been rejected. The American theatre producer and Russian traveller Norris Houghton reflected on this change as early as 1938:

> Now with the predominance of socialistic realism to the gradual exclusion of all other art forms, this variety, which was not only a stimulation of the foreigners but a powerful catalytic agent within the Soviet theatre itself, has given place to uniformity.[222]

Interestingly, any potential resolution between the stylised avant-garde and the linear verisimilitude of realism could only occur far away from the geographical space that had spawned them. While remaining within the confines of the European continent, Griffith and Baron's plays illustrate James Harding and John Rouse's assertion that the avant-garde (and I borrow this term advisedly for use in this book) is defined by contested edges: in their words, 'ambiguous territorial boundaries'.[223] In the case of these plays, the edges of contestation are both geographical and artistic; they are British plays and yet focus on Russia and, formally, they appear balanced on a border between realism and something more synthetic. Consequently, they disturb typical linear models of theatre historiography by illustrating the re-emergence of modes, absent from their original spaces of creation, in new geographical locations. In these plays, realism and stylisation clash along a contested artistic edge; simultaneously they draw attention to national identities and borders while advocating a transnational sense of solidarity. Ultimately, I claim, Russian realism and 1920s revolutionary experimentation lived on despite the juggernaut of socialist realism. But rather than Moscow or St Petersburg providing the contextual backdrop it was London and Leeds.

## Notes

1. J.M. Nikonov, 'Theatre' in *Art in the USSR*, ed. C.G. Holme (London: Studio Limited, 1935), 91.
2. A.Y. Arosev, 'Introduction' in *Art in the USSR*, ed. Holme, 11.

3. Young, 'Non-Chekhov Russian and Soviet Drama' in *Russia in Britain*, eds Beasley and Bullock, 106.
4. Young, 'Non-Chekhov Russian and Soviet Drama' in *Russia in Britain*, eds Beasley and Bullock, 110–11. For a full list of Moscow Art Theatre Prague Group's performances and performers see Sergei Ostrovsky's 'Appendix 2' in Senelick, *Wandering Stars*, 216–18.
5. Laurence Senelick, 'The Accidental Evolution of the Moscow Art Theatre Prague Group', *New Theatre Quarterly*, 30.2 (May 2014): 164.
6. Qtd in Senelick, 'Accidental Evolution', 159.
7. Maria Guermanova, 'Moscow Art Theatre', *The Times*, 17 April 1928, 12.
8. Alma Law, 'Balieff and the Chauve-Souris' in *Wandering Stars*, ed. Senelick, 19.
9. Senelick, *Historical Dictionary of Russian Theater*, 36.
10. 'Programme of Chauve-Souris', Strand Theatre, 1925–6, Cadbury Research Library, University of Birmingham, MS38/3090.
11. 'Chauve-Souris at The Coliseum', *The Times*, 15 November 1921, 7.
12. The Chauve-Souris could trace its origins back to Baliev's first Letuchaya mysh cabaret company with its 'living doll' productions in which live actors pretended to be marionettes, dolls or puppets, formed inanimate tableaux and came alive at various points in the performance to sing, dance or recite. For further information on this pre-Chauve-Souris innovation see Harold B. Segel, *Pinocchio's Progeny: Puppets, Marionettes, Automatons and Robots in Modernist and Avant-Garde Drama* (Baltimore: The Johns Hopkins Press, 1995), 72–4.
13. Law, 'Balieff and the Chauve-Souris', 21.
14. 'La Chauve-Souris', *The Times*, 25 November 1924, 12.
15. James Ross Moore, 'Girl Crazy: Musicals and Revue Between the Wars' in *British Theatre Between the Wars, 1918–1939*, eds Clive Barker and Maggie B. Gale (Cambridge UP, 2000), 101.
16. A.P. Herbert and Nigel Playfair, *Riverside Nights* (London: T. Fisher Unwin, 1926), 73.
17. Herbert and Playfair, *Riverside Nights*, 75.
18. 'Programme of Chauve-Souris', Strand Theatre, 1925–6.
19. *The Observer*, 2 May 1926, Cadbury Research Library, University of Birmingham, MS38/5226.
20. *The Stage*, 20 May 1926, and *Sunday Pictorial*, 2 May 1926, Cadbury Research Library, University of Birmingham, MS38/5226.
21. David Shirley, 'Stanislavsky's Passage into the British Conservatoire' in *Russians in Britain*, ed. Pitches, 40.
22. Basil Dean, 'Between the Public and Ourselves' (1926), 7.
23. Van Gyseghem, *Theatre in Soviet Russia*, 44.
24. Shirley, 'Stanislavsky's Passage' in *Russians in Britain*, ed. Pitches, 42.

25. Ctd in *Unity Theatre Newsletter*, 16 January 1939, Unity Theatre Archive, V&A, 2.
26. Van Gyseghem, *Theatre in Soviet Russia*, 51.
27. See Patrick Miles, *Chekhov on the British Stage* (Cambridge UP, 1993) and Laurence Senelick, *The Chekhov Theatre: A Century of the Plays in Performance* (Cambridge UP, 1997) for two fascinating starting points.
28. Ctd in Miles, *Chekhov on the British Stage*, 29.
29. Senelick, *The Chekhov Theatre: A Century of the Plays in Performance*, 131.
30. Percy Lubbock, *George Calderon: A Sketch from Memory* (London: Grant Richards, 1921), 40.
31. Senelick, 'For God, for Czar, for Fatherland: Russians on the British Stage from Napoleon to the Great War' in *Russia in Britain*, eds Beasley and Bullock, 32.
32. George Calderon, *Two Plays by Tchekof: The Seagull and The Cherry Orchard* (London: Grant Richards, 1912), 13.
33. Calderon, *Two Plays by Tchekof*, 10.
34. George Calderon, *The Little Stone House: A Play in One Act* (London: Sidgwick and Jackson, 1913), 32.
35. Senelick, 'For God, for Czar, for Fatherland' in *Russia in Britain*, eds Beasley and Bullock, 33.
36. Calderon, *The Little Stone House*, 21.
37. Calderon, *The Little Stone House*, 13.
38. Calderon, *The Little Stone House*, 9.
39. Miles, *Chekhov on the British Stage*, 41.
40. James Loehlin, *Chekhov: The Cherry Orchard* (Cambridge UP, 2006), 96.
41. Gielgud remained fascinated by Chekhov throughout his life, even playing the Russian playwright in the 1968 film *From Chekhov with Love*.
42. Ibid.
43. Milly S. Barranger, *Margaret Webster: A Life in the Theater* (Ann Arbor: Michigan UP, 2004), 226.
44. 'Lyric Theatre, Hammersmith', *The Times*, 26 May 1925, 14.
45. Loehlin, *The Cherry Orchard*, 99.
46. *Punch*, 9 March 1927, 274, Cadbury Research Library, University of Birmingham, MS38/4811.
47. Philip Godfrey, *Back-Stage* (London: George Harrap, 1933), 101.
48. With thanks to my grandparents who must have rescued Fen's *A Girl Grew Up in Russia* from a second-hand bookshop somewhere, and to my mum for digging it out of their substantial book collection while clearing their house! Without them I would not have stumbled upon Fen's amazing body of work.
49. Elisaveta Fen, 'Introduction' in *Plays*, Anton Chekhov (London: Penguin, 1951), 8.

50. Fen in *Plays*, Chekhov, 9.
51. Calderon, *Two Plays by Tchekof*, 18.
52. Maurice Baring, *An Outline of Russian Literature* (London: Williams and Norgate, 1914), prologue.
53. Baring, *An Outline of Russian Literature*, 246–7.
54. Maurice Baring, *What I Saw in Russia* (London: William Heinemann, 1927), 4, 193.
55. Maurice Baring, *The Puppet Show of Memory* (London: William Heinemann, 1922), 265.
56. Maurice Baring, *The Grey Stocking and Other Plays* (London: Constable and Company, 1911), 8.
57. Baring, *The Grey Stocking*, 31.
58. Baring, *The Grey Stocking*, 33.
59. Senelick in *Russia in Britain*, eds Beasley and Bullock, 34.
60. Maurice Baring, *The Double Game* in Baring, *The Grey Stocking*, 272.
61. Senelick in *Russia in Britain*, 34.
62. *The Playgoer and Society Illustrated*, vol. 6: 31–36 (London: Kingshurst, 1912), 87.
63. Evgeny Vakhtangov, 'From Notebooks' in *The Vakhtangov Sourcebook*, ed. Andrei Malaev-Babel (Abingdon: Routledge, 2011), 231.
64. Baring, *What I Saw in Russia*, 4.
65. George Bernard Shaw, *Heartbreak House* (1916), accessed 3 July 2015, http://www.gutenberg.org/files/3543/3543-h/3543-h.htm.
66. Shaw, *Heartbreak House*, prologue.
67. Ibid.
68. Shaw, *Heartbreak House*, act 3.
69. Miriam Handley, 'Chekhov Translated: Shaw's Use of Sound Effects in *Heartbreak House*', *Modern Drama*, 42 (Winter 1999): 567.
70. Shaw, *Heartbreak House*, act 3.
71. Handley, 'Chekhov Translated', 573.
72. Olga Soboleva and Angus Wrenn, *The Only Hope of the World: George Bernard Shaw and Russia* (Oxford: Peter Lang, 2012), 80–1.
73. Soboleva and Wrenn, *The Only Hope of the World*, 92.
74. Chambers ed., *The Continuum Companion to Twentieth Century Theatre*, 325.
75. Chambers, *The Story of Unity Theatre*, 281.
76. Robert Mitchell interviewed by Jack Mitchell, 1967, ctd in Bill Findlay, 'By Policy a Native Theatre: Glasgow Unity and the Significance of Robert Mitchell's Scottish Adaptation of *The Lower Depths*', *International Journal of Scottish Theatre*, 2.1 (2001), accessed 17 July 2015, http://journals.qmu.ac.uk/index.php/IJoST/article/view/74/html.
77. Findlay, 'By Policy a Native Theatre'.

78. George Bernard Shaw, *Annajanska: The Bolshevik Empress* (1917), accessed 3 July 2015, http://www.gutenberg.org/files/3485/3485-h/3485-h.htm.
79. Ibid.
80. Matthew Taunton, 'Angus Wrenn and Olga Soboleva Speaking about George Bernard Shaw on Russia', 10 October 2012, accessed 10 July 2015, https://soundcloud.com/matthew-taunton/george-bernard-shaw-on-russia.
81. George Bernard Shaw, 'Back from Moscow', *Observer*, 2 August 1932, 9.
82. Soboleva and Wrenn, *The Only Hope of the World*, 149–50.
83. Eugene Lyons, *Assignment in Utopia* (New York: Harcourt, Brace and Company, 1937), 428.
84. Lyons, *Assignment in Utopia*, 430.
85. 'My Reply', *Daily Express*, 13 June 1932, ctd in Soboleva and Wrenn, *The Only Hope of the World*, 165.
86. For a thorough reading of productions of Shaw's plays in Russia see Laurence Senelick, 'More Looked at Than Listened to: Shaw on the Prerevolutionary Russian Stage', *SHAW: The Annual of Bernard Shaw Studies*, 27 (2007).
87. Iurii Sobolev, 'Pigmalion', *Rampa I zhizn*, 6.45, 9 November 1914, 3, trans. Laurence Senelick in 'More Looked at Than Listened to', Senelick, 96.
88. Robert Benchley, 'Vienna Letter' (1925) in *The Soviet Theater*, eds Senelick and Ostrovsky, 184–5.
89. James Agate, *Contemporary Theatre* (London: Chapman and Hall, 1927), 68.
90. Agate, *Contemporary Theatre*, 71.
91. Ibid.
92. Isadora Duncan, *My Life* (New York: Norton, 2013), 140.
93. Elizabeth Souritz, 'Isadora Duncan's Influence on Dance in Russia', *Dance Chronicle*, 18.2 (1995): 282.
94. 'Letter from Stanislavski to Isadora', January 1908, in *The Moscow Art Theatre Letters*, ed. Jean Benedetti (New York: Routledge, 1991), 261.
95. Edward Gordon Craig, 'Hamlet in Moscow: Notes for a Short Address to the Actors of the Moscow Art Theatre', *The Mask* 7, 2 (May 1915) in *Gordon Craig's Moscow* Hamlet: *A Reconstruction*, Laurence Senelick (Westport: Greenwood, 1982), 193.
96. At the end of this article Craig writes 'this is the gist of what I wanted to say to the actors of the Moscow Art Theatre. But on seeing their kind faces and wrinkled brows I had not the heart to add one more wrinkle' (Craig, 'Hamlet in Moscow' in *Gordon Craig's Moscow* Hamlet, Senelick, 196).
97. Innes, *Edward Gordon Craig: A Vision of the Theatre*, 162.
98. Craig, *On the Art of Theatre*, 70.

99. Edward Gordon Craig, 'The True Hamlet' (1908) in *The Theatre – Advancing*, Edward Gordon Craig (Boston: Little Brown and Company, 1919), 270.
100. Jean Benedetti, *Stanislavski and the Actor* (New York: Routledge, 2013), 134.
101. Em. Veskin, 'Gamlet v shirmakh', *Rannee Utro*, 28 December 1911 in *Gordon Craig's Moscow* Hamlet, Senelick, 175.
102. John Semar (Edward Gordon Craig), *The Mask*, 4 April 1912 in *Gordon Craig's Moscow* Hamlet, Senelick, 179.
103. Senelick, *Gordon Craig's Moscow* Hamlet, 184.
104. 'Mr Craig's Designs for Hamlet', *The Times*, 10 September 1912, 56.
105. Konstantin Stanislavsky, *My Life in Art*, trans. Jean Benedetti (London: Routledge, 2008), 295.
106. Innes, *Edward Gordon Craig*, 168.
107. Ibid.
108. Stanislavsky, *My Life in Art*, 296.
109. Edward Gordon Craig, 'Stanislavsky's System' (1937) in *Craig on Theatre*, ed. J. Michael Walton, (London: Methuen, 1999), 89.
110. Senelick, *Gordon Craig's Moscow* Hamlet, xvi.
111. Marie-Christine Autant-Mathien and Yana Meerson eds, *The Routledge Companion to Michael Chekhov* (Abingdon: Routledge, 2015), 147.
112. Michael Chekhov, *To the Actor* (London: Routledge, 2003), 1.
113. Chekhov, *To the Actor*, 71.
114. Chamberlain, *Michael Chekhov*, 72.
115. Senelick, *Gordon Craig's Moscow* Hamlet, 72.
116. Edward Braun, *Meyerhold: A Revolution in Theatre* (London: Methuen, 1998), 285.
117. Vsevolod Meyerhold, 'The Solitude of Stanislavsky' (1921) in *Meyerhold on Theatre*, ed. Edward Braun (London: Methuen, 1998), 179.
118. Vsevolod Meyerhold, 'Speech at Open Debate on *The Dawn*' (1920) in *Meyerhold on Theatre*, ed. Braun, 174.
119. Launcelot Lawton, 'An Interview with Meyerhold at the Theatre of Revolution' (1924) in *Meyerhold, Eisenstein and Biomechanics: Actor Training in Revolutionary Russia*, eds Alma Law and Mel Gordon (London: McFarland, 1996), 227.
120. Dean, 'Between the Public and Ourselves', 7.
121. Dean, 'Roast Beef and Caviare', 90.
122. Ashley Dukes, *The Scene Is Changed* (London: MacMillan, 1942), 72.
123. Ibid.
124. Dukes, *The Scene Is Changed*, 120.
125. Edward Braun, *Meyerhold: A Revolution in Theatre* (London: Bloomsbury, 1998), 213.

126. Rudnitsky, *Russian and Soviet Theatre*, 117.
127. Ibid.
128. Rudnitsky, *Russian and Soviet Theatre*, 179.
129. Van Gyseghem, *Theatre in Soviet Russia*, 18.
130. Van Gyseghem, *Theatre in Soviet Russia*, 18.
131. Van Gyseghem, *Theatre in Soviet Russia*, 20.
132. Van Gyseghem, *Theatre in Soviet Russia*, 32.
133. Van Gyseghem, *Theatre in Soviet Russia*, 35.
134. Amy Skinner, 'Riding the Waves: Uncovering Biomechanics in Britain' in *Russians in Britain*, ed. Pitches, 103.
135. Van Gyseghem, *Theatre in Soviet Russia*, 30.
136. Van Gyseghem, *Theatre in Soviet Russia*, 30.
137. *Daily Telegraph*, 24 May 1932, Cadbury Research Library, University of Birmingham, MS38/1123.
138. *Sunday Times*, 29 May 1932, Cadbury Research Library, University of Birmingham, MS38/1123. 'Grock' here means 'clown-like'.
139. *The National Graphic*, 2 June 1932, Cadbury Research Library, University of Birmingham, MS38/1123.
140. *Observer*, 29 May 1932, Cadbury Research Library, University of Birmingham, MS38/1123.
141. Saville, Introduction, *Ideas, Forms and Developments in the British Workers' Theatre, 1925–1935*.
142. Stourac and McCreery, *Theatre as a Weapon*, 201.
143. Stephen Schofield, *The Judge of All the Earth* (London: Labour Publishing Company, 1927), viii.
144. John Stokes, 'Rebecca West at the Theatre' in *The Edwardian Theatre: Essays in Performance and the Stage*, eds Michael Booth and Joel Kaplan (Cambridge UP, 1996), 198.
145. Braun, *Meyerhold: A Revolution in Theatre*, 260.
146. Braun, *Meyerhold: A Revolution in Theatre*, 261.
147. Senelick, *Historical Dictionary of Russian Theater*, 228, 52.
148. Van Gyseghem, *Theatre in Soviet Russia*, 121.
149. Ibid.
150. Pavel Markov, 'The Actor and the Revolution' (September 1936) in *Theatre Arts on Acting*, ed. Laurence Senelick (London: Routledge, 2013), 192.
151. Marshall, *The Pictorial History of Russian Theatre*, 148.
152. Julian and Margaret Bullard eds, *Inside Stalin's Russia: The Diaries of Reader Bullard 1930–1934*, ctd in *The Soviet Theater*, eds Senelick and Ostrovsky, 359.
153. Marshall, *The Pictorial History of Russian Theatre*, 148.
154. Marshall, *The Other Theatre*, 196. Actually this is an intentional slight misquote for pithiness sake. The accurate quote is 'I know nothing about this playwright but he is everywhere'.

155. *Unity Theatre Newsletter* 7, 1944, Unity Theatre Archive, V&A, THM 9/4/1/10.
156. John Hallett, 'The Soviets Through Soviet Eyes', *Spectator*, 13 September 1934, 22.
157. P.A. Markov, *The Soviet Theatre* (New York: G.P. Putnam's and Sons, 1934), 170.
158. Joseph Macleod, *A Soviet Theatre Sketchbook* (London: George Allen and Unwin, 1951), 79.
159. Macleod, *A Soviet Theatre Sketchbook*, 83.
160. Terence Gray, *Dance-Drama: Experiments in the Art of Theatre* (Cambridge: Heffer and Sons, 1926), 27.
161. Cornwall, *Only by Failure*, 283.
162. Cornwall, *Only by Failure*, 290.
163. Cornwall, *Only by Failure*, 296.
164. Joseph Macleod, *The New Soviet Theatre* (London: George Allen and Unwin Ltd, 1943), 8.
165. Macleod, *A Soviet Theatre Sketchbook*, 118.
166. Macleod, *A Soviet Theatre Sketchbook*, 76.
167. Macleod, *A Soviet Theatre Sketchbook*, 73, 128.
168. Joseph Macleod, *Actors Cross the Volga: A Study of Nineteenth Century Russian Theatre and of Soviet Theatres in War* (London: George Unwin, 1946), 52.
169. Anon, 'Editorial: Russian/Modernist Connections', *International Journal of Scottish Literature*, 2, 2009, accessed 1 July 2015, http://www.ijsl.stir.ac.uk/issue5/editorial.htm.
170. Macleod, *The New Soviet Theatre*, 98.
171. Macleod, *The New Soviet Theatre*, 93.
172. Macleod, *Actors Cross the Volga*, 219.
173. Macleod, *Actors Cross the Volga*, 267.
174. Macleod, *Actors Cross the Volga*, 268–9.
175. Macleod, *Actors Cross the Volga*, 45.
176. *Daily Telegraph*, 11 July 1940, Cuttings *Distant Point*, Unity Theatre Archive, V&A, THM 9/4/5/20.
177. Alexander Afinogenev, *Distant Point* (London: Pushkin, 1941), 84.
178. Basil Wright, 'The Theatre', *Spectator*, 7 November 1941, 10.
179. *Daily Worker*, 19 October 1947, 3, Unity Theatre Archive, V&A, THM 9/4/5/54.
180. Joan Skipsey, 'The Russian Question', *Illustrated*, 8 November 1947, Unity Theatre Archive, V&A, THM 9/4/5/54.
181. Chambers, *The Story of Unity Theatre*, 329.
182. Griffith, *Seeing Soviet Russia*, vii.
183. Griffith, *Seeing Soviet Russia*, 177.
184. Burton, *Travel Narrative and the Ends of Modernity*, 23.

185. Griffith, *Seeing Soviet Russia*, 77, 154, 144.
186. Maurice Hindus, *Mother Russia* (London: Collins, 1943), 369.
187. Griffith, *Seeing Soviet Russia*, 196.
188. Hubert Griffith, *This Is Russia* (London: Hammond, 1943), 11.
189. Griffith, *This Is Russia*, 45.
190. Steve Nicholson, 'Censoring Revolution: The Lord Chamberlain and the Soviet Union', *New Theatre Quarterly*, 8.32 (November 1992): 308.
191. Hubert Griffith, 'Letter to the Editor of The Times', *The Times*, 3 July 1929, 17.
192. Hubert Griffith, 'Preface', *Red Sunday* (London: Cayme Press, 1929), x.
193. Griffith, *Seeing Soviet Russia*, 2.
194. Griffith, *Red Sunday*, 88.
195. For a further, more detailed reading of Griffith and his work see Claire Warden, 'Moscow, Saint Petersburg, London: Hubert Griffith and the Search for a Russian Truth', *Comparative Drama*, 49.1 (Spring 2015): 1–21.
196. Nicholson, *British Theatre and the Red Peril*, 78.
197. Griffith, *Red Sunday*, 77.
198. James Purves-Stewart, *A Physician's Tour in Soviet Russia* (Woking: Unwin, 1933), 62.
199. Griffith, *Red Sunday*, 73.
200. Jonathan Pitches, *Vsevolod Meyerhold* (London: Routledge, 2003), 102.
201. Griffith, *Red Sunday*, 31.
202. Griffith, *Red Sunday*, 58.
203. *The Stage*, 14 July 1929, Cadbury Research Library, University of Birmingham, MS38/236.
204. Theodor Komisarjevsky, *Myself and the Theatre* (London: Heinemann, 1929), 140–1.
205. Komisarjevsky, *Myself*, 156. So far this is the only image I have found of this production.
206. *The Stage*, 14 July 1929, Cadbury Research Library, University of Birmingham, MS38/236.
207. V.E. Borovsky, *A Triptych of Russian Theatre: The Komissarzhevskys* (London: Hurst, 2001), 349.
208. Hubert Griffith, *European Encounters* (London: John Lane, 1931), 241.
209. Griffith, *European Encounters*, 242.
210. Naomi Mitchison, 'Pages from a Russian Diary' (1932) in *Modernism and Nationalism: Literature and Society in Scotland 1918–1939*, ed. Margery Palmer McCulloch (Glasgow: Association for Scottish Literary Studies, 2004), 211.
211. Hubert Griffith, *The People's Court* (London: Rich and Cowan, 1933), 17.
212. Nicholson, *British Theatre and the Red Peril*, 88.

213. Alec Baron, *I Was There*, unpublished autobiography, 1. Beginnings. With thanks to Alec's family for so generously sharing his unpublished manuscript.
214. Ibid.
215. Alec Baron and Kate Plenty, *Comrade Enemy* (1942), BC Ms 20c Theatre, Baron, Brotherton Collection, University of Leeds.
216. Baron, *I Was There*, 4. Unity Theatre. Baron also suggests here that Sybil Thorndike watched the performance and wanted to get it produced professionally in London. Nothing came of this as far as I can tell and, although there is no substantive evidence of Thorndike's involvement with *Comrade Enemy*, her connection with Unity Theatre and her commitment to encouraging leftist theatre work makes this anecdote most probable.
217. Baron and Plenty, *Comrade Enemy*, 3.1.
218. Miles Tomalin, Comments from London Unity (29/10/41), BC Ms 20c Theatre, Baron.
219. Baron and Plenty, *Comrade Enemy*, 2.2.
220. Lord Chamberlain's notes on *Comrade Enemy*, BC Ms 20c Theatre, Baron [held alongside the play]
221. Griffith, *Seeing Soviet Russia*, 182.
222. Norris Houghton, *Moscow Rehearsals* (London: George Allen and Unwin, 1938), 285. British audiences and practitioners were certainly aware of Houghton's work. Indeed, *Moscow Rehearsals* is mentioned in the *WTM Bulletin* of September 1938 with a promotional quote from Michel Saint-Denis: 'the most complete and intelligent account of the different methods of production which have been used in the Soviet Union' (*WTM Bulletin*, September 1938, Unity Theatre Archive, V&A, THM 9/4/1/9).
223. James Harding, 'From Cutting Edge to Rough Edges: On the Transnational Foundations of Avant-Garde Performance' in *Not the Other Avant-Garde: The Transnational Foundations of Avant-garde Performance*, eds James Harding and John Rouse (Ann Arbor: Michigan UP, 2006), 27.

CHAPTER 4

# Images and Montage: Russian Cinema and the British Stage

In the same year as Laurence Olivier appeared in *Salute to the Red Army* he took the lead role in a new film entitled *The Demi-Paradise* (1943), directed by Anthony Asquith and produced by Anatole de Grunwald with music by Russian émigré Nicholas Brodsky.[1] He plays a Russian engineer and inventor Ivan Kouznetsoff who tells two errant British sailors (one is Scottish, the other from the south coast of England) how he learnt English. He first arrived in England in 1939, he recalls, with a revolutionary new design for a ship's propeller to share with English ship-building companies. It is a tale of misunderstandings and cultural differences, from the etiquette of asking questions to the way one conducts business. Kouznetsoff spends much of the first half of his recalled narrative in bemused confusion, while the English characters around him are either frightened of the Russian or else presume his conversation (conducted in broken English) is frightfully rude. Two of these misapprehensions occur at theatrical events, the first at a revue show in London where Kouznetsoff is disgusted at the prices, bemoans his restricted-view seat behind a pillar and is thoroughly perplexed by the comedian's supposedly hilarious butchering of one of Rachmaninoff's piano *Preludes*. The second theatrical misadventure occurs in Barchester, home of Ann Tisdall, who rather takes him under her wing, and her grandfather, Mr Runalow, manager of the ship-building company. Under Rowanna Ventnor's indomitable leadership the town produces a pageant, Ventnor resembling Miss La Trobe in Virginia Woolf's 1941 *Between the Acts*. Kouznetsoff is confused by the unnerving historical focus and eventually excuses himself with the criticism 'you're living in the past'.



C. Warden, *Migrating Modernist Performance*,
DOI 10.1057/978-1-137-38570-3_5

Kouznetsoff and his English friends begin to understand one another a little better as the narrative progresses. As he is attempting to fix the propeller in 1941, Germany invades Russia, and, crowded round the radio in Barchester, Kouznetsoff and the family listen to Winston Churchill proclaim 'we shall give whatever help we can to the Russian people'. From this point, the two countries are allies. Kouznetsoff continues to work on the propeller, with the help of local Russophile worker Tom and his comrades. He successfully finds a solution to his engineering problem by staring into the ripples of a cup of tea, importantly taken with milk: the English way. Miss Ventnor puts on the pageant once again, collecting money for Kouznetsoff's hometown, but changes the finale so that the Roman Occupation of Britain and the Battle of Waterloo lead into a celebration of international cooperation with military groups entering the stage with flags. In the final scene they launch the ship, named 'Druzhba' ('Friendship'), and Kouznetsoff gives a rousing speech in which he encourages everyone to 'fight together in the years to come and then laugh together in the years afterwards'. The film then returns to Kouznetsoff with the two British sailors, pointing out Druzhba sailing in the Russian waters.

*The Demi-Paradise* speaks directly to the central themes of *Migrating Modernist Performance*. It stars Laurence Olivier, who performed in a number of Russian-focused works (including *Salute to the Red Army*) and was produced by a Russian émigré who had fled his native land in 1910. It is based on two central migratory journeys: the British soldiers to Russia and Kouznetsoff (twice) to Britain. Although most of the narrative takes place in Britain, the framing story is situated in Russia as Kouznetsoff recounts his experiences to the British sailors. This slightly clunky device is easy to forget as it acts as bookends, appearing at the beginning and end of the film but otherwise not interfering with the linear tale. The film details the various misunderstandings on both sides of the national divide, moving from comedic love story to serious wartime propaganda, encouraging friendship and cooperation between the two countries against the Nazi threat. It confirms the importance of travel in dispelling erroneous assumptions about other nationalities. However, the images of both countries – Russia as a community-focused place of workers' rights, nearly full employment and cheap theatre tickets, and an England (and it is specifically *England*) of pageants, tea, stiff upper lips and stoic refusal to give up – are decidedly stereotypical, in keeping with the highly propagandistic message. This is a film, then, that simultaneously bashes down and raises up national clichés.

Furthermore, *The Demi-Paradise* affirms cinema as a vital medium for discussions of British and Russian culture in the first half of the twentieth century. Film is a defining emblem of modernity; as Lara Feigel convincingly confirms, the structures and characteristics of film reflect the 'painfully abrupt contrasts of the capitalist city' – the speed, the 'distracted spectatorship', the shock of vertiginous schisms, whether aesthetic or socio-political.[2] Importantly for my purposes, cinema is also intricately connected with notions of travel. In *The Demi-Paradise*, Kouznetsoff's two train journeys to Britain are visually and audibly layered with, first, Russians telling him about the horrid English weather and the unfriendly English people, and then, on his second trip, German predictions of Britain's imminent collapse. Of course, the Lumière Brothers played up the associations between travel and film in the early cinematic experiment, *Arrival of a Train at La Ciotat Station* (1896). However, the motif recurs throughout the history of cinema. In 1930, British filmmaker and editor of the journal *Close Up* Kenneth MacPherson was still using this train motif in *Borderline*.[3]

Travel, particularly train travel, and modernity are interlinked concepts, but methods of modern travel also transform one's perception of place. According to Lynne Kirkby 'the railroad gave us our first mass vehicle of deception – based on a fundamental perceptual shift in which speed and the visual framed every encounter with the Other. The cinema gave us our second such vehicle'.[4] As Kirkby confirms, modern travel and the cinema both distort our perceptions of the world: skipping quickly between places, allowing rapid views but not the opportunity to rest one's eyes on a scene, altering our understanding of time, culture and landscape. Travel and cinema are also engaged with issues of accessibility; trains can transport the masses literally, while cinema can do so figuratively. The body has formed a central connective motif in this book so far and it is as important to modernist cinema as it is to the experience of travel or the presentation of live performance. Tim Armstrong claims 'film also allows the exploration of motion and even the spaces of the body in new ways'.[5] In fact, Armstrong re-emphasises the central concern of this book when he describes the 'cinematicized' body (that is, the body embedded in filmic motion, sound and modern mechanisation) as having 'migratory status' in that it reappears in many other artistic genres.[6]

Alongside films from Germany and France, Russian cinema took a particularly aspirational position in British understanding of filmic methods. In fact, this can be identified in the opening example of this chapter. The layered images Kouznetsoff experiences on the train, with the Russian and German faces speaking through the image of the landscape rushing past, are reminiscent of decidedly Russian montage effects. Asquith was certainly aware of European avant-garde film, particular the innovations of the Russian cinematographers and German expressionists.[7] He even attended Sergei Eisenstein's London lectures of 1929.[8] Montage, propagated in differing forms by Russian figures such as Eisenstein, Vsevolod Pudovkin and Dziga Vertov (all of whom had significant influence over the burgeoning British film scene) haunts this later British popular film in a direct way.

This chapter does not attempt to address the importance of Russian cinema in a British context. Instead it has a very specific intention: to uncover some of the ways Soviet cinema affected live stage performance in Britain. This is not a simple one-way appropriation of technique. Rather, the overlaps and shared characteristics of the media prove most fascinating. In identifying a more circumlocutory sharing of practices I follow the lead of scholars like David Trotter in *Cinema and Modernism* (2007) and Andrew Shail in *The Cinema and the Origins of Literary Modernism* (2012) who break away from easy genealogies of influence towards a more fluid model. These important studies focus specifically on literature but behind this chapter is also the impetus of contemporary performance studies, a field that is, in Diana Taylor's words, challenging the 'disciplinary compartmentalization of the arts'.[9] Accordingly, the chapter grapples with ongoing discussions around temporality and liveness, mediation and immediacy, issues that divide performance scholars. What is the relationship between the live theatrical performance and film?[10] Here I've focused on a number of little-known performances, contextualising them through the regular discussions of Russian film in journals and the presentation of Russian films by societies across the country. The performances mentioned are also all embedded in the Russian travels of their creators, reconnecting the train and the cinema as explicated by Kirby above. What emerges is a collection of esoteric, sometimes rather awkward, experiments, created by some of the most influential British travellers to Russia.

## Providing a Context: Russian Cinema in Britain

The theatrical performances that form the bulk of this chapter require initial framing within a broader understanding of Russian film in Britain. It is particularly important to note the way that Soviet cinematics migrated to Britain through cinema clubs, journals and direct communication between practitioners, including through the arrival of Russian filmmakers. It should be remembered that only particular Russian films appeared in Britain, generally the most aesthetically impressive. This gave British audiences a rather skewed reading of Russian cinema. British doctor James Purves-Stewart, who travelled throughout the Soviet Union in 1932, substantiated this warning after attending a cinema in Kiev:

> Then there was a series of topical pictures showing the anniversary demonstrations held this very day in celebration of the Young Communist party. The leading orators were filmed, haranguing the crowd. I never saw a more degraded or malignant type of faces – almost bestial – than in these orators. Such films would be excellent anti-communist propaganda for exhibition before an ordinary civilized audience.[11]

Given that Purves-Stewart's medically focused narrative is fairly balanced throughout, this response to Russian film stands out as very strong indeed. Such crude propaganda was not what most of the admiring British audiences thought of when they eulogised the Russian cinematic experiment.

Russian film made its way to Britain through the myriad of small film societies that arose across Britain. These can be read as two separate, though interconnected, initiatives: the groups organised by university-educated or more aesthetically driven societies (the London Film Society being the most influential and fruitful), and those associated with working-class communities propagating leftist political views. While the intentions and characteristics of these two lineages differed, actually they shared personnel (as I shall show, Ivor Montagu provides a specific link here) and, as Laura Marcus has claimed, in the minds of the censors and government bodies at least, every medium for presenting or promoting Soviet cinema was regarded as part of the same propaganda exercise.[12] Russian films did not always dominate the programming of these groups (between 1925 and 1939 the London Film Society showed 41 Russian films out of a total of approximately 500),[13] but certainly Russian cinema engendered the most press coverage and controversy, due partly to aesthetics and partly to politics.

In addition to this burgeoning collection of groups and societies, journals and magazines simultaneously exposed British readers to the techniques and innovations of Soviet cinema. *Close Up* (1927–1933), for example, a short-lived magazine founded in Switzerland and edited by Britons Kenneth Macpherson and his wife, Bryher, regularly mentioned Russian cinema. Its September 1928 volume was even set up as 'A Russian number' and provides a concise reflection of the way this influential journal (and British audiences in general) responded to Russian film. In his introduction to the volume, MacPherson does not unequivocally praise Russian cinema (he considers a film about Pushkin entitled *Tzar and Poet* to be 'one of the really boring hours I have spent in a projection room')[14] but, broadly speaking, he sets up the Soviet film industry as an institution to emulate:

> The Russian method uses [the camera] not as an eye, but as a *brain*. It darts surely and exactly from one vital thing to another vital thing. Its penetration is acute and deep, and very rarely (in its best films never) led astray by side-issues or sentimentality.[15]

For MacPherson these innovative Russian methods sharply contrast with film techniques in Britain. He laments, 'if Russia is going to continue as it has started, and we are going to continue as we have been going on, we will be in the same relation to modern existence as The Doomsday Book was to Queen Elizabeth'.[16] The rest of this special edition explores the importance of Soviet cinema and often alludes to the difference between the British and Russian film industries. HD, for example, suggests that Russian and British cinema actually share similar technical challenges but, while the latter relies on star appeal, 'Russia has taught us that every man, every woman and every child is a "star"'.[17] If British filmmakers could approach their work in similar ways to their Russian counterparts, providing a vehicle for the stories and images of the working population, then, says HD, they might truly produce films 'by the people'.[18] In the final article of the volume (entitled 'Dope or Stimulus'), Bryher (who wrote a 1929 book entitled *Film Problems of Soviet Russia*) criticises British popular culture for being anti-intellectual and facile, 'destructive because it is used as a cover to prevent real consideration of problems, artistic, or sociological'.[19] In many ways this edition seems be as much about the inadequacies of the British film scene as the vibrancy of the Russian.

The next edition of the journal, from the following month, is not a self-professed Russian number, but does carry on the focus on Soviet cinema, particularly through an article by Eisenstein, Pudovkin and Alexandroff on the turn towards sound rather than silent cinema. They express concern about this innovation, identifying its potential to destroy the artistic progress made, before coming to the conclusion that it might be possible to resist the inevitable clutches of the corporate machine and produce a film effect that extends the montage methods by simply using sound as another layered aesthetic element rather than as a tool for explaining (and, inevitably, reducing) the image.[20] Throughout its history *Close Up*, while recognising that there are good and bad films in every country, held Russian cinema up as a pinnacle of artistic excellence and as a model for British cinema to emulate. Further, Anne Friedberg describes *Close Up* as a 'form of "literary montage" – a serial project with the random architecture of juxtaposition, an exhibit of documents'.[21] In this it mirrored the visual characteristics of Russian film, swiftly moving from one impression to the next, conscious of the need to discuss transnational art that engaged with contemporary aesthetic and political issues. So, as well as focusing on Russian cinema, its 'montage of attractions' structure resembled *Battleship Potemkin* or *October*.

Russian cinema's marginal but significant influence in Britain was, then, partly due to the promotion of Russian film in local clubs and groups, and the availability of journals and magazines that provided a British readership with a sense of Soviet cinematic innovation. But, in addition to the migration of text and film, Soviet cinema was transported to Britain through the travels of individuals. One of the most influential voices in this British desire to learn more about Russian film was Huntly Carter, a journalist and cultural commentator who travelled to Russia on numerous occasions between 1921 and 1938; he wrote a number of books on his perceptions of European theatre for Anglophone audiences. After his first trip Carter produced articles for the journal *The New Age*. They are relatively balanced, reflecting on a country still in chaos after the First World War and subsequent Civil War. He concludes his final article of 17 November 1921 with the hopeful proclamation, 'given the opportunity the Youth of Russia will do more to regenerate Russia in a few years than the elders can do in ten centuries'.[22] He bases his analysis in these articles on objects he has picked up on his first trip such as propaganda posters and productivity charts.

Carter's later books are detailed and expansive, firmly connecting cultural history to contextual politics. His explanations of Russian theatre are sympathetic and reverent, while never uncritically laudatory. Like so many others, Carter placed considerable emphasis on the experiential importance of travel. At the start of *The New Spirit in the Russian Theatre, 1917–1928* (1929) Carter makes the following proclamation:

> Only writers who, like myself, have entered Russia from time to time since 1917 and have systematically collected material for books on theatre as a whole, can boast of being in a position to tell the complete story of the New theatre.[23]

Carter's varied experiences of the Russian theatre alongside his tireless scholarship means *The New Spirit in the Russian Theatre* provides first-hand descriptions of (as he terms them) 'Master Builders' like Tairov, Stanislavsky and Meyerhold, and 'Lesser Builders' like the Blue Blouse movement and TRAM. He takes each chronological period in turn, splitting the history of Soviet Theatre into four epochs: 1917–1922 when, despite war, famine and economic troubles, the new Bolshevik government recognised the importance of art; 1923–1928, a period of growth and innovation; today's theatre, by which Carter means the 1926–1928 seasons; and the theatre of tomorrow.

However, it is the final section of this book that opens up the discussion of this chapter. Here, in a book ostensibly about live performance, Carter focuses on the development of Russian cinema alongside theatre (and radio). During the 1920s many artists wrote comprehensibly about the difficult relationship between theatre and cinema. Russophile Virginia Woolf, for instance, basing her 1926 article for *The New Republic* on the idea of dramatising Tolstoy's *Anna Karenina*, praised the potential of the cinematic and yet remained troubled by film's immaturity: 'while all the other arts were born naked, this, the youngest has been born fully clothed. It can say everything before it has anything to say.'[24] Russian traveller George Bernard Shaw focused on the potential theatrical benefits of the growth in cinema: 'in short, the cinema takes from the theatre only those plays that have no business there; and the resultant pressure on the theatres to find plays with some brains in them is of incalculable benefit to the drama.'[25] In a recent study Anthony Paraskeva, indicating the importance of the body – a motif vital to the narrative of this book – attempts to unravel the intricate relationship between film and theatre:

> Cinema emerges from theatre by transforming presence into mediated technological representation, eliminating the auratic presence of the actor and bringing it closer to writing; yet it remains haunted by theatre, and by the representation of the performative body which originates in theatre.[26]

So while they are different beasts in terms of aesthetics and audiences, and embroiled in issues of class, gender and location in different ways, theatre and cinema are, nevertheless, inextricably connected. Extending Paraskeva's description here, the examples below illustrate that cinema and theatre exist in a perpetual relationship of haunting and emerging: an intermingled aesthetic bricolage.

Carter acknowledged this interconnection but expressed it in an alternative way; theatre has a duty to address socio-political contextual concerns, he suggests, and cinema 'promised in fact to shoulder some of the responsibilities of the theatre without interfering with its indispensable birthrights'.[27] Despite contradictions, cinema could not only act as theatre's collaborator but also present ideas in ways deemed impossible on a live stage. Carter embraces the differences, challenging the perceived rivalry between the forms and, instead, posits a mutually supportive relationship:

> The cardinal constructive principle of the plan is mass production – mass philosophy, sentiment, action, necessary to prepare the people as a whole to undertake the mass work of the epoch. Owing to its limitation the Theatre cannot fulfil such a gigantic task alone. It needs a partner.[28]

His explanation focuses on the political responsibilities of art and seems more immediately relevant to Soviet Russian society than to British. However, Carter's methodology posed a utopian challenge to the 1920s British cinema industry so exasperatingly criticised by Bryher in *Close Up*.

Though Carter was perhaps the most prominent traveller to engage with Russian film, he was by no means alone. In 1927 Ivor Montagu (son of a baron, committed communist and, later, leading figure in the Society for Cultural Relations with Russia) travelled to the Soviet Union to witness the Revolution for himself. One can partly piece together his journey by studying his address book and photograph album. The former is tricky to decipher but mentions two theatres of note to visit: Meyerhold's theatre and the Bolshoi. In naming these two theatrical institutions, Montagu confirms both his diverse interests in the Russian stage, and, on a broader note, points to the unique nature of 1920s Russian theatre, where the establishment Bolshoi and the revolutionary Meyerhold coexisted in an albeit fraught theatre scene.[29] The details of his trip become clearer when read through the images in his photograph album. The latter begins with an image of the Latvian-Russian frontier, taken by Montagu from the train carriage as he passed a military hut and a lone soldier. There are photos of Moscow (including a number of the Bolshoi theatre) and Leningrad, but between images of these two urban centres are photographs of rural Georgia and the Northern Caucasus, and of less well-travelled cities like Rostov and Baku. The photographs confirm Montagu as an adventurous traveller, committed to overcoming the dangers, restrictions and challenges of journeying through the Soviet Union during this period. Many years later, in 1949, Montagu returned to Russia and, while chatting with a Russian naval officer, was reminded of his earlier trip: 'I tell him of my first visit to Peterhof, long ago, of how a friend and I came out by train and foot when the revolution was still young.'[30] With his new officer friend he returned to the beach where he swam in 1927 and where, notably, in an imaginative transnational layering, he suggested the children played with 'Butlins abandon'.[31] During this visit Montagu thought back to the period between the wars when 'in every town and working class centre [in Britain] persons existed and were well-known who had visited the Soviet Union and founded their admiration on the sight of their own eyes'.[32] Once again, the experiential exposure to Russian culture through travel remained a defining method of cross-cultural understanding. Montagu advocated a migratory relationship between Britain and Russia throughout his career, hoping that Russian visitors would also journey to Britain, as he imagined misunderstandings and misrepresentations could better be overcome by direct congenial conversation and hand-shaking than by the written word, which could so often be misconstrued.[33] But Montagu was also aware of the difficulties in interacting with Soviet culture and critical of those, like Bertrand Russell, who entered Russia with preconceived ideas:

> I think such intellectuals were completely deceived by surface appearances. They came from a society in which mental activity had become so divorced from physical toil that the glorification of toil and toiler that they found in the USSR scared them out of their wits and certainly out of their judgement and sense of proportion. The sweat of fear started out upon their foreheads much more readily than the sweat of hard physical work.[34]

Montagu accuses other travellers of being so engrained in (at least what he, as a communist, imagined to be) the attitudes of class-ridden, capitalist Britain that they were unable to appreciate the true nature of Russian society. While this perhaps feels a touch unfair, Montagu's allegations reveal again the potential difficulties of travel.

As well as being an exponent of table tennis, introducing the game to players all over the world (he is, according to Nicholas Griffin's recent study, 'the reason – the only reason – that 300 million Chinese play table tennis every week'),[35] Montagu was instrumental in the importing of Russian films to Britain, leading in the setting up of the Film Society in London, one of the most important conduits for bringing innovative filmmaking to Britain. This collective consciously mirrored the Stage Society's commitment to innovation and the importing of foreign artworks, and claimed a direct influence from the more established theatrical group that, as this book has discussed, introduced British audiences to a range of Russian playwrights including Gorky and Chekhov.[36]

Parallelling the situation in the theatre, the presentation of Soviet film was hampered by vigorous censorship. In his 1929 pamphlet *The Political Censorship of Film*, Montagu points to the Censor's objections to *Battleship Potemkin* and *Mother* as examples of British governmental attitudes to the importing of foreign films. The Censor's objections, according to Montagu's pamphlet, seemed to rest on the fact that these films were ostensibly Russian in nature and clearly showed Russian politics. Despite Montagu's suggestion that 'their exhibition might tend to a better understanding of the situation in Russia in the present day' such films were still regarded with suspicion.[37] As with groups like the Stage Society or Unity Theatre, Montagu's Film Society provided a way round the censors as private, subscription clubs came under less scrutiny than more public, open forums.

Montagu also translated Pudovkin's writing into English, prefacing his 1953 version of *Film Technique and Film Acting* (a translation work originally published in abbreviated form in 1929) with a 'personal memoir'. This prologue is particularly intimate, based less on Pudovkin's reputation as a filmmaker than his travels from Russia to Britain, and Montagu's own journeys the opposite way. The latter's recollection of Pudovkin's 'joy at discovering how easy it was to speak to his wife in Moscow by the telephone at my flat, his delight in shopping to buy English clothes – not in the least from snobbery, but because they were exotic and English, as a London visitor to Moscow might buy an embroidered cap or shirt' firmly grounds this study of film technique in transnational friendship.[38] Pudovkin showed a particular interest in British film. In a letter (which we can broadly date from the four 1948 films he mentions) from Pudovkin to the Society for Cultural Relations with Russia, the filmmaker confirmed 'my film colleagues and I are particularly keen to become acquainted with the work of the English film masters, to see if only one of the latest English films: "Oliver Twist", "Hamlet", "Great Expectations", and especially "Anna Karenina"'.[39] Again, Russian practitioners seemed as interested in sharing practice as their British counterparts.

In his preface to *Film Technique and Film Acting*, Montagu mentions film critic and biographer Marie Seton who, apparently, helped Pudovkin improve his English.[40] In addition to acting as Pudovkin's language coach,

Seton also wrote a biography of Sergei Eisenstein, partly based on conversations she had with him. It is a celebratory piece which recognises Eisenstein as 'one of the most important artists of the $20^{th}$ century'.[41] Reproductions of Eisenstein's 1929 London lectures can be found in Appendix 2. In these lectures (as transcribed by documentary filmmaker Basil Wright) Eisenstein details the characteristics of montage film, suggesting that 'in montage ALWAYS CHOOSE PIECES WHICH DO NOT FIT'. The shock or surprise of these layered images define Eisenstein's concept here. Importantly he understands the film and live theatre experiences as intrinsically mirroring one another:

> The theatre and the spielfilm [dramatic film] are definitely connected: the spielfilm has several (or unlimited) proscenium openings as a result of camera mobility.[42]

Despite the difference in number of proscenium openings, Eisenstein appears to be suggesting that both media aim to open up the space within (or beyond) to the spectator.

In 1934 Seton travelled to Moscow with actor and singer Paul Robeson and his wife, Essie. Though American by birth, Robeson significantly influenced the British theatre scene, and indeed worked with a number of figures mentioned in this book, including van Gyseghem, who directed him in Eugene O'Neill's *All God's Chillun Got Wings* (1933). He remained committed to the project of Unity Theatre, appearing in one of the collective's most successful productions, *Plant in the Sun*, in 1938.[43] This production is important to this book's argument because it was directed by Herbert Marshall, whom Robeson met in Russia in 1934. The origin of this performance, then, lay in Russian travels. Further, Robeson turned down the opportunity to perform in Basil Dean's *The Sun Never Sets* at Drury Lane in order to star in *Plant in the Sun* and fulfil his commitment to Unity, a collective that appealed to him politically as well as aesthetically.[44]

Robeson could speak Russian and enjoyed fruitful conversations with Eisenstein during this 1934 trip. He returned in the summer of 1936. Robeson, like so many other African-American artists, appreciated what he saw as Soviet Russia's open attitude to race and colour. While he experienced significant prejudice in America (including, much later, being blacklisted by the government and having his passport confiscated), he, like other Harlem Renaissance figures such as Claude McKay, Langston

Hughes and W.E.B. Dubois, found a far less discriminatory society in Russia.[45] He did not ignore the violence of the Soviet system, and was aware of the tense political situation during his visits, but Russia's opposition to racism (at least as he saw it) meant he remained an ardent supporter of the Soviet project.

This brief overview of just some of the migratory exchanges between Soviet and British film illustrates the vibrancy of this transnational relationship. Indeed, it is an increasingly well-documented field of study. The relationship was deeply embedded in travelled experience, in the direct communication of practitioners and commentators. But this does not yet answer the central question of this chapter: how did Russian film influence British theatre, if at all? Further, returning to Paraskeva's explanation, I have yet to explain how theatre and cinema haunted and emerged from one another, particularly as part of a migratory, transnational network of artists. The recollections and practices of a selection of British theatrical travellers to Russia provide a series of recourses.

## The British Stage and Russian Cinematics: *Aristocrats*, *Brain* and the Living Newspaper

One of the recurring stars of this book, André van Gyseghem, reserved the final chapter of his 1943 *Theatre in Soviet Russia* for a practitioner he praises as creating 'the most interesting theatre in Moscow... I believe him to have made the most significant move yet towards a "new" theatre'.[46] Van Gyseghem is referring to the head of the Realistic Theatre, Nikolai Okhlopkov, who initiated a rather remarkable experiment in stage realism. Van Gyseghem's description is detailed, imaginative and intense, based on his direct work with Okhlopkov. He chronicles a 'theatre more full of sound than was the crowded foyer' with 'no stage at all as we know it':

> We, the audience, represent their comrades, and the actors flood the theatre, the iron stream breaks over us, our hands are clasped by the gnarled hands of bearded peasants, women greet women with a warm embrace and the children dart in among the seats, throwing themselves at us with cries of delight. Actors and audience are still one – and we applaud each other.[47]

In the previous chapter I complicated the notion of realism through Russian theatrical experiment and equivalent British responses. Here is another type of realism: a realism of visceral communication, of tangible embodied experience, of body-to-body engagement. Van Gyseghem describes this theatre as creating a bond between actor and audience: 'the barriers between us are broken down; the path to our hearts is open and the actors take that path.'[48] He illustrates his celebration of Okhlopkov's theatre by focusing particularly on the Realistic Theatre's 1935 performance of Nikolai Pogodin's *Aristocrats.*

*Aristocrats* is ostensibly a socialist realist play about the construction of the White Sea-Baltic Canal by a motley crew of prisoners. They are mostly work-shy anti-revolutionists, committed only to personal gain and comfort rather than to any collective sense of society. Gradually, however, they individually come to realise their responsibility to the community, and strive to build a new society and escape from their felonious pasts. At the end, The Captain, one of the main criminal ringleaders, proclaims a 'Red Banner Collective'[49] and Gromov makes a rousing speech:

> Why will the White Sea Canal be famous? Because here the forces that have drawn people like Sadovsky and Dorokhov to participate in socialist work, are operating with unheard-of daring, with true Bolshevik austerity, and on the broad scale Comrade Stalin has taught us. These people, once rejected by society, outcasts, lost, and even enemies, are today recognized and highly valued by their country.[50]

Actually, it is not the most inspiring or artistically creative play, stuck as it is in socialist realist linear structures. It contains far too many characters, making it difficult to connect with them individually (presumably this is the point, but it doesn't make for a particularly interesting theatrical experience) and the moral is awkwardly didactic. The difficulty, then, is how to stage this rather plodding text. Okhlopkov turned it into what he called a 'carnival play', encouraging spectators and actors alike to, in his words, 'laugh the victors' laugh of energetic joy'.[51] Reviews picked up on Okhlopkov's imaginative rendering of the play. Actors began by throwing white confetti over the audience, simulating a blizzard in the desolate far north of Russia. Then came a series of short vignettes or 'poetic picture[s]', scenes which drew the audience in, relying on its imaginative response. Ultimately, says a reviewer, Okhlopkov was 'attracted to broad epic canvases'.[52] Remarkably, Okhlopkov managed to transform this piece of socialist realism into a celebratory pageant that seemed to truly engage spectators. Witnessing the spectacle, van Gyseghem regarded it as a culmination of Okhlopkov's style, focusing in his book on two particular scenes. The first is a young girl skiing, a scene performed physically using music with an accelerating tempo. Van Gyseghem expresses his admiration for this visceral interpretation of the action.[53] The second scene is the drowning of renegade Kostia in which his body is washed up on the shore. Okhlopkov mimicked the water using canvas cloth, cut at intervals to allow actors' limbs to poke through. According to van Gyseghem's recollections, at the end of this scene, Kostia's body appeared lifeless from beneath the canvas.[54]

Three years later, Pogodin's *Aristocrats* appeared in translation at Unity Theatre. It marked the company's transition from amateur collective to a paid subscription society. In a letter to members describing this change (dated 28 November 1937) we find the first mention of the forthcoming production:

> 'ARISTOCRATS' is one of the world's great plays, and we think our production will be a landmark in the history of the Working Class Theatre, and in every way is a magnificent play with which to open our new theatre.[55]

Although *Aristocrats* was supposed to welcome the professional theatre's foundation, its performance history at Unity was less than congenial, leading to a significant falling out between Herbert Marshall (not to be confused with the more famous Hollywood actor of the same name) and Nelson Illingworth, an opera-trained Australian voice coach who, working with Unity, Theatre Workshop and Group Theatre, became a significant connecting point for British modernist avant-garde theatre.[56] The directorial influences of deposed Illingworth and new creative head Marshall are rather tricky to untangle. However, the latter's first-hand experience in Russia can certainly be discerned in descriptions and extant photographs of the 1938 production.

Marshall travelled to Moscow on a scholarship from the Higher Film Institute in the mid 1930s, and worked with Eisenstein, Meyerhold and, indeed, Okhlopkov. In addition he helped to organise the 1933 Moscow Olympiad where the jury so vilified the British efforts.[57] Marshall claimed that the first Russian film director he ever met in person was Dziga Vertov. In 1929 Vertov attended the International Avant-Garde Film and Photo Conference in Stuttgart as part of a larger European tour.[58] There he met Marshall who (in his 1983 retrospective *Masters of the Soviet Cinema: Crippled Creative Biographies*) gushed that Vertov, along with Pudovkin, 'definitely influenced my whole life'.[59] Accompanying Marshall was his friend (and Russian speaker) Lionel Britton.[60]

Britton remains a rather mysterious figure as Tony Shaw's recent scholarship has identified.[61] Writer, novelist, linguist and translator, he certainly travelled to Russia in the 1930s, and wrote the communist novel *Hunger and Love* (1931) and the play *Spacetime Inn* in 1932, which, according to his archive at the Southern Illinois University in Carbondale, was performed at the House of Commons.[62] In 1930, months after he and Marshall met Vertov in Stuttgart, Britton wrote a strange play entitled *Brain: A Play of the Whole Earth*. It was performed by the Masses Stage and Film Guild at the Savoy Theatre in April of that year and caused very few ripples in the theatrical world. After criticising it as wholly inconceivable and incomprehensible, an *Observer* reviewer concluded '"Brain" was a drama not easy to forget or to forgive, a depressive ending to what had been, climatically, a perfect day'.[63] Certainly the play has issues but, after reading it, Bernard Shaw apparently claimed the playwright 'can deliver the goods', and though Britton conducted much of his work in obscurity, *Brain* certainly warrants a proper analysis.[64] I want to resurrect *Brain* as an example of cinematic theatre, written after meeting Vertov in Stuttgart and, I suggest, perhaps reflecting the Russian's ideas. This is a rather speculative analysis, of course, but the evidence certainly points towards a connection, despite Vertov's rejection of theatre in favour of cinema, describing the former as 'almost always just a lousy imitation of that same life, plus an idiotic conglomerate of balletic affectation, musical squeaks, tricks of lighting, stage sets'.[65] After listening to Vertov's speech in Stuttgart Marshall summed up the Russian's practice: 'these fragments of life he puts together – mounts – montage – in various rhythmic ways, using all the possibilities of montage, of cutting.'[66] *Brain* partly reflects this sort of aesthetic structuring and also uses filmed material as part of the play.

*Brain* begins in the present with a Professor and Librarian discussing the possibility of building a giant mechanical brain in the Sahara Desert, an entity which could capture 'all the isolated activities and energies of the world inter-related and interlocking, isolated no longer, forming one single conscious unit'.[67] They write a manuscript to this effect and then promptly die. The rest of the play narrates what happens to the manuscript, the creation of the brain (a development that leads some to panic and others to work for it) and, eventually, the end of the world in the year 50,000,000. It is a science fiction thriller, a dystopian play to be read alongside Karel Čapek's *R.U.R.*, written some ten years earlier.

*Brain* is tricky to perform, not least because of the remarkable (for the time) amount of onstage nudity, but also due to its sense of aesthetic ambition. By way of example: the deaths of the manuscript writers are theatricalised in act 1, scene 1b, a short interlude with two possible performance methods. Britton first suggests presenting their deaths using a 'cinematograph' in five episodes: (1) the undertaker's cart, (2) the mound in the cemetery, (3) funeral, (4) grave, (5) a close-up on the manuscript with subtitles added – 'And What Became of the Manuscript?', 'Well – ', 'Who Knows?'[68] It is a clear example of Vertov's fragments of life, described by Marshall after the Stuttgart conference. However, Britton recognised that such innovative stage devices, combining live theatre and filmed material, might prove impossible for under-resourced theatre companies, so he provides an alternative: three short scenes containing a Bishop and undertakers. It is far more obvious than the symbolic, image-led filmed sequence – the undertakers confirm that the manuscript has been sent to the British Museum – perhaps suggesting that it is easier to remain ambiguous (and still take your audience with you) when the visuals are so true-to-life (as in the film) than it is with the rather more obscure artistry of live theatre. This latter episode also markedly resembles the 'cross-class montage' of Vertov's *The Man With the Movie Camera* (1929), in which the director cuts between a middle-class lady putting on makeup and a woman hard at work.[69] In *Brain* the Bishop's highbrow religious mumblings are interrupted (or cross-cut) by the cockney gravediggers discussing the manuscript and whether they are going to get lucky that evening. At the end of this scene Britton writes 'the three scenes all merge quickly into the other and are really a single scene'.[70] This theatrical montage, though using live bodies on the stage, works in much the same way as cinematic montage.

There is also the sense that the more enigmatic passages of the play were influenced, in part, by cinematic visuality. Take act 2, scene 3: 'an Impressionist presentation of the final frenzied effort of what is now termed the "earth"'.[71] The set is draped in black and, from behind these curtains, characters appear and disappear, lit by angled lights. As in an agitprop play, these figures are stock characters, able to change their identity simply by putting on another hat. The term 'impressionism' stands out here; Britton does not advocate a constructivist, expressionist or cubist presentation as might be expected. 'Impressionism' here seems to be an incongruous nineteenth-century throwback. However, in cinematic terms, it is associated with Vertov, either as a (largely) celebratory description of Vertov's visuality from Viktor Shklovsky[72] or as a rather accusatory term as in Eisenstein's charge that his compatriot's methods relate '*to one of the least valuable expressions in ideological terms, to primitive Impressionism*'.[73] Despite Vertov's proclamation that he and his comrades were cleansing the cinema of 'foreign matter – of music, literature, and theater',[74] this scene from *Brain* certainly produces a cinematic, impressionistic montage effect that can be read alongside the Russian's innovations if not in a direct relationship of influence.

In 1977, many years after his experiences at the Stuttgart conference with Britton and his 1930s Russian escapades, Marshall published *The Pictorial History of the Russian Theatre*, one of the most comprehensive Anglophone renderings of Russian theatre from the Middle Ages onwards, with particular focus on the twentieth century. Marshall split his book into short sections, each one focusing on a company, collective or artist. This means that, rather than maintaining a strict chronological narrative, the book concentrates on the developing history of particular companies. He also introduces readers to a range of practitioners and techniques rarely mentioned in English-language analyses of Russian theatre: the revolving sets of Isaak Rabinovich, for example, or the Stanislavsky- and Vakhtangov-influenced Zavadsky Studio.[75] *The Pictorial History of the Russian Theatre* stands in sharp contrast to a fictionalised narrative like Macleod's *A Soviet Theatre Sketchbook*, or even van Gyseghem's *Theatre in Soviet Russia* with its prominent empirical undertone. Despite Marshall's undoubted first-hand experience of Russian theatre, his book feels far more like an academic study, perhaps unsurprisingly given his 20-year tenure at the Center for Soviet and East European Studies in Performing Arts at Southern Illinois University in Carbondale.[76]

As well as a theatre-maker, Marshall was a polymath and translator. His most significant contribution was translating the poems of Vladimir Mayakovsky, the instigator of Russian futurism, who he described as a 'revolutionary poet, in form and content. His satire was unmerciful, his irony biting, his sweep tremendous'.[77] In the foreword to Marshall's 1965 translations of Mayakovsky's work, C.M. Bowra confirms 'his [Marshall's] tone of voice is almost uncannily like that of Mayakovsky';[78] the accuracy of translation is important but, in the translation of poetry, it is the tone, the rhythms, the rhymes that take precedence. Marshall alludes to this in his introduction when he proclaims, 'translating Mayakovsky is a tough job, but my feeling is that he fits more easily into the English language than into any other except his own'.[79] Marshall's description of the translation process chimes with the experience of other British translators of Russian modernist texts; Constance Garnett, for example, proclaims, 'Tolstoy's simple style goes straight into English without any trouble'.[80] For these translators, though working with decidedly different texts, English and Russian seem to share particular characteristics, making the translation process more organic.

Marshall mentions Okhlopkov's version of *Aristocrats* very briefly in *The Pictorial History of the Russian Theatre*. His lack of real study is initially surprising given that he produced the play for Unity immediately after arriving back from his period in Russia. Alongside his brief analysis he includes some remarkable pictures of *Aristocrats*, almost certainly unavailable to Anglophone audiences before. However, his description is somewhat tempered:

> He [Okhlopkov] portrayed the romantic aspects of Stalin's Soviet prison camps' 'rehabilitation' programs (this was before the true nature of the gulag became known).[81]

Marshall here identifies an issue for many of the travellers mentioned in this book. Arriving in Russia, mesmerised by the vibrancy of the Russian stage and/or sheltered by the on-message leaders of Intourist trips, British travellers often did not see (or maybe overlooked) Soviet oppression of the Russian people. Only later were they able, sometimes in a rather embarrassed way, as perhaps Marshall shows here, to really comprehend the horrors of the Soviet system.

However, back in 1938, Marshall threw himself wholeheartedly into the Unity production of *Aristocrats*, directing, designing, lighting and, possibly, translating the play.[82] The programme description reveals the production's intentions:

> 'ARISTOCRATS' by Nicholai [sic] Pogodin is Unity's contribution to the anniversary of the Soviet Union, and is the first play produced in this country which deals with the other side of Soviet life – the construction of great works and the reconstruction of human beings. The play, based entirely on fact; it is the story of the building of the White Sea Canal, and deals with the problem of crime and criminals – problems that have to be faced in our own country. It stands in significant contrast to our own wretched prison systems.[83]

*Aristocrats* is a decidedly Russian play about specifically Russian issues and circumstances, and yet Unity's programme attempts to expound its relevance for British audiences. Like *Salute to the Red Army* some years later, Unity's production of *Aristocrats* celebrated an anniversary, a chance to pay tribute to the advances of the Soviet Union and, simultaneously, show transnational solidarity. It also provided a different view of Soviet life, an alternative perspective not explored on the British stage up to that point; it dealt with the problem of crime, an issue as relevant to Britain as to Soviet Russia. And it showed an alternative prison system, one which challenged the cheerless places of incarceration and punishment apparently so prevalent in Britain. Reading this now with the benefit of hindsight, one can see why Marshall framed his later brief description of Okhlopkov's version of *Aristocrats* in such apologetic terms.

Reviews of Unity's performance, such as there were, were celebratory and complimentary. The *Manchester Guardian*, for example, describes the production as an 'elaborately formless play, with its twenty-six changes of scene [that] would strain the resources of the most professional theatre. This unprofessional little theatre tackles its proposition astonishingly well'.[84] The review challenges the reading of this play as socialist realism by noting the fragmentation of narrative. This was a characteristic of both the Russian and British versions. In a sense, Okhlopkov's production technique mirrored the montage effects of Eisenstein or Pudovkin; van Gyseghem includes Okhlopkov's own words to describe this technique:

> We have introduced 'montage action'… In doing this we have not copied cinema montage, though we have carefully studied it together with the montage of the ancient Greek theatre.[85]

Interestingly here, Okhlopkov's montage has both cinematic and theatrical origins. Again, it is not that theatre slavishly borrowed from its newer, brasher cousin; rather, such montage effects had a long, theatrical history. Marshall confirms Okhlopkov's use of montage in *The Pictorial History of the Russian Theatre*:

> For a cinematic montage style he resorted to Meyerhold's and Eisenstein's theories of spatial organization, utilizing the entire theatre. This enabled him to present scenes simultaneously or in quick succession, while achieving closer intimacy between performer and audience.[86]

For Marshall also, Okhlopkov's montage had theatrical and cinematic sources, permitting a stronger sense of unity (aesthetically and, by extension, politically) in the theatre space.

Marshall's British version of *Aristocrats* built on the montage effects embedded in Okhlopkov's original by bringing cinema directly onto the stage. Not only did the production maintain the episodic style of Okhlopkov's rendering, it actually used cinematic techniques in the production. The play was performed in front of three screens set up on a scaffold. This mirrors Okhlopkov's version which used three painted backdrops to suggest the changes in the seasons. On Marshall's screens were projected images that imaginatively suggested place (e.g. a cabin) as well as maps and architectural impressions of the canal. Apparently (though sadly there do not appear to be any extant photographs of this event), in the finale the scaffold opened like canal lock gates and, using projection, the 'water' poured on to the audience.[87] This was an extremely ambitious production, embedded in the first-hand travel experiences of its director, Marshall.

As well as taking on challenging plays like *Aristocrats*, Unity also developed a strong tradition of political revue, pantomime and living newspaper. The latter emanated in part from an American source through the visit of New York playwright Arthur Arent and van Gyseghem's tour of the US.[88] The living newspaper received particularly high-profile backing across the Atlantic; in 1935, Hallie Flanagan set up the Federal Theatre Project (FTP), part of Franklin D. Roosevelt's New Deal scheme, designed to promote American economic recovery. But the transnational genesis of this technique is more complicated, as Colin Chambers suggests:

> The idea of the Living Newspaper – a live representation, drawing on documentary sources, of an important, contemporary issue – had come from the Russian revolution via America, though distant antecedents can be traced in popular nineteenth-century British theatre.[89]

Like the pageant form, mid 1930s living newspapers partly emanated from British cabaret and music hall (in its fragmented vibrancy if not its political efficacy), and partly from a more recent complex, migratory network of documentary theatre-making. The intricate interweaving of influences can be seen in a piece such as the 1942 Unity living newspaper *Get Cracking*. The programme clarified the performance's intentions, saying 'Unity believes in the theatre as a social force. That is why our revue is entitled "Get Cracking" – we feel it is a phrase on the lips of the people; we have turned it into a gay revue – with a serious message'.[90] The description slips between political commitment and unadulterated enjoyment.

The living newspaper had a particular cinematic etymology, a characteristic recognised by the leading members of Unity as evidenced by this reflection on their 1938 *Busmen*:

> A variety of scene is made dramatically possible by the cinematic continuity of the staging. A formal constructional set employing a number of different levels is used and different parts of the stage are spot-lighted and blacked-out as required, thus effectively speeding up the action.[91]

This type of theatrical construction can be clearly noted in Unity's 1938 play *Crisis*, a living newspaper produced by Russian traveller Herbert Marshall in the same year he took on the challenge of *Aristocrats*. *Crisis* discusses the political situation in Czechoslovakia, and was written and performed in days, without months of rehearsal or planning. Its immediacy, political urgency and stylised, fragmented structure differed from *Aristocrats*' more linear, character-led (even if those characters were emblematic rather than particularly developed) narrative. Yet, like *Aristocrats* (and like living newspapers in general) the cinematic prevailed. *Crisis* is written in 26 episodes and, in a distinct montage effect, moves from one to the next without the need for explanation. The fragments – geographically, chronologically and tonally contrasting – coexist amicably in this episodic style. Furthermore, *Crisis* is, at its heart, a transnational piece, using these fragments to take audience members to places like Nuremberg, Prague, Versailles and London. This sense of geographic freedom, made possible by the cinematic structure, exemplifies the central transnational intention of the piece. As so often with living newspapers, a leading narrator voice provides some clues, challenging the 'Chamberlain-apologist Air Warden' who suggests British people should accept war with stoicism. Instead the voice (called, imaginatively, 'Voice of the Living Newspaper') says that 'War can be stopped. Not by spreading panic and dread of war, but by the truth. Democracy is strong! Together, the peoples of democratic countries are a force no bullying dictator can dare attack': included in his list of 'democratic countries' are 'Russia, France, Czecho-Slovakia, Republican Spain, etc'.[92] Ultimately this living newspaper is about the development of transnational partnerships in order to prevent an oncoming war. Russia and Britain, as so-called 'democratic countries', could be part of this network. Unity performed it first on the day Chamberlain flew to Munich (29 September 1938) and changed it constantly to reflect the developing political situation: when the First Lord of the Admiralty resigned, for example, *Crisis* reported the news that evening.[93]

Unity's living newspapers were often constructed collaboratively, though occasionally particular figures were named on scripts as playwrights. Australian-born Jack Lindsay was one of those playwrights. He moved to Britain in the mid 1920s and remained a consistent supporter of the Soviet Union, regarding it as both a barrier to fascist expansionism and a leader for a transnational working-class collective. By 1941, when Lindsay wrote *Socialist Russia? A New Social Order*, the landscape of the world had been significantly altered by worldwide conflict. Lindsay imagined the Soviet Union, which, he claimed, 'has always stood for peace',[94] as leader in the chaotic socio-political atmosphere of the Second World War. He suggests, in problematically one-sided terms, that Russia provides a 'voice of just working-class retribution'.[95]

This conviction remained after the war when, in 1949, he journeyed to the Soviet Union for the celebrations to mark the 150th anniversary of Pushkin's birth. Artists from across the world joined him: Pablo Neruda, Paul Robeson, Halldór Laxness (Iceland) and Emi Siao (China), among others. Lindsay spent his time talking with writers, travelling the country, speaking with local people and, inevitably, attending theatre. His reflections are contained in his 1950 book *A World Ahead: Journal of a Soviet Journey*, a travel narrative reminiscent of the Webbs' *Soviet Communism: A New Civilisation?* (a book I mentioned in the introduction) in its almost whimsical romanticism. He criticises the drab, 'naturalistic' (his term) paintings on the walls of a crèche, but otherwise admires and valorises every aspect of Russian society.[96] In fact, as with so many of his fellow travellers (artistically and politically) mentioned in this book, Soviet Russia represents a vibrant alternative to Britain, not just theatrically, but politically, culturally and socially:

> In the arm-linked lovers I see the silent apotheosis of all lyric songs. I want to ask them if they know how blest they are, inheritors of an uncontaminated earth where the dancers within the song at last cast no shadows... I seem as strange as a mortal man who has landed on the moon, I who come from a cruel and bitter world, where wolves slaver out of the forests of newsprint and an ancient ape-evil speaks to me when I turn the wireless on.[97]

This flowery poeticism recurs time and again in his travelogue. Everything Lindsay saw and experienced during his 1949 trip seemed to delight him.

He is amazed by the speed and beauty of the rebuilding process in the wake of the war, inspired by the work ethic of the people he meets (from the writers in Moscow to the collective farmers in the Ukraine), astonished at the seeming abundance of excellent food. He is particularly enthused by his theatrical experiences: the 'masterly' verse-drama of Pushkin's *Boris Godunov*, the MAT's production of *Three Sisters*, which compels him to conclude that 'the English idea of Chekhov as a melancholy atmospheric-painter hasn't even the beginning of the right approach', a deeply affecting version of *The Lower Depths* and some beautiful ballet (though he preferred the newer Soviet *The Bronze Horseman* to the more conventional *Swan Lake*).[98]

While in Russia, Lindsay also shared some of his own work, discussing his performance poems *Cry of Greece* and the more well-known *On Guard for Spain*, which had been presented by Unity Theatre in 1937 to raise awareness of the Spanish Civil War and the ongoing fight against fascist expansion. Lindsay saw considerable benefits in such mass declamation poetry; in a similar way to its artistic cousins, the living newspaper and the political pageant, it could create a sense of community between actor and audience, and educate spectators about particular political issues.[99] While *On Guard for Spain* was the most popular and influential, Lindsay continued to experiment with this form, producing two with particular Russian themes: *We Need Russia* and *Salute the Soviet Union*, both first produced by Unity just before the Second World War.

A study of the latter enables a more thorough understanding of the workings of Lindsay's mass declamations and the way Unity responded to them in performance. The annotated script from Leeds Unity gives some sense of the way *Salute the Soviet Union* might have been performed. First, the script seems to be significantly cut. Lindsay's mass declamations tend to be wordy and, at times, tricky to decipher, so, in performance, cuts are vital. Yet, many significant poetic stanzas remain; this poem celebrates the Soviet Union as a global saviour, an antidote to world history that has tended to celebrate the rich and powerful, and suppress the poor or politically revolutionary. 'The Soviet star leaped in the sky of man' is the recurring sentiment.[100] Leeds Unity used group choruses and solo voices to bring some sense of tonal shading. So, in the final section, the four repetitive entreaties to 'defend' the Soviet Union and, in turn, 'defend' the British working class are spoken by individually numbered voices, while the concluding line – 'Salute the Soviet Union' – is performed in unison.[101] The aesthetic connections with agitprop are clear. In the Leeds version the actors were given particular roles: a nurse, a worker in dungarees holding a spanner, a farmer with a rake.[102] These are both individualised characters and representative symbols. The sense of transnational solidarity is as central to this piece as to *Crisis*; the script mentions places like Guernica, Malaga and Almeria. Interestingly, in the Leeds version, these are crossed out in pencil, replaced by London, Paris, Warsaw, Moscow, presumably in light of changing politics as the world's focus moved from Spain to Europe more generally. Only the city of Shanghai remains from the original list.[103]

As war began in earnest, Lindsay returned to the cinematic living newspaper form to entertain and educate audiences as part of the ABCA Play Unit, set up in 1944 by former head of the Westminster Theatre Michael MacOwen. The collective included some of Unity's central personnel, including two British-Russian travellers in van Gyseghem and Lindsay.[104] ABCA living newspaper plays focused on a range of issues including post-war reconstruction and the trouble of accepting American aid. Andrew Davies's description of the Unit's theatrical process illustrates its filmic style:

> It came up with a form of presentation that was almost cinematic in the speed and excitement by which it continually surprised the audience – for instance, there were speakers placed in the auditorium and even staged fights… as well as innovative lighting effects which directed the spectators' attention towards one spot and then another.[105]

In 1947 Montagu Slater (political playwright and, later, librettist for Benjamin Britten) wrote a historiographical narrative (starting with André Obey's *Le Viol de Lucrèce* in 1930) for *Documentary News Letter* that sought to reassess 'the interaction of stage and screen'. The living newspaper is a key element of his narrative, and he points to ABCA's work in this genre while noting 'that the ABCA unit dropped the title "Living Newspaper", finding it was misleading and called their productions "Documentary Plays"'.[106] Slater doesn't specify the reason for the change but presumably the latter proved more aesthetically expansive (documentary plays could have a more historical focus) and, perhaps, politically expedient given governmental concerns about the Play Unit's perceived revolutionary nature. Despite this semantic change the Unit's beginnings can be clearly seen in the 1930s migratory network of living newspapers in which influence, ideas and techniques transferred back and forth between Europe and the US.

## 'Better' in the Cinema? *Tsar Lenin*

Fifteen years after Hubert Griffith put Lenin and Trotsky on the stage in *Red Sunday*, the Stage Society attempted a new play with a similar focus: Ossia Trilling and Emanuel Wax's 'English version' of French playwright François Porché's *Tsar Lenin*. This play is a highly expressionistic rendering of Russian history, with various members of Soviet society (from an aristocrat to a peasant) transformed into chess pieces for Lenin to sweep off the board, and a danced version of the Bolshevik's rise to power.[107] This play (which concludes with Death saluting Lenin as a 'peerless grave-maker')[108] opened in 1937 at the Westminster and the reviewer from *The Times* gave his verdict:

> It is a difficult study, and the symbolic figures are used to make clear the movement of Lenin's mind and the movement of events in Russia. The device works well while it is revealing the man; less well when it is called upon to differentiate the contending groups of the Russia of 1917 and to show a revolution in progress. Then the play is in danger of becoming at once abstract and hysterical, and we are inclined to remember how much better the same thing has been done by the Russian films.[109]

Despite praise for individual performances, the reviewer has the nagging feeling that such a story might be told better by cinema than theatre.

Trilling was born in 1913 in Bialystok, Poland (then part of the Russian Empire) and could speak a number of languages, including Russian.[110] As editor of *Theatre Newsletter* from 1946 and joint honorary secretary of the British Theatre Conference, Trilling had significant influence over the academic study of theatre in Britain. In 1949 he co-edited one of the first post-Second World War volumes on world theatre: *International Theatre*. It is a volume that brings together contributions from a variety of British travellers to Russia – van Gyseghem, Seton, Marshall and Priestley – and includes two chapters on Soviet theatre from van Gyseghem who is described as 'Producer of ABCA Play Unit'.[111] The first focuses on theatre in Moscow, in which he compares the theatre scene of Russia's capital to its equivalent in London and New York:

> The theatres of London and New York ring a few beautifully modulated changes of the single bell of naturalism; Moscow reverberates to a full peal with the booming bass of realism dominating at the moment.[112]

The chapter discusses the socialist realist performances of Moscow and, like much of the rest of the book, is celebratory; indeed, the whole collection feels like a reconciliatory gesture, an exposition of international theatre that attempts to heal broader political rifts. While van Gyseghem mentions that Meyerhold has fallen out of favour, he also makes the wholly fallacious claim that 'Meyerhold, the director, is still at work in other theatres, much respected and as brilliant as ever'.[113] Meyerhold had been murdered by the state some nine years earlier so van Gyseghem's erroneous comment appears ludicrous. It perhaps says something about the difficulty of transmitting accurate information between two countries, particularly with the added barriers of Stalin's paranoid dictatorship and worldwide conflict, both of which made a significant difference to the ability of British theatre-makers to actually travel to Russia.

J.B. Priestley's postscript is a little more balanced, written just a couple of years after his visit to Russia. He asserts that 'the most successfully organised national theatre... is that of the Soviet Union',[114] but he also concedes that Soviet playwrights have less freedom than writers in other countries and that modern Russian plays are tricky to perform. He also, acknowledging two of his fellow travellers, criticises their quality:

> Although I will go all the way with enthusiasts like André van Gyseghem and Joseph Macleod when they praise the directing and acting in the Soviet theatre, and ask us to admire and copy the way in which it is organised, I cannot help feeling that they overestimate the value of contemporary Soviet Drama itself, which is not offering the world the major playwrights it might be expected to produce.[115]

Priestley's assessment of Russian theatre once again points to the challenge posed by the turn to socialist realism.

*The Times*' reviewer was not the only critic to understand Trilling and Wax's rendering of *Tsar Lenin* in cinematic terms. From the *Observer*:

> M Porché has taken the easy line of the very modern dramatist who, unable to build a scene, does not try to do so, but simply bombards his audience with a volley of bits and pieces and knows that his audience, being used to films, will not notice his slackness or incompetence.[116]

Criticisms of *Tsar Lenin* here centre on its relationship to the cinema. Porché's use of cinematic technique in his script seemed to be a conscious decision; he certainly understood the potentially fruitful relationship between cinema and theatre, though he maintained that theatre must not simply ape cinema but rather adapt and translate filmic techniques in its own way.[117] The montage techniques used in *Tsar Lenin*, however, are (for these two reviewers at least) confirmation of a troublesome relationship between theatre and the cinematic, a prime example of disciplinary disconnect. This final example reveals that, far from being resolved, the transnational intermingling of live performance and filmed performance (just as for contemporary performance studies scholars) remains fraught and troublesome.

## Notes

1. *The Demi-Paradise*, Anthony Asquith dir., Two Cities Films, 1943.
2. Lara Feigel, *Literature, Cinema and Politics, 1930–1945: Reading Between the Frames* (Edinburgh UP, 2010), 5.
3. For a full reading of this film in connection with its Russian roots see Maclean, *Vogue for Russia*, 151–7.
4. Lynne Kirkby, *Parallel Track: The Railroad and Silent Cinema* (Exeter UP, 1997), 251.
5. Armstrong, *Modernism, Technology and the Body*, 220.
6. Armstrong, *Modernism, Technology and the Body*, 221.
7. Tom Ryall, *Anthony Asquith* (Manchester UP, 2005), 40.
8. Maclean, *Vogue for Russia*, 146.
9. Taylor, *The Archive and the Repertoire*, 27.
10. This is an enormous area of research but for more about these debates see Elin Diamond's edited collection *Performance and Cultural Politics* (London: Routledge, 1996), Peggy Phelan's *The Politics of Performance* (London: Routledge, 1993), Philip Auslander's *Liveness: Performance in a Mediatized Culture* (Abingdon: Routledge, 2008) or Janelle Reinelt and Joseph Roach's *Critical Theory and Performance* (Michigan UP, 2007). Although not directly citing these texts, this chapter is indebted to the discussions to be found in their pages.
11. Purves-Stewart, *A Physician's Tour of Soviet Russia*, 162.
12. Laura Marcus, 'The Tempo of Revolution: British Film Culture and Soviet Cinema in the 1920s' in *Russia in Britain*, eds Beasley and Bullock, 230.
13. Maclean, *The Vogue for Russia*, 143.
14. Kenneth MacPherson, 'As Is: By the Editor', *Close Up*, 3.3 (September 1928): 13.
15. Ibid.
16. McPherson, 'As Is', 7.

17. HD, 'Russian Films', *Close Up*, 3.3 (September 1928): 27.
18. HD, 'Russian Films', 29.
19. Bryher, 'Dope or Stimulus', *Close Up*, 3.3 (September 1928): 61.
20. S.M. Eisenstein, W.I. Pudovkin and G.V. Alexandroff, 'The Sound Film', *Close Up*, 3.4 (October 1928): 12.
21. Anne Friedberg, 'Reading *Close Up*, 1927–1933' in *Close Up: 1927–1933: Cinema and Modernism*, eds James Donald, Anne Friedberg and Laura Marcus (New Jersey: Princeton UP, 1998), 4.
22. Huntly Carter, 'The New Russia' *The New Age* (17 November 1921), 27. The other articles appear in previous volumes from September and October of the same year.
23. Carter, *The New Spirit in Russian Theatre, 1917–1928*, xviii.
24. Virginia Woolf, 'The Movies and Reality', *New Republic* (4 August 1926), accessed 4 September 2015, http://www.newrepublic.com/article/120389/virginia-woolf-movies-and-reality.
25. George Bernard Shaw, 'Plays With Brains: Mr G.B. Shaw on Effect of Cinema Competition' (28 October 1923) in *Bernard Shaw on Cinema*, ed. Bernard Dukore (Southern Illinois UP, 1997), 38.
26. Anthony Paraskeva, *The Speech-Gesture Complex: Modernism, Theatre, Cinema* (Oxford UP, 2013), 25.
27. Carter, *The New Spirit in Russian Theatre*, 278.
28. Carter, *The New Spirit in Russian Theatre*, 281.
29. Ivor Montagu, 'Address Book and Notes from Visit to Soviet Union' (1927), CP/IND/MONT/2/7, Labour History Archive.
30. Ivor Montagu, 'Meeting with Vasily and Others' (u.d.), CP/IND/MONT/3/2, Labour History Archive, 4.
31. Ibid. Given that Butlins holiday camps were not founded until 1936, such a reflection must have occurred to him far later than the original travelling experience.
32. Ivor Montagu, 'Letter from England' (1949), CP/IND/MONT/3/3, Labour History Archive, 18.
33. Montagu, 'Letter from England', 21.
34. Ivor Montagu, 'Soviet Writers and the War' (u.d.), CP/IND/MONT/3/2, Labour History Archive, 3.
35. Nicholas Griffin, *Ping-Pong Diplomacy: Ivor Montagu and the Astonishing Story Behind the Game that Changed the World* (London: Simon and Schuster, 2014), prologue.
36. Laura Marcus, *The Tenth Muse: Writing About Cinema in the Modernist Period* (Oxford UP, 2007), 261.
37. Ivor Montagu, *The Political Censorship of Films* (London: Victor Gollancz, 1929), 14.
38. V.I. Pudovkin, *Film Technique and Film Acting*, trans. Ivor Montagu (London: Vision, 1968), 15.

39. V.I. Pudovkin, letter to Society for Cultural Relations with Russia Film Section (u.d.), CP/IND/MONT/9/1, Labour History Archive.
40. Pudovkin, *Film Technique*, 14.
41. Marie Seton, *Sergei Eisenstein: A Biography* (New York: Grove Press, 1960), 15.
42. Seton, *Sergei Eisenstein*, 482.
43. For more on Robeson's success in *Plant in the Sun* see Sheila Tully Boyle and Andrew Bunie, *Paul Robeson: The Years of Promise and Achievement* (Boston: Massachusetts UP, 2001), 394–5.
44. Paul Robeson Jnr, *The Undiscovered Paul Robeson: An Artist's Journey, 1898–1939* (New York: John Wiley, 2001), 295.
45. Joy Gleason Carew, *Blacks, Reds and Russians: Sojourners in Search of the Soviet Promise* (Rutgers UP, 2008), 5.
46. Van Gyseghem, *Theatre in Soviet Russia*, 205.
47. Van Gyseghem, *Theatre in Soviet Russia*, 192.
48. Ibid.
49. Nikolai Pogodin, *Aristocrats*, trans. Anthony Wixley and Robert S. Carr (London: Lawrence and Wishart, 1937), 284.
50. Pogodin, *Aristocrats*, 303–4.
51. Nikolay Okhlopkov, 'Aristocrats at the Realistic Theater', *Rabochaya Moskva* (3 November 1934) in *The Soviet Theater*, eds Senelick and Ostrovsky, 417.
52. Yu. Yuzovsky, 'A Festive Play: *Aristocrats* at the Realistic Theater', *Literaturnaya Gazeta*, 2 February 1935 in *The Soviet Theater*, eds Senelick and Ostrovsky, 419.
53. Van Gyseghem, *Theatre in Soviet Russia*, 203.
54. Van Gyseghem, *Theatre in Soviet Russia*, 204.
55. Unity Theatre, letter to members, 28 November 1937, Unity Theatre Archive, V&A, THM 9/471/1.
56. Claire Warden, *British Avant-Garde Theatre* (Basingstoke: Palgrave MacMillan, 2012), 98–9.
57. Chambers, *The Story of Unity Theatre*, 134.
58. For more details about Vertov's international travels see Malte Hagener, 'Mushrooms, Ant Paths and Tactics: The Topography of the European Film Avant-Garde' in *Decentring the Avant-Garde*, eds Per Bäckström and Benedikt Hjartarson (London: Rodopi, 2014), 152–3.
59. Herbert Marshall, *Masters of the Soviet Cinema: Crippled Creative Biographies* (Oxon: Routledge, 2014[1983]), 61.
60. Ibid.
61. Shaw has begun to redeem Britton from total obscurity. See his comprehensive blog post situating Britton in a history of working-class novelists: accessed 25 September 2015, http://tonyshaw3.blogspot.com/2008/11/working-class-fiction-and-lionel.html.

62. See Lionel Britton Papers, accessed 25 September 2015, http://archives.lib.siu.edu/?p=collections/findingaid&id=2165&q=&rootcontentid=50080.
63. 'Brain by Lionel Britton', *Observer*, 4 May 1930, 15.
64. St John Ervine, 'At the Play', *Observer*, 21 September 1930, 15.
65. Dziga Vertov, 'Kinoks: A Revolution' (1923) in *Kino-Eye: The Writings of Dziga Vertov*, Dziga Vertov, ed. Annette Mendelson, trans. Kevin O'Brien (Berkeley: California UP, 1984), 19–20.
66. Marshall, *Masters of Soviet Cinema*, 61.
67. Lionel Britton, *Brain: A Play of the Whole Earth* (London: G.P. Putnam's, 1930), act 1, sc.1.
68. Britton, *Brain*, act 1, sc.1b.
69. Feigel, *Literature, Cinema and Politics*, 26.
70. Britton, *Brain*, act 1 sc.1b.
71. Britton, *Brain*, act 2, sc. 3.
72. Viktor Shlovsky, 'Where Is Dziga Vertov Striding?' (1926) in *The Film Factory: Russian and Soviet Cinema in Documents*, eds Ian Christie and Richard Taylor (Abingdon: Routledge, 2002), 152.
73. Sergei Eisenstein, 'The Problem of the Materialist Approach to Form' (1925) in *The Eisenstein Reader*, Sergei Eisenstein, ed. Richard Taylor (London: BFI, 1998), 57.
74. Dziga Vertov, 'We: Variant of a Manifesto' (1922) in *Kino-Eye*, Vertov, 7.
75. Marshall, *The Pictorial History of the Russian Theatre*, 95, 153.
76. Herbert Marshall Archive, Southern Illinois University, accessed 29 December 2015, http://archives.lib.siu.edu/?p=creators/creator&id=374.
77. Herbert Marshall, 'Notes on Mayakovsky', *Anglo-Soviet Journal*, April, 1940, 105.
78. C.M. Bowra, 'Foreword' in *Mayakovsky*, Vladimir Mayakovsky, trans. Herbert Marshall (London: Dennis Dobson, 1965), 15.
79. Herbert Marshall, 'Introduction' in *Mayakovsky*, Mayakovsky, 47.
80. Qtd in Beasley and Bullock, 'Introduction' in *Translation and Literature* 20 (2011): 287.
81. Marshall, *The Pictorial History of the Russian Theatre*, 158.
82. Chambers, *The Story of Unity Theatre*, 136.
83. Unity Theatre, *Aristocrats* programme (1937), Unity Theatre Archive, V&A, THM 9/4/7/1.
84. *Manchester Guardian*, 15 December 1937, Unity Theatre Archive, V&A, THM 9/4/5/5.
85. Van Gyseghem, *Theatre in Soviet Russia*, 194.
86. Marshall, *A Pictorial History of the Russian Theatre*, 156.
87. Chambers, *The Story of Unity Theatre*, 136.
88. Chambers, *The Story of Unity Theatre*, 141.

89. Ibid.
90. Unity Theatre, programme for *Get Cracking* (1942), THMS/9/7/110, V&A Theatre Archive.
91. Unity Theatre, 'Living Newspaper: Unity Theatre's Unique Production' (February 1938), THM/9/4/5/6 *Busmen*, V&A Theatre Archive.
92. Unity Theatre, *Crisis* (1938), Southern Illinois University Archive at Carbondale, MSS029, Box 6, Folder 1, 4.
93. Chambers, *The Story of Unity Theatre*, 165.
94. Jack Lindsay, *Socialist Russia? A New World Order* (Labor Council of NSW, c1941), 4.
95. Lindsay, *Socialist Russia?* 15.
96. Jack Lindsay, *A World Ahead: Journal of a Soviet Journey* (London: Fore, 1950), 102.
97. Lindsay, *A World Ahead*, 40–1.
98. Lindsay, *A World Ahead*, 45, 51, 92, 131.
99. Chambers, *The Story of Unity Theatre*, 82.
100. Jack Lindsay, *Salute the Soviet Union* (1938–9), Alec Baron Archive, University of Leeds, section 2.
101. Lindsay, *Salute the Soviet Union*, section 7.
102. Lindsay, *Salute the Soviet Union*, misc. handwritten notes.
103. Lindsay, *Salute the Soviet Union*, section 7.
104. Rebecca D'Monté, *British Theatre and Performance, 1900–1950* (London: Bloomsbury, 2015), 155.
105. Andrew Davies, 'The War Years' in *Theatre and Performance, 1933–1945: Performance in Extremis*, ed. Michael Balfour (New York: Berghahn, 2001), 60.
106. Montagu Slater, 'Documentary Theatre', *Documentary News Letter* (January–February 1947, London: Film Centre): 18.
107. Steve Nicholson, 'Irritating Tricks: Aesthetic Experiment and Political Theatre' in *Rewriting the Thirties: Modernism and After*, eds Keith Williams and Steven Matthews (London: Longman, 1997), 154.
108. Qtd in Nicholson, 'Irritating Tricks', 155.
109. 'Stage Society', *The Times*, 28 June 1937, 12.
110. 'Ossia Trilling', *Encyclopedia Britannica*, accessed 2 October 2015, http://www.britannica.com/biography/Ossia-Trilling.
111. John Andrews and Ossia Trilling eds, *International Theatre* (London: Sampson Low, 1949), 94.
112. André van Gyseghem, 'Theatre in Moscow' in *International Theatre*, eds Andrews and Trilling, 95.
113. Van Gyseghem, 'Theatre in Moscow' in *International Theatre*, eds Andrews and Trilling, 101.

114. J.B. Priestley, 'Postscript' in *International Theatre*, eds Andrews and Trilling, 207.
115. Priestley, 'Postscript' in *International Theatre*, eds Andrews and Trilling, 208.
116. 'Tsar Lenin', *Observer*, 4 July 1937, 17.
117. Qtd in Nicholson, 'Irritating Tricks' in *Rewriting the Thirties: Modernism and After*, eds Williams and Matthews, 157.

# Conclusion: Migratory Gossiping

On January 22 1946 the Dorland Hall, London hosted a new exhibition, opened by the wife of the Soviet Ambassador, Madame Gusev, and the president of the Society for Cultural Relations with Russia (Theatre Section) Edith Evans. With help from practitioners and officials in Moscow the exhibition imported a vast array of materials—sets, models, designs, costumes and photographs—documenting Russian theatre practice from 1898 to 1944. It was a unique opportunity for British audiences to experience Russian theatre. Visitors could browse designs from the Bolshoi, models from the Maly Theatre, Kamerny and MAT, photographs of the innovative five-pointed star design of the Central Theatre of the Red Army. The exhibition was, allegedly, as popular with committed theatregoers as with housewives looking for 'new colour schemes for interior decoration'![1] In fact, such was the demand for this exhibition that it toured around the country to various art galleries; as Evans was writing her reflective analysis for the Summer 1946 edition of *The Anglo-Soviet Journal*, the collection was apparently welcoming 31,000 visitors in a three-week Glasgow residency.[2] J.B. Priestley, having recently returned from Russia, wrote in the catalogue, 'the Soviet Theatre is not perfect. It does not do everything better than any other theatre does. But taking both quality and quantity into consideration, it must be judged the best theatre in the world'.[3]

But this is not the end of the story. In 1948 Evans was invited to Russia by VOKS (The Soviet Union Society for Cultural Relations with



C. Warden, *Migrating Modernist Performance*,
DOI 10.1057/978-1-137-38570-3_6

Foreign Countries). Her diary of the trip, printed again in *The Anglo-Soviet Journal*, is full of descriptions of the theatres she visited and productions she saw – the Little Theatre's *School for Scandal*, the Bolshoi's versions of *Cinderella* and *The Queen of Spades*, MAT's *The Forest*, the Children's Theatre, *Madame Bovary* at the Tairov Theatre (where she 'gossiped with Mr Tairov and his partners, who spoke English fluently'), the Red Army Theatre's *The Dancing Master*.[4] Evans seemed to thoroughly enjoy her packed schedule: 'I met mostly people of my own profession and, of course, experienced that feeling of being completely at home, which we actors always feel with one another.'[5] While in Moscow Evans opened another exhibition, this one organised by the Theatre Section of the Society for Cultural Relations with Russia (in conjunction with the Arts Council). The exhibition was entitled 'A History of Shakespearean Production in England' and Evans launched it alongside the president of VOKS (a figure she called her 'opposite number'), Alexei Popov.[6] Like the Soviet Theatre Exhibition, 'A History of Shakespearean Production in England' aimed to give local theatregoers an opportunity to witness the designs and costumes of another nation's theatre history.

This final example illustrates the central themes of this book: here are two transnational attempts to expose foreign audiences to the innovations and performance histories of their respective theatres. At the heart of this exchange is migratory British performer Edith Evans. Her presence at these events acts as a connecting point, as a witness and participant in both exhibitions. In both cases there is the strong sense of theatre as a connecting node, a way of overcoming preconceptions and creating a bond of friendship that is larger and more far-reaching than aesthetics.

In addition, Evans premises her first article on her identity as an actor; she imagines a unique friendliness, an innate sense of understanding and mutual appreciation. This book focuses on the intertwined dramatic histories of Britain and Russia, uncovering modernist precursors to the continuing British interest in Russian performance, exemplified by events such as the 2014 UK-Russia Year of Culture, the Victoria and Albert Museum's Russian Avant-Garde Theatre exhibition (2014), the Royal Court's commitment to Russian new writing (including presentation of plays from Vassily Sigarev and the Presnyakov Brothers), and the continuing work of figures such as Katie Mitchell, Declan Donnellan and Michael Boyd.[7] It therefore expands British theatre history by uncovering 'lost' work or reimagining better-known examples in an expansive, transnational historiography of British performance. However, my initial impulse came out of a broader driving concern: to place performance (and the parlance and experience of performance) into the increasingly (and welcomingly) prevalent new modernist studies narratives of transnationalism, migration, cosmopolitanism and travel. The aim, borrowing Carrie Preston's beautifully expansive phrase, is to 'dislodge [...] definitions of modernism from fixed positions and shape [...] a version that can accommodate seeming opposites'.[8] This is, I suggest, an effect produced whenever performance in general (not only dance as Preston discusses) is incorporated into modernist narratives; suddenly here is a tangible object, a moving body that physically and cognitively experiences its surroundings. The uniqueness of the live experience; the energy and interconnectedness of bodies in space; the concepts of spectacle and spectator; the acts of interpretation (of the physicalised as well as the textual) – these are elements embedded in the approaches of performance studies. As both modernist studies and performance studies continue to expand, fracture and migrate, I hope that the two will converse with all the excitement and enthusiasm of Evans and Tairov 'gossiping' in a corner after the performance of *Madame Bovary*.

## Notes

1. Dame Edith Evans, 'Soviet Theatre Exhibition: 22nd January to 28th February, 1946', *Anglo-Soviet Journal* (Summer 1946): 37.
2. Evans, 'Soviet Theatre Exhibition', 38.
3. Evans, 'Soviet Theatre Exhibition', 37.
4. Dame Edith Evans, 'My Russian Diary', *Anglo-Soviet Journal* (Summer 1948): 31–2.
5. Evans, 'My Russian Diary', 32.
6. Society for Cultural Relations with Russia, Draft Annual Report, 1947/8, CP/IND/MONT/9/1, Labour History Archive.
7. See the final chapter of Pitches ed., *Russians in Britain*, for further information about these three important British theatre-makers.
8. Preston, 'Introduction', *Modernist Cultures*, 5.

# Bibliography

Afinogenev, Alexander. *Distant Point*. London: Pushkin, 1941.

Agate, James. *Contemporary Theatre*. London: Chapman and Hall, 1927.

Andrews, Geoff, Nina Fishman, and Kevin Morgan. *Opening the Books: Essays on the Social and Cultural History of British Communism*. London: Pluto, 1995.

Andrews, John and Ossia Trilling eds. *International Theatre*. London: Sampson Low, 1949.

Andreyev, Leonid. *The Dear Departing*. London: Henderson's, 1916.

Anon. "Russia and Ourselves." *Daily Mail*, Monday, February 22, 1943.

Anon. *The Daily Graphic*, February 22, 1926. Cadbury Research Library, University of Birmingham, MS38/2427.

Anon. "Russia's Day." *The Times*, November 19, 1915.

Anon. "The Theatre of the Soul." *The Times*, December 4, 1915.

Anon. *The Daily Mirror*, November 4, 1926. Cadbury Research Library, University of Birmingham, MS38/5304.

Anon. *Sporting and Dramatic News*, March 16, 1929. Cadbury Research Library, University of Birmingham, MS38/235.

Anon. *The Sketch*, March 13, 1929. Cadbury Research Library, University of Birmingham, MS38/235.

Anon. *Sunday Graphic and Sunday Herald*, March 3, 1929. Cadbury Research Library, University of Birmingham, MS38/235.

Anon. "Savoy Theatre." *The Times*, June 8, 1932.

Anon. *Tatler*, November 10, 1937. Cadbury Research Library, University of Birmingham, MS38/594.

Anon. *The Stage*, October 10, 1937. Cadbury Research Library, University of Birmingham, MS38/594.



C. Warden, *Migrating Modernist Performance*,
DOI 10.1057/978-1-137-38570-3

Anon. *A Communist Policy for Theatre*. London: Farleigh Press, 1948.

Anon. "Salute to the Red Army: Impressive Pageantry." *The Times*, February 22, 1943.

Anon. *Sydney Morning Herald*, October 26, 1932.

Anon. "Editorial: Russian/Modernist Connections." *International Journal of Scottish Literature*, 2, 2009, accessed July 1, 2015, http://www.ijsl.stir.ac.uk/issue5/editorial.htm

Antiff, Mark and Scott W. Klein eds. *Vorticism: New Perspectives*. Oxford: Oxford UP, 2013.

Armstrong, Tim. *Modernism, Technology and the Body*. Cambridge: Cambridge UP, 1998.

Asquith, Anthony dir. *The Demi-Paradise*. Two Cities Films, 1943.

Auden, W.H. and Christopher Isherwood. *Plays and Other Dramatic Writings 1928–1938*, ed. Edward Mendelson. London: Faber and Faber, 1989.

Auslander, Philip. *Liveness: Performance in a Mediatized Culture*. Abingdon: Routledge, 2008.

Autant-Mathien, Marie-Christine and Yana Meerson eds. *The Routledge Companion to Michael Chekhov*. Abingdon: Routledge, 2015.

Bäckström, Per and Benedikt Hjartarson eds. *Decentring the Avant-Garde*. London: Rodopi, 2014.

Banks, George. "Petrouchka – the Russian Ballet." *Rhythm* 6 (July 1912).

Barker, Clive and Maggie B. Gale eds. *British Theatre Between the Wars, 1918–1939*. Cambridge: Cambridge UP, 2000.

Baron, Alec. *I Was There*. Unpublished autobiography.

Baron, Alec and Kate Plenty. *Comrade Enemy* (1942). BC Ms 20c Theatre, Baron, Brotherton Collection, University of Leeds.

Barranger, Milly S. *Margaret Webster: A Life in the Theater*. Ann Arbor: Michigan UP, 2004.

Baubock, Rainer and Thomas Faist eds. *Diaspora and Transnationalism: Concepts, Theories and Methods*. Amsterdam: Amsterdam UP, 2010.

Bakshy, Alexander. *The Path of the Modern Russian Stage and Other Essays*. London: Cecil Palmer and Hayward, 1916.

Balfour, Michael ed. *Theatre and Performance, 1933–1945: Performance in Extremis*. New York: Berghahn, 2001.

Baring, Maurice. *An Outline of Russian Literature*. London: Williams and Norgate, 1914.

—— *What I Saw in Russia*. London: William Heinemann, 1927.

—— *The Puppet Show of Memory*. London: William Heinemann, 1922.

—— *The Grey Stocking and Other Plays*. London: Constable and Company, 1911.

Barrie, J.M. *The Truth About Russian Dancers*. New York: Dance Perspectives, 1962.

Beachcomber. "Russian Pickwick." *Daily Express*, December 17, 1928.

Beasley, Rebecca and Philip Ross Bullock eds. *Russia in Britain 1880*–1940. Oxford: Oxford UP, 2013.

Beasley, Rebecca and Philip Ross Bullock. "Introduction: The Illusion of Transparency." *Translation and Literature*, 20 (2011).

Bellow, Juliet. *Modernism on Stage: The Ballets Russes and the Parisian Avant-Garde*. Farnham: Ashgate, 2013.

Benedetti, Jean ed. *The Moscow Art Theatre Letters*. New York: Routledge, 1991.

Benedetti, Jean. *Stanislavski and the Actor*. New York: Routledge, 2013.

Bigliazzi, Silvia, Peter Kofler and Paola Ambrosi. *Theatre Translation in Performance*. Abingdon: Routledge, 2013.

Blanton, Casey. *Travel Writing: The Self and the World*. New York: Routledge, 2002.

Boleslawskaia, Madame. Letter to Basil Dean. October 15, 1926, DEA 1/1/327-335, Basil Dean Archive.

Booth, Michael and Joel Kaplan eds. *The Edwardian Theatre: Essays in Performance and the Stage*. Cambridge UP, 1996.

Borovsky, V.E. *A Triptych of Russian Theatre: The Komissarzhevskys*. London: Hurst, 2001.

Boyle, Sheila Tully and Andrew Bunie. *Paul Robeson: The Years of Promise and Achievement*. Boston: Massachusetts UP, 2001.

Bracken, Brendan. Letter to Basil Dean. February 24, 1943, DEA 5/3/4, Basil Dean Archive.

"Brain by Lionel Britton." *The Observer*, May 4, 1930.

Braun, Edward. *Meyerhold: A Revolution in Theatre*. London: Methuen, 1998.

Britton, Lionel. *Brain: A Play of the Whole Earth*. London: G.P. Putnam's, 1930.

Brooker, Peter and Andrew Thacker eds. *Geographies of Modernism*. Abingdon: Routledge, 2005.

Brooker, Peter, Sascha Bru, Andrew Thacker and Christian Weikop eds. *The Oxford Critical and Cultural History of Modernist Magazines vol III 1880–1940*. Oxford: Oxford UP, 2013.

Bryher. "Dope or Stimulus." *Close Up* 3:3 (September 1928).

Burden, Robert. *Travel, Modernism and Modernity*. Farnham: Ashgate, 2015.

Burton, Stacy. *Travel Narrative and the Ends of Modernity*. Cambridge: Cambridge UP, 2014.

Calderon, George. *Two Plays by Tchekof: The Seagull and The Cherry Orchard*. London: Grant Richards, 1912.

—— *The Little Stone House: A Play in One Act*. London: Sidgwick and Jackson, 1913.

Carlson, Marvin. *The Haunted Stage: The Theatre as Memory Machine*. Ann Arbor: Michigan UP, 2003.

Carter, Huntly. *The New Spirit in the Russian Theatre, 1917–1928*. London: Arno, 1929.

—— *The New Spirit in the European Theatre, 1914–1924*. London: Benn, 1925.

—— "The New Russia." *The New Age*, November 17, 1921.

Certeau, Michel de. *The Practice of Everyday Life*, trans. Steven F. Rendell. Berkeley: California UP, 1988.

Chambers, Colin. *The Story of Unity Theatre*. London: Lawrence and Wishart, 1989.

Chambers, Colin ed. *The Continuum Companion to Twentieth-Century Theatre*. London: Continuum, 2002.

"Chauve-Souris at The Coliseum." *The Times*, November 15, 1921.

Chekhov, Anton. *Plays*. London: Penguin, 1951.

Chekhov, Michael. *To the Actor*. London: Routledge, 2003.

Chinitz, David. *T.S. Eliot and the Cultural Divide*. Chicago: Chicago UP, 2003.

Christie, Ian and Richard Taylor eds. *The Film Factory: Russian and Soviet Cinema in Documents*. Abingdon: Routledge, 2002.

Clayton, Martin and Bennett Zon eds. *Music and Orientalism in the British Empire, 1780s-1940s: Portrayal of the East*. Farnham: Ashgate, 2007.

Clayton, Michelle. "Modernism's Moving Bodies." *Modernist Cultures* 9.1 (2014).

Cohen, Brigid. *Stefan Wolfe and the Avant-Garde Diaspora*. Cambridge: Cambridge UP, 2012.

Cornwall, Peter. *Only by Failure: The Many Faces of the Impossible Life of Terence Gray*. Cambridge: Salt, 2004.

Cox, Emma. *Theatre and Migration*. London: Palgrave MacMillan, 2014.

Craig, Edward Gordon. *On the Art of the Theatre*, ed. Franc Chamberlain. London: Routledge, 2009.

—— *Craig on Theatre*, ed. J. Michael Walton. London: Methuen, 1999.

—— *Craig on Movement and Dance*, ed. Arnold Rood. London: Dance Books, 1977.

—— *The Theatre – Advancing*. Boston: Little Brown and Company, 1919.

Croall, Jonathan. *Gielgud: A Theatrical Life*. London: Continuum, 2001.

Cross, Anthony ed. *A People Passing Rude: British Responses to Russian Culture*. London: Open Book, 2012.

Cummings, E.E. *Eimi: A Journey Through Russia*. New York: Liveright, 2007.

Curtin, Adrian. *Avant-Garde Theatre Sound: Staging Sonic Modernity*. New York: Palgrave MacMillan, 2014.

D'Monté, Rebecca. *British Theatre and Performance, 1900–1950*. London: Bloomsbury, 2015.

*Daily Worker*. October 19, 1947. Unity Theatre Archive, V&A, THM 9/4/5/54.

Dana, H.W.L. "Yellow Rust: The History of a Crime." *New Masses: A Magazine of Workers Art and Literature* (April 1930).

Davison, Clare. *Translation as Collaboration: Virginia Woolf, Katherine Mansfield and S.S. Koteliansky*. Edinburgh UP, 2014.

de Valois, Ninette. *Come Dance With Me: A Memoir 1898–1956*. Dublin: Lilliput Press, 1992.

Dean, Basil. "Address to Nottinghamshire Playgoers Club." January 1926, DEA 12/1/28, Basil Dean Archive.

—— *Seven Ages: An Autobiography 1888–1927*. London: Hutchinson, 1970.

—— *Mind's Eye: An Autobiography 1927–1932.* London: Hutchinson, 1973.
—— *The Theatre at War.* London: Harrap, 1956.
—— Letter to Mr [Dmitri] Bogomoloff, January 1926, DEA 1/2/210, Basil Dean Archive.
—— "Roast Beef and Caviare [sic]: Reflections upon the Theatre in England and Russia." *Soviet Union Monthly* (May 1926): 90–1, DEA 12/1/31, Basil Dean Archive.
—— "The Actor and His Workshop" (lecture presented at the Victoria and Albert Museum During the International Theatre Exhibition, July 1922), DEA 12/1/16, Basil Dean Archive.
—— "The Machine Artists: Notes on a Recent Visit to the Russian Theatre." *The Sphere*, August 28, 1926, DEA 12/1/35, Basil Dean Archive.
—— "My Aims in the Theatre." November 1928, DEA 12/1/45, Basil Dean Archive.
—— "Interview with Hubert Griffith." October 25, 1938, DEA 12/1/80, Basil Dean Archive.
—— Letter to Madame Boleslavsky. February 15, 1927, DEA 1/2/215, Basil Dean Archive.
Dean, Basil and Margaret Kennedy. *The Constant Nymph.* prompt copy, DEA 6/8, Basil Dean Archive.
—— *Programmes*, DEA 10/6/119, Basil Dean Archive.
—— Letter to Fenner Brockway. March 11, 1929, DEA 1/2/297-315, Basil Dean Archive.
—— Letter to Alexei Granovsky. January 10, 1927, DEA 1/2/738, Basil Dean Archive.
—— *The Theatre of War.* London: George Harrap, 1956.
—— *The changing theatre.* BBC Radio. The British Library csf. 846985 (17 December 1969).
—— "Between the Public and Ourselves." DEA 12/1/29, Basil Dean Archive.
—— "The Theatre as a National Asset (1938)." DEA 12/1/29, Basil Dean Archive.
Diamond, Elin. *Performance and Cultural Politics.* London: Routledge, 1996.
Donald, James, Anne Friedberg and Laura Marcus eds. *Close Up: 1927–1933: Cinema and Modernism.* New Jersey: Princeton UP, 1998.
Doyle, Laura and Laura Winkiel eds. *Geomodernisms: Race, Modernism, Modernity.* Bloomington: Indiana UP, 2005.
Duncan, Isadora. *My Life.* New York: Norton, 2013.
Dukes, Ashley. *The Scene is Changed.* London: MacMillan, 1942.
Eisenstein, S.M., W.I. Pudovkin and G.V. Alexandroff. "The Sound Film." *Close Up* 3:4 (October 1928).
Eisenstein, Sergei. *The Eisenstein Reader*, ed. Richard Taylor. London: BFI, 1998.
Ervine, St John. "At the Play." *The Observer*, September 21, 1930.
Evans, Edith. "Soviet Theatre Exhibition: 22nd January to 28th February, 1946." *The Anglo-Soviet Journal* (Summer 1946).

—— "My Russian Diary." *The Anglo-Soviet Journal* (Summer 1948).

Evreinov, Nikolai. *The Theatre of the Soul*, trans. Marie Potapenko and Christopher St John. London: Hendersons, 1915.

Feigel, Lara. *Literature, Cinema and Politics, 1930–1945: Reading Between the Frames*. Edinburgh UP, 2010.

Findlay, Bill. "By Policy a Native Theatre: Glasgow Unity and the Significance of Robert Mitchell's Scottish Adaptation of *The Lower Depths*." *International Journal of Scottish Theatre*, 2:1 (2001), accessed July 17, 2015, http://journals.qmu.ac.uk/index.php/IJoST/article/view/74/html

Fischer-Lichte, Erika and Benjamin Wihstutz eds. *Performance and the Politics of Space: Theatre and Topology*. Abingdon: Routledge, 2013.

Ford, Ford Madox. *The Soul of London: A Survey of a Modern City*. London: Alston Rivers, 1905.

Foulkes, Richard. *Repertory at the Royal*. Northampton: Northampton Repertory Players, 1992.

Gale, Maggie. *J.B. Priestley*. London: Routledge, 2008.

Garafola, Lynn. *Diaghilev's Ballet Russes*. Oxford: Oxford UP, 1993.

—— *Legacies of Twentieth-Century Dance*. Middletown: Wesleyan UP, 2005.

Garrington, Abbie. *Haptic Modernism: Touch and the Tactile in Modernist Writing*. Edinburgh: Edinburgh UP, 2013.

Gayle, David ed. *An English Ballet*. London: Oberon, 2011.

Geldern, James von. *Bolshevik festivals, 1917–1920*. Berkeley: California UP, 1993.

Gikandi, Simon. "Preface: Modernism in the World." *Modernism/Modernity* 13:3 (September 2006).

Gleason Carew, Joy. *Blacks, Reds and Russians: Sojourners in Search of the Soviet Promise*. Rutgers UP, 2008.

Godfrey, Philip. *Back-Stage*. London: George Harrap, 1933.

Goebel, Walter and Saskia Schabio eds. *Locating Transnational Ideals*. London: Routledge, 2010.

Goorney, Howard and Ewan MacColl eds. *Agit-prop to Theatre Workshop: Political Playscripts, 1930–50*. Manchester UP, 1986.

Gorchakov, Nikolai. *The Theater in Soviet Russia*. New York: Columbia UP, 1957.

Gordon, Mel. "Granovsky's Tragic Carnival: Night in the Old Market." *The Drama Review* 29: 4 (Winter 1985).

Granovsky, Alexis. Letter to Basil Dean. November 13, 1926, Basil Dean Archive, John Rylands Library, DEA 1/1/995-1036.

—— *Night in the Old Market* (photograph) (1925), DEA 9/3/69, Basil Dean Archive.

Granovsky, Alexis and Joseph Gordon. "Night in the Old Market: A Mystery in Two Parts After I. L. Peretz." *The Drama Review* 29: 4 (Winter 1985).

Gray, Terence. *Dance-Drama: Experiments in the Art of Theatre*. Cambridge: Heffer and Sons, 1926.

Griffin, Nicholas. *Ping-Pong Diplomacy: Ivor Montagu and the Astonishing Story Behind the Game that Changed the World*. London: Simon and Schuster, 2014.

Griffith, Hubert. *European Encounters*. London: John Lane, 1931.

—— *Seeing Soviet Russia: An Informative Record of the Cheapest Trip in Europe*. London: John Lane, 1932.

—— *This is Russia*. London: Hammond, 1943.

—— "Letter to the Editor of The Times." *The Times*, July 3, 1929.

—— *Red Sunday*. London: Cayme Press, 1929.

—— *The People's Court*. London: Rich and Cowan, 1933.

Guermanova, Maria. "Moscow Art Theatre." *The Times*, April 17, 1928.

Herbert, A.P. and Nigel Playfair. *Riverside Nights*. London: T. Fisher Unwin, 1926.

Hallett, John. "The Soviets Through Soviet Eyes." *The Spectator*, September 13, 1934.

Hamilton, Cicely. *Modern Russia as Seen by an Englishwoman*. London: E.P. Dutton, 1934.

—— *A Pageant of Great Women*. The Suffrage Shop, 1910.

Handley, Miriam. "Chekhov Translated: Shaw's Use of Sound Effects in *Heartbreak House*." *Modern Drama*, 42 (Winter 1999).

Harding, James and John Rouse eds. *Not the Other Avant-Garde: The Transnational Foundations of Avant-Garde Performance*. Ann Arbor: Michigan UP, 2006.

Harris, George. *George W Harris*. London: Nisbet, 1930.

Harrison, Jane. *Reminiscences of a Student's Life*. London: Hogarth Press, 1925.

—— *Ancient Art and Ritual*. Oxford: Oxford UP, 1948.

HD. "Russian Films." *Close Up* 3:3 (September 1928).

Hindus, Maurice. *Mother Russia*. London: Collins, 1943.

Holdsworth, Nadine ed. *Theatre and National Identity: Re-Imagining Conceptions of Nation*. London: Routledge, 2014.

Holme, C.G. ed. *Art in the USSR*. London: Studio Limited, 1935.

Hope, John Francis. "Drama." *The New Age* 15:8 (June 19, 1919).

Houghton, Norris. *Moscow Rehearsals*. London: George Allen and Unwin, 1938.

Innes, Christopher. *Edward Gordon Craig: A Vision of the Theatre*. Abingdon: Routledge, 2004.

Jones, Susan. *Literature, Modernism and Dance*. Oxford: Oxford UP, 2013.

Kelly, Brigitte. *'Mim': A Personal Memoir of Marie Rambert*. Alton: Dance Books, 2009.

Kirkby, Lynne. *Parallel Track: The Railroad and Silent Cinema*. Exeter: Exeter UP, 1997.

Komisarjevsky, Theodore. *Myself and the Theatre*. London: Heinemann, 1929.

"La Chauve-Souris." *The Times*, November 25, 1924.

Landen Odom, Selma. "The Dalcroze Method, Marie Rambert and *Le Sacre du printemps*." *Modernist Cultures* 9.1 (2014).

Lau, Meghan. "Performing History: The War-Time Pageants of Louis Napoleon Parker." *Modern Drama* 54:3 (Fall 2011).

Law, Alma and Mel Gordon eds. *Meyerhold, Eisenstein and Biomechanics: Actor Training in Revolutionary Russia.* London: McFarland, 1996.

Leach, Robert. *Vsevolod Meyerhold.* Cambridge: Cambridge UP, 1999.

—— *Revolutionary Theatre.* London: Routledge, 1994.

Leach, Robert and Victor Borovsky eds. *A History of Russian Theatre.* Cambridge: Cambridge UP, 1999.

Lindsay, Jack. *Socialist Russia? A New World Order.* Labor Council of NSW, c1941.

—— *A World Ahead: Journal of a Soviet Journey.* London: Fore, 1950.

—— *Salute the Soviet Union* (1938–9). Alec Baron Archive, University of Leeds, section 2.

Livak, Leonard. *How It Was Done in Paris: Russian émigré literature and French modernism.* Madison: Wisconsin UP, 2003.

Loehlin, James. *Chekhov: The Cherry Orchard.* Cambridge UP, 2006.

Lubbock, Percy. *George Calderon: A Sketch from Memory.* London: Grant Richards, 1921.

Lyons, Eugene. *Assignment in Utopia.* New York: Harcourt, Bruce and Company, 1937.

Lykiardopulos, Michael. Letter to Basil Dean. March 1913, DEA 1/1/2429-30, Basil Dean Archive.

"Lyric Theatre, Hammersmith." *The Times*, May 26, 1925.

MacColl, Ewan. *Journeyman.* London: Sidgwick and Jackson, 1990.

MacDonald, Nesta. *Diaghilev Observed by Critics in England and the United States, 1911–1929.* New York: Dance Horizons, 1975.

Maclean, Caroline. *The Vogue for Russia: Modernism and the Unseen in Britain, 1900–1930.* Edinburgh UP, 2015.

Macleod, Joseph. *A Soviet Theatre Sketchbook.* London: George Allen and Unwin, 1951.

—— *The New Soviet Theatre.* London: George Allen and Unwin Ltd, 1943.

—— *Actors Cross the Volga: A Study of Nineteenth Century Russian Theatre and of Soviet Theatres in War.* London: George Unwin, 1946.

MacPherson, Kenneth. "As Is: By the Editor." *Close Up* 3:3 (September 1928).

Malaev-Babel, Andrei ed. *The Vakhtangov Sourcebook.* Abingdon: Routledge, 2011.

Mao, Douglas and Rebecca L. Walkowitz. "The New Modernist Studies." *PMLA* 123:3 (2008).

Marcus, Laura. *The Tenth Muse: Writing About Cinema in the Modernist Period.* Oxford: Oxford UP, 2007.

Markov, P.A. *The Soviet Theatre.* New York: G.P. Putnam's and Sons, 1934.

Marshall, Herbert. *The Pictorial History of the Russian Theatre.* New York: Crown, 1977.

—— *Masters of the Soviet Cinema: Crippled Creative Biographies.* Oxon: Routledge, 2014[1983].

—— "Notes on Mayakovsky." *The Anglo-Soviet Journal.* April, 1940.

Marshall, Norman. *The Other Theatre.* London: John Lehmann, 1947.

Mayakovsky, Vladimir. *Mayakovsky,* trans. Herbert Marshall. London: Dennis Dobson, 1965.

Mazower, David. *Yiddish Theatre in London.* London: The Jewish Museum, 1987.

Merwin, Ted. "Jew-Face: Non-Jews Playing Jews on the American Stage." *Cultural and Social History: The Journal of the Social History Society* 4:2 (2007).

Messel, Oliver. *In the Theatre of Design,* ed. Thomas Messel. New York: Rizzoli, 2011.

Meyerhold, Vsevolod. *Meyerhold on Theatre,* ed. Edward Braun. London: Methuen, 1998.

Miles, Patrick. *Chekhov on the British Stage.* Cambridge: Cambridge UP, 1993.

Mirsky, D.S. *Jane Harrison and Russia.* Cambridge: W Heffer and Sons, 1930.

Montagu, Ivor. "Address Book and Notes from Visit to Soviet Union" (1927). CP/IND/MONT/2/7, Labour History Archive.

—— "Meeting with Vasily and Others" (u.d.). CP/IND/MONT/3/2, Labour History Archive.

—— "Letter from England" (1949). CP/IND/MONT/3/3, Labour History Archive.

—— "Soviet Writers and the War" (u.d.). CP/IND/MONT/3/2, Labour History Archive.

—— *The Political Censorship of Films.* London: Victor Gollancz, 1929.

Montagu-Nathan, M. "Translations of Russian Fiction." *The Egoist* 2:9 (September 1, 1915).

Morgan, Kevin. *Against Fascism and War: Ruptures and Continuities in British Communist Politics, 1935–41.* Manchester UP, 1989.

Mountbatten, Edwina. Letter to Basil Dean. February 24, 1943, DEA 5/3/8, Basil Dean Archive.

"Mr Craig's Designs for Hamlet." *The Times,* September 10, 1912.

Nicholls, Peter. *Modernisms: A Literary Guide.* Basingstoke: Palgrave MacMillan, 2009.

Nicholson, Steve. *British Theatre and the Red Peril: The Portrayal of Communism 1917–1945.* Exeter: Exeter UP, 1999.

—— "Theatrical Pageants of the Second World War." *Theatre Research International* 18:3 (1993).

—— "Censoring Revolution: The Lord Chamberlain and the Soviet Union." *New Theatre Quarterly* 8:32 (November 1992).

Nugent, Lt Col. Letter to Basil Dean. February 22, 1943, DEA 5/3/9, Basil Dean Archive.

O'Neill, Eugene. *The Unknown O'Neill: Unpublished or Unfamiliar Writings of Eugene O'Neill.* New Haven: Yale UP, 1988.

—— *Ah Wilderness! and Other Plays.* Harmondsworth: Penguin, 1966.

"Ossia Trilling," *Encyclopedia Britannica*, accessed October 2, 2015, http://www.britannica.com/biography/Ossia-Trilling

Palmer McCulloch, Margery ed. *Modernism and Nationalism: Literature and Society in Scotland 1918–1939.* Glasgow: Association for Scottish Literary Studies, 2004.

Paraskeva, Anthony. *The Speech-Gesture Complex: Modernism, Theatre, Cinema.* Oxford: Oxford UP, 2013.

Parker, Louis Napoleon. *Drake.* London: John Lane, 1912.

—— *Joseph and His Brethren: A Pageant Play.* London: John Lane, 1913.

Pathé films. *Salute to the Red Army*, accessed August 31, 2012, http://www.britishpathe.com/video/salute-to-the-red-army/query/01285200

Peacock, Lieutenant RNVR. Letter to Basil Dean, DEA 5/3/10, Basil Dean Archive.

Phelan, Peggy and Jill Lane eds. *The Ends of Performance.* New York: New York UP, 1998.

Phelan, Peggy. *The Politics of Performance.* London: Routledge, 1993.

Pitches, Jonathan ed. *Russians in Britain: British Theatre and the Tradition of Russian Actor Training.* London: Routledge, 2012.

Pitches, Jonathan. *Vsevolod Meyerhold.* London: Routledge, 2003.

Pogodin, Nikolai. *Aristocrats*, trans. Anthony Wixley and Robert S. Carr. London: Lawrence and Wishart, 1937.

Postlewait, Thomas. *The Cambridge Introduction to Theatre Historiography.* Cambridge: Cambridge UP, 2009.

Preston, Carrie. "Introduction: Modernism and Dance." *Modernist Cultures* 9:1 (2014).

Priestley, J.B. *Russian Journey.* London: Writers Group of the Society for Cultural Relations with the U.S.S.R., 1946.

—— *Time and the Conways and Other Plays.* London: Penguin, 1987.

"Programme of Chauve-Souris." Strand Theatre, 1925–6. Cadbury Research Library, University of Birmingham, MS38/3090.

Pudovkin, V.I. *Film Technique and Film Acting*, trans. Ivor Montagu. London: Vision, 1968.

—— Letter to Society for Cultural Relations with Russia Film Section (u.d.). CP/IND/MONT/9/1, Labour History Archive.

*Punch*, March 9, 1927. Cadbury Research Library, University of Birmingham, MS38/4811.

Purves-Stewart, James. *A Physician's Tour in Soviet Russia.* Woking: Unwin, 1933.

Rae, Paul. "Where is the Cosmopolitan Stage?" *Contemporary Theatre Review* 16:1 (2006).

Rambert, Marie. *Quicksilver.* London: MacMillan, 1972.

Ransome, Arthur. *Six Weeks in Russia in 1919.* London: George Allen and Unwin, 1919.

Riley, Matthew ed. *British Music and Modernism, 1895–1960.* Farnham: Ashgate, 2010.

Ross, Stephen and Allana Lindgren eds. *The Modernist World*. London: Routledge, 2015.

Rabaté, Jean Michel. *A Handbook of Modernist Studies*. Boston: Wiley Blackwell, 2013.

Reed, John. *Ten Days that Shook the World*. Harmondsworth: Penguin, 1977.

Roach, Joseph. *Critical Theory and Performance*. Ann Arbor: Michigan UP, 2007.

Robeson Jnr, Paul. *The Undiscovered Paul Robeson: An Artist's Journey, 1898–1939*. New York: John Wiley, 2001.

Rudnitsky, Konstantin. *Russian and Soviet Theatre: Tradition and the Avant-Garde*. London: Thames and Hudson, 2000.

Russell, Robert. "An English Influence on Russian Revolutionary Festivals." *Theatre Notebook* 40:3 (1986).

Ryall, Tom. *Anthony Asquith*. Manchester: Manchester UP, 2005.

Samuel, Raphael, Ewan MacColl and Stuart Cosgrove eds. *Theatres of the Left, 1880–1935*. London: Routledge and Kegan Paul, 1985.

Saville, Ian. "Ideas, Forms and Developments in the British Workers' Theatre, 1925–1935" (PhD diss, City University, 1990), accessed April 5, 2013, http://www.redmagic.co.uk/sites/default/files/documents/THESIS.pdf

Sayler, Oliver. *The Russian Theatre Under the Revolution*. Boston: Little, Brown and Company, 1920.

Schechner, Richard. *Performance Studies: An Introduction*. Abingdon: Routledge, 2013.

Schedler, Christopher. *Border Modernism*. New York: Routledge, 2002.

Schofield, Stephen. *The Judge of All the Earth*. London: Labour Publishing Company, 1927.

Segel, Harold B. *Pinocchio's Progeny: Puppets, Marionettes, Automatons and Robots in Modernist and Avant-Garde Drama*. Baltimore: The Johns Hopkins Press, 1995.

Senelick, Laurence and Sergei Ostrovsky ed. *The Soviet Theater: A Documentary History*. New Haven: Yale UP, 2014.

Senelick, Laurence ed. *Wandering Stars: Russian Émigré Theatre, 1905–1940*. Iowa UP, 1992.

—— *Theatre Arts on Acting*. London: Routledge, 2013.

Senelick, Laurence. *Historical Dictionary of Russian Theater*. Lanham: Scarecrow, 2007.

—— *Gordon Craig's Moscow* Hamlet: *A Reconstruction*. Westport: Greenwood, 1982.

—— *The Chekhov Theatre: A Century of the Plays in Performance*. Cambridge: Cambridge UP, 1997.

—— "The Accidental Evolution of the Moscow Art Theatre Prague Group." *New Theatre Quarterly* 30:2 (May 2014).

—— "More Looked at than Listened to: Shaw on the Prerevolutionary Russian Stage." *SHAW: The Annual of Bernard Shaw Studies* 27 (2007).

Seton, Marie. *Sergei Eisenstein: A Biography*. New York: Grove Press, 1960.

Shaw, George Bernard. *Heartbreak House* (1916), accessed July 3, 2015, http://www.gutenberg.org/files/3543/3543-h/3543-h.htm

—— *Annajanska: The Bolshevik Empress* (1917), accessed July 3, 2015, http://www.gutenberg.org/files/3485/3485-h/3485-h.htm

—— "Back from Moscow." *The Observer*, August 2, 1932.

—— *Bernard Shaw on Cinema*, ed. Bernard Dukore. Carbondale: Southern Illinois UP, 1997.

Sidnell, Michael. *Dances of Death: The Group Theatre of London in the Thirties.* London: Faber and Faber, 1984.

Sitwell, Osbert. *Laughter in the Next Room.* London: MacMillan, 1949.

Skipsey, Joan. "The Russian Question." *Illustrated*, November 8, 1947. Unity Theatre Archive, V&A, THM 9/4/5/54.

Slater, Montagu. "Documentary Theatre." *Documentary News Letter* (January-February 1947). London: Film Centre.

Soboleva, Olga and Angus Wrenn. *The Only Hope of the World: George Bernard Shaw and Russia.* Oxford: Peter Lang, 2012.

"Society for Cultural Relations with Russia, Draft Annual Report." 1947/8. CP/IND/MONT/9/1, Labour History Archive.

Souritz, Elizabeth. "Isadora Duncan's Influence on Dance in Russia." *Dance Chronicle* 18:2 (1995).

Stanford Friedman, Susan. "Planetarity: Musing Modernist Studies." *Modernism/Modernity*, 17:3 (September 2010).

—— "Bodies on the Move: A Poetics of Home and Diaspora." *Tulsa Studies in Women's Literature* 23:2 (Fall 2004).

Stanislavsky, Konstantin. *My Life in Art*, trans. Jean Benedetti. London: Routledge, 2008.

Stephens, Winifred ed. *The Soul of Russia.* London: MacMillan, 1916.

Stourac, Richard and Kathleen McCreery. *Theatre as a Weapon: Workers' Theatre in the Soviet Union, Germany and Britain, 1917–1934.* London: Routledge, 1986.

Sudakova, Elena ed. *See USSR: Intourist Posters and the Marketing of the Soviet Union.* London: GRAD, 2013.

*Sunday Pictorial*, May 2, 1926. Cadbury Research Library, University of Birmingham, MS38/5226.

Tairov, Alexander. *Notes of a Director*, trans. William Kuhlke. Florida: Miami UP, 1969.

—— *Das Entfesselte Theater.* Potsdam: Gustav Kiepenheuer Verlag, 1923.

—— Photograph, DEA 9/3/57, Basil Dean Archive.

—— Photograph of *The Hairy Ape* (1926), DEA 9/3/63, Basil Dean Archive.

Taylor, A.J.P. *English History 1914–1945.* Oxford: Oxford University Press, 1965.

Taylor, Diana. *The Archive and the Repertoire.* Durham: Duke UP, 2005.

Taunton, Matthew. "Angus Wrenn and Olga Soboleva Speaking About George Bernard Shaw on Russia." October 10, 2012, accessed July 10, 2015, https://soundcloud.com/matthew-taunton/george-bernard-shaw-on-russia

Taxidou, Olga. *Modernism and Performance: Jarry to Brecht*. Basingstoke: Palgrave MacMillan, 2007.

Terry, Ellen. *The Russian Ballet* (1913), accessed April 24, 2015, http://www.gutenberg.org/files/45299/45299-h/45299-h.htm

Thacker, Andrew. *Moving Through Modernity: Space and Geography in Modernism*. Manchester: Manchester UP, 2003.

*The Daily Telegraph*, May 24, 1932. Cadbury Research Library, University of Birmingham, MS38/1123.

*The Daily Telegraph*, July 11, 1940. Cuttings *Distant Point*, Unity Theatre Archive, V&A, THM 9/4/5/20.

*The National Graphic*, June 2, 1932. Cadbury Research Library, University of Birmingham, MS38/1123.

*The Observer*, May 29, 1932. Cadbury Research Library, University of Birmingham, MS38/1123.

*The Observer*, May 2, 1926. Cadbury Research Library, University of Birmingham, MS38/5226.

*The Playgoer and Society Illustrated*, vol 6: 31–36. London: Kingshurst, 1912.

*The Stage*, July 14, 1929. Cadbury Research Library, University of Birmingham, MS38/236.

*The Stage*, May 20, 1926. Cadbury Research Library, University of Birmingham, MS38/5226.

*The Sunday Times*, May 29, 1932. Cadbury Research Library, University of Birmingham, MS38/1123.

The Unnamed Society. *The Unnamed Book*. Manchester: Sherratt and Hughes, 1924. Manchester Central Library Archive, TH792 094273Ma27.

"The Workers' Theatre Movement Bulletin (December 1932)." Unity Theatre Archive, V&A Theatre Archive, THM 9/6/2/1.

"The Workers' Theatre Movement Bulletin (March 1934)." Unity Theatre Archive, V&A Theatre Archive, THM 9/6/2/1.

Thomas, Tom. *The Ragged Trousered Philanthropists*. London: Richards, 1936.

Thorndike, Sybil. "Scrapbook." Sybil Thorndike/Lewis Casson archive, V&A, THM 33/1/5.

Tomalin, Miles. Comments from London Unity (29/10/41). BC Ms 20c Theatre, Baron, Brotherton Collection, University of Leeds.

Tretiakov, Sergei. *Roar China*, trans. F. Polianovska and Barbara Nixon. London: Martin Lawrence, 1931.

"Tsar Lenin." *The Observer*, July 4, 1937.

*Unity Theatre Newsletter*, January 16, 1939. Unity Theatre Archive V&A, THM 9/4/1/10.

*Unity Theatre Newsletter* 7, 1944. Unity Theatre Archive V&A, THM 9/4/1/10.

Unity Theatre. Letter to Members. November 28, 1937, Unity Theatre Archive, V&A, THM 9/471/1.

Unity Theatre. Programme for *Get Cracking* (1942). THMS/9/7/110, Unity Theatre Archive, V&A.

Unity Theatre. "Living Newspaper: Unity Theatre's Unique Production" (February 1938). THM/9/4/5/6 *Busmen*, V&A Theatre Archive.

Unity Theatre. *Crisis* (1938). Southern Illinois University Archive at Carbondale, MSS029, Box 6, Folder 1.

Van Gyseghem, André. *Theatre in Soviet Russia*. London: Faber and Faber, 1943.

—— *The Theatre is Our Weapon*. London: Russia-Today Society, u.d.

Vertov, Dziga. *Kino-Eye: The Writings of Dziga Vertov*, ed. Annette Mendelson, trans. Kevin O'Brien. Berkeley: California UP, 1984.

Wallis, Mick. "Pageantry and the Popular Front: Ideological Production in the Thirties." *New Theatre Quarterly* 10:38 (May 1994).

Walkowitz, Rebecca. *Cosmopolitan Style*. New York: Columbia UP, 2006.

Warden, Claire. "Moscow, Saint Petersburg, London: Hubert Griffith and the Search for a Russian Truth." *Comparative Drama* 49:1 (Spring 2015): 1–21.

—— *British Avant-Garde Theatre*. Basingstoke: Palgrave MacMillan, 2012.

Webb, Sidney and Beatrice. *The Truth About Soviet Russia*. London: Longmans, 1942.

Weinstein, Katherine. "Towards a Theatre of Creative Imagination: Alexander Tairov's O'Neill Productions." *Eugene O'Neill Review* 22:1/2 (Spring/Fall 1998).

Wells, H.G. *Russia in the Shadows*. New York: George H. Doran, 1921.

Whitworth, Michael ed. *Modernism*. Oxford: Blackwell, 2007.

Wicksteed, Alexander. *Life Under the Soviets*. London: John Lane, 1928.

Williams, Keith and Steven Matthews eds. *Rewriting the Thirties: Modernism and After*. London: Longman, 1997.

Wollaeger, Mark ed. *The Oxford Handbook of Global Modernisms*. Oxford: Oxford UP, 2012.

Woolf, Virginia. "The Russian Point of View" in *The Common Reader* (1925), Virginia Woolf, chapter 16, accessed August 25, 2012, https://ebooks.adelaide.edu.au/w/woolf/virginia/w91c/chapter16.html

—— "The Movies and Reality." *The New Republic* (August 4, 1926), accessed September 4, 2015, http://www.newrepublic.com/article/120389/virginia-woolf-movies-and-reality

Worrall, Nick. *Modernism to Realism on the Soviet Stage: Tairov, Vakhtangov, Okhlopkov*. Cambridge: Cambridge UP, 1989.

Wright, Basil. "The Theatre." *The Spectator*. November 7, 1941.

WTM. *Red Stage* (January 1932) Working Class Movement Library Archives, Salford, 31000484/AG/TheatreBox1/A.

WTM. *Red Stage* (November 1931) Working Class Movement Library Archives, Salford, 31000484/AG/TheatreBox1/A.
WTM. *Red Stage* (April/May 1932) Working Class Movement Library Archives, Salford, 31000484/AG/TheatreBox1/A.
WTM. *New Red Stage* (September 1932) Working Class Movement Library Archives, Salford, 31000484/AG/TheatreBox1/A.
"Yiddish Theatre in London." Jewish Museum London, accessed June 6, 2015, http://exhibitions.europeana.eu/exhibits/show/yiddish-theatre-en/theatres/hebrew-dramatic-club
Youngs, Tim. *The Cambridge Introduction to Travel Writing*. Cambridge: Cambridge UP, 2013.
Zangwill, Israel and Edna Nahshon. *From the Ghetto to the Melting Pot: Israel Zangwill's Jewish Plays*. Detroit: Wayne State UP, 2006.
Zangwill, Israel. "The Doom of Drama." *Canadian Jewish Chronicle* (June 25 1920).
—— *The Melting-Pot*, act 2, accessed June 17, 2015, http://www.gutenberg.org/files/23893/23893-h/23893-h.htm

# Index





C. Warden, *Migrating Modernist Performance*,
DOI 10.1057/978-1-137-38570-3

Printed by Printforce, the Netherlands